Unready Kilowatts

Unready Kilowatts

The High-Tension Politics of Ecology

Gary Farmer

Open Court   La Salle, Illinois

Printed in the United States of America

Library of Congress Cataloging in Publication Data

Farmer, Gary, 1923—
    Unready kilowatts.

    Includes bibliographical references.
    1. Atomic power-plants—Environmental aspects. 2. Energy policy.
3. Environmental policy.
I. Title.
TD195.E4F37   363.6   74-13372
ISBN O-87548-296-1

Contents

Chapter I
The Ecological Police State

There is every reason to believe that Americans today want a clean and pleasant environment. A flood of articles, news stories, television reports, films, and legislative debates in the last few years has made us all aware of the problems of pollution in the air we breathe, in the land that gives us food, in the water we drink. We all agree that something must be done to improve and protect our environment. And almost all of us agree that the steps we take to clean up our surroundings must be reasonable, effective, and within our means.

A small minority take a different view. They act as if protecting the environment were not only important, but more important than anything else in life: more important than our standard of living, our economic future, our freedom. They carry any and every environmental question to its extremes, and beyond. They voice opposition to almost every sort of economic activity and progress on environmental grounds. You find them at public hearings and in court trying to block a road or a dam or a pipeline. You find them lobbying in Congress and the legislatures for restrictive and amazingly expensive antipollution laws. They do not offer reasonable solutions or constructive alternatives; they just say "stop!" The motive underlying their activities, as will be seen, is not so much a concern for the environment as a relentless hostility to America's way of life, free institutions, and private enterprise. I call them environmental extremists, and extremists indeed they are.

As I will show in these pages, the environmental extremists have already caused billions of dollars of damage to America. Their activities have done much to aggravate and perpetuate the energy crisis. They have inflicted a terrible overburden of bureaucratic regulations, repressive laws, and taxes on the business and industry that sustain our basic standard of living. They have greatly discouraged capital investment in vital industries such as forestry, automobile, electric power, mining, and a host of others, so that our future economic progress is uncertain and dim. As consumer and taxpayer, you pay the bill for their crusading activities.

More and more of our leading commentators, reporters, and authorities are now talking of the environmental extremists and how they have been instrumental in bringing about the erosion of the base for generating capital, with a goal of modifying the private enterprise system. This book is a sincere attempt to present the real environmental extremist and is intended to be helpful in alerting Americans to the true purpose of these zealots. After all the social benefits and risks are weighed, the conclusion is presented for the reader's disposition. The case will be made that the environmental extremist has no interest in workable and reasonable procedures to guarantee clean air, water, and land. This simply isn't part of his lexicon. The environmental extremist is, rather, interested only in throttling down our growth. If governmental entities must be incapacitated or destroyed to attain stasis, this destruction is undertaken.

There are environmentalist leaders in each region or community, and they can be easily identified. The zealot is the one in the news spotlight who is using the courts to block a needed hydroelectric project or nuclear power-er plant one day and assailing the corporations and utili-ties for the energy shortage the next. On the national scene are Ralph Nader, Sheldon Novick, David Brower, Senator Mike Gravel, Senator Ed Muskie, and Dr. John Gofman. Rachel Carson was the first of the activists.

As Irving Kristol recently wrote, "If people today are especially concerned about clean air and clean water, then economic analysis can show them different ways, with different costs and benefits, of getting varying de-grees of clean air and clean water. But it turns out that your zealous environmentalists do not want to be shown anything of the sort. They are not really interested in clean air or clean water at all. What does interest them is modern industrial society and modern technological civilization, toward which they have profoundly hostile sentiments. . . . What environmentalists really want is very simple: They want the authority, the power, to create an 'environment' which pleases them; and this 'environment' will be a society where the rulers will not want to 'think economically' and the ruled will not be permitted to do so. Something similar is going on with the 'consumers protection movement,' whose true aim is not to 'protect' the consumer but rather to circum-scribe, and ultimately abolish, his 'sovereignty.' The 'consumers protection movement,' like the 'environ-mentalist' movement, is a revulsion against the kind of civilization that common men create when they are giv-en the power, which a market economy does uniquely give them, to shape the world in which they wish to live."[1]

The environmental extremist's negative personality has driven the nation's governmental agencies and much of industry toward a point of administrative breakdown and eventual financial collapse. Before this happens, Americans must wake up to the fact that money, both public and private, which had been earmarked for urgently needed expansion of energy and food production, as well as national defense, has not been used for these purposes. Rather, they will find it has either been wasted on meaningless administrative and bureaucratic delays or bungling, or that it has been spent for over-designed and ill-conceived environmental control gadgetry and nonsense.

Three or four years ago in direct confrontations with environmental extremists, many of us attempted to find out what they wanted, so we could comply with their wishes, if possible, and get on with completing needed projects. However, it was difficult to determine what they wanted other than to stop work and bring a halt to industrial growth. In a debate on goals at that time, they finally declared their ultimate end was a change in the present system, accompanied by a redistribution of the wealth and a new order. This clearly suicidal objective has now largely disappeared from their stated demands, though they are still bent on halting and obstructing projects. They now talk vaguely of "excessive corporate profits," or of the necessity of restricting the "multinationals," or of developing exotic energy sources; but they are unwilling or unable to offer concrete solutions to the problems confronting society today. Their universal cry is stop—or else.

The New Age of Fact-Pollution

An activist environmental group subsists solely on the financial support of others. These groups produce no wealth: they plant no trees, generate no power, clean no highways, change no ghettos, dispose of no wastes, and possess no viable means to accomplish environmental improvement objectives. They rely on a program of negative criticism and attack. The most serious, baffling, and overlooked deficiency of the environmental extremist is his lack of knowledge to support the assertions he makes. Environmental extremists readily pose as experts on any issue, including nuclear fission, thermonuclear fusion, the Alaskan permafrost, or the oceans. These problem areas should be treated seriously and with great thought, but the extremists obstruct and detract rather than contribute to the proper achievement of sound environmental protection.

They seem unwilling or unable to accept important advances in social, scientific, and technical issues. Either through lack of education, aptitude, knowledge, intelligence, or perhaps only from noninvolvement in the issue at hand, they have failed to keep abreast. To fulfil their authoritarian instincts, they inject themselves into controversies. By forcing halts to major projects they gain personal recognition. That their actions may inconvenience or needlessly disrupt entire regions or communities seems of no concern to them.

The extremists' tactics vary and some new ones have been perfected. One of the favorite and most innovative is the court injunction. Another even more effective method is a public hearing, for it appears to have a certain acceptance that other tactics lack and still can be dominated by the environmental extremist and his vocal supporters. During a profusion of public hearings throughout the country they have made any number of demands, including changes in commission memberships, free legal services, publication of confidential records, etc. They usually demand copies of all private documents and correspondence on the issues, including side issues, for their personal use. These often go back several years and have no bearing on the subject under discussion. There are not enough people with the pertinent expertise available to evaluate all the documents they demand, even if given years to do so. Yet the demands continue, and projects are suspended. A typical demand was made by Mr. Townsend Belzer of South Carolina, who wanted to see AEC files filling many four-drawer filing cabinets and covering several years' correspondence with Duke Power and Light.

The extremists very often formulate their ideas from secondhand or hearsay information. For instance, using the statements and reports of a self-proclaimed expert, they may attempt to build a case against nuclear energy. The support of others with similar political views is elicited next, rather than those with adequate scientific knowledge, experience, or common sense. Most are quite well equipped to debate. They eagerly seize information from anyone who agrees with them politically and include it in their repertoire. But there is a lack of substance to their assertions since these zealots have no facility for developing new knowledge beyond a superficial point. The work and data of others are paraphrased or reinterpreted.

When challenged by bona fide experts the environmental extremist argues that not enough is known of the subject. This simply avoids the issue. It can be argued that not enough is known of anything, especially some of the biological functions which are part of the ecological scene. It is an unreasonable position, since enough may never be known about many systems in nature to satisfy such critics.

Very little was known of electricity when it was first proposed for use commercially. Electric power almost was not allowed to be used. A review of headlines of the 1890s reveals that a massive campaign was mounted to prevent electricity from being transmitted into homes and businesses. This was on the basis of electrocutions, explosions with ozone in the air, fire, cost, etc. Only by the successful electric lighting of the Chicago World's Fair of 1893 was it proved that these fears were fabrications of the environmental extremists of those days, like the extremists' assertions today about nuclear-electric generating plants.

In fact, there is much we do not understand today about electricity, but this does not mean we should discontinue its use until all the i's are dotted and the t's are crossed. We must not allow the fanatic to force us into hibernation until all his questions have been answered and he is satisfied. He never will be, for his objective is not to learn but to obstruct.

Dr. Phillip Abelson, editor of *Science,* and president of the Carnegie Institute and one of the nation's leading scientists, explained recently that the environment campaign is being oversold. Dr. Abelson asks: "How far down the path of pollution abatement do we go? There are those who demand that no emissions or effluents be permitted. This is unrealistic, for if no man lived on earth, the air and water would still contain materials we classify as pollutants. Abating the first 50 per cent is usually not very costly, after that the costs escalate rapidly. In many cases it costs as much to achieve a further 5 per cent as it did to get the first 50 per cent. Costs of an environmental program will be far greater than the public dreams and will hit everyone, especially the poor. What will we get? In spite of scare headlines, it would be difficult to prove that any more than a minor fraction of our people had suffered more than minimal effects from pollution. True, some annoyance as in smog, but no real damage. The documented cases where air pollution has increased morbidity are few. . . . Many people are predisposed to accepting the view that irresponsible devils are trying to poison them. They have been encouraged in this belief by the environmental zealots."[2]

Environmental crusading has already consumed vast resources of capital, materials, and the services of highly trained people required to comply with recent air and water emissions standards. There are not enough engineers, biologists, and ecologists in the nation to prepare properly the required environmental impact statements now being demanded, nor are there counterparts in government to evaluate properly those submitted. The elaborate—and unheeded—Environmental Impact Statement on the Tussock Moth problem in the Northwest forests or the Alaskan pipeline illustrates the futility and wastefulness of these documents. The scientific content of many of these reports is overruled by trivial and frivolous fads, politics, and emotion. Precise scientific fact and scientists themselves have been badly maligned.

It has become faddish to attack science and technology and to quote Harold Laski, who asserted thirty or forty years ago, "experts should be on tap, not on top." This is absurd, yet many have agreed with the statement. The decision-making process has been transferred from the scientific community to politicians and bureaucrats, many of whom are bound to err on the side of indiscretion, at best. Most scientists and technologists are logical and reasonable people, willing to work with and listen to politicians. Unfortunately the reverse is not true. Zealous politicians have been able to keep our best scientists at arm's length, and as a result, disastrous political decisions have been made (Tussock Moth, DDT, DES, cyclamates, etc.). The public must insist that proper decisions be made now and be based on science and technology rather than by scientifically inept politicians and ideologues.

The environmental extremist rejects the proposition that man can draw from his store of experience to provide new ways of forestalling the transformation of technology from a good servant to a bad master. Individually, very few hesitate in the rush to embrace "technological doom." As C. P. Snow has written in *The Two Cultures*, "It is all very well for one as a personal choice to reject industrialization, do a modern Walden if you like, and if you go without much food, see most of your children die in infancy, despise the comforts of literacy, accept twenty years off your life; then I respect you for the strength of your esthetic revulsion, but I don't respect you in the slightest if even passively you try to impose the same choice on others, who are now free to choose; in fact, we know what their choice will be, for with singular unanimity, in any country where they have had the choice, and the chance, the poor have walked off the land into the factories as fast as the factories could take them."[3] Science and technology are in fact the only means we have to provide the additional capital and know-how to do the job.

Many extremists, when challenged for solutions to our problems, choose to cure environmental ills and solve the energy crisis by limiting growth. This approach received its greatest support from the book, *The Limits To Growth*, sponsored by the Club of Rome. As most knowledgeable scientists predicted, the proposition was rejected by reviewers in *Foreign Affairs;* the prestigious British scientific publication, *Nature; New York Times Book Review*, and numerous others, including Richard B. Carroll: "Along the same lines, Marxists, Neo-Marxists, and Romantics blame technology for environmental ills and the fuel shortage. One of their favorite myths is that manufacture of plastics, paints,

man-made fibers, and such from petroleum uses up vast
quantities of fuel, thereby exacerbating the energy crisis. That proposition is just not true: excluding carbon
black, only about 5 per cent of fuel consumed goes into
such products. As a matter of fact continued development and application of technology are necessary to
some energy and environmental problems. Without limiting desirable growth, we do need to conserve energy.... The present piecemeal approach in which
solutions to these problems are entrusted to bureaucrats
watched over by fanatics simply will not do. The cries
of some demagogues,. the misguided, and the misinformed, on these issues have already exacted their toll.
Legislators and the public must wise up, even to the extent of repealing the harsh and debilitating portions of
the environmental legislation recently enacted."[4]

Throughout the environmental movement, there are
sprinkled a number of scientists and professional people
to whom the others turn or point as lending credence to
their position. Some of the more significant are Linus
Pauling, Barry Commoner, Paul Ehrlich, and various
members of Congress, including Senators Kennedy,
Muskie, and Gravel. Many have the credentials to speak
as bona fide scientists, but frequently they speak on subjects outside their area of expertise. Dr. Pauling received the Nobel Prize in chemistry but speaks freely as
an "expert" in medicine (vitamin C), nutrition, or nuclear energy. His theories failed to receive the approval
of the American Medical Association, Health Physics
Society, American Nuclear Society, or any other body
having responsibility for the scientific and technical
areas he invades. The public should always question the
validity of claims made counter to well-known authorities or professional bodies, especially when such claims
have been evaluated and declared invalid.

An evaluation of the qualifications of Larry Bogart, Myron Cherry, Sheldon Novick, Elizabeth Hogan, Leo Goodman or Richard Curtis should cause anyone to become skeptical of zealots posing as environmentalists or safety experts. These environmental extremists assume that any environmental impact is irreversible, which simply is not true. It does not take nature long to reclaim unused highways or open spaces. Reclamation may be costly and time-consuming but less so than the cost and waste of natural resources which result from obstructive actions of environmental extremists.

Many techniques used during hearings are more or less standard for the environmental extremist. Testimony is given by anyone: self-appointed experts, pseudo-scientists (perhaps with a hand in biology), a "concerned citizen," or anyone willing to speak. Facts and supporting data are welcome but in no way necessary. Old testimony is circulated from group to group across the nation and may apply to an entirely different subject. Information commonly originates in newspapers, written by freelance writers such as Roger Rapoport who have very special interests on one side of the issue.

A standardized rhetoric can be heard from California to New York to South Carolina. Quotes from Sternglass, Commoner, Ehrlich, Bogart, or Gofman make the rounds in about three or four weeks. These are filed for future use even though proven false in the interim. Many citizens and public officials are caught off guard by these charges, which cast doubt and cause alarm. By the time accurate scientific data is publicized to disprove them, the zealots have discarded them and substituted a new series of allegations received in the meantime for circulation and use in upcoming hearings.

This requires that the responsible members of the community remain constantly vigilant. They must work

hard in presenting the facts again and again to counter
new rumors and keep the record straight. This is not
easy, for no one is beyond discreditation by the environmental extremists. Well-known scientists including Dr.
Glenn Seaborg, Dr. Norman Borlaug, and Dr. Victor
Bond have been denounced. The extremists steadfastly
maintain their own jackleg experts, while established experts, leaders in the field for years, are branded liars. If
one follows hearings from one section of a state to another over a period of three or four years, one hears the
same old arguments verbatim. The new spokesman has
"rediscovered the wheel" once again. He may be most
eloquent in describing the type of life he desires for *others*; as for himself, there is some doubt. For example,
the president of the Oregon-based Committee for Conservation of Energy, a vociferous opponent of a nuclear
power plant, advocated rationing electricity, using more
natural gas, and building alternate energy sources. It
was then revealed that he had an electric home and had
increased his consumption of electricity consistently
over the past several years.

A Curious Disregard

Perhaps the most puzzling and alarming trait in the
character of the environmental extremist is his curious
disregard for truth, honesty, and integrity in factual discussions of issues. The code of ethics of the environmental extremist seems to permit the use of any means
to obtain his ends. Senator Proxmire even stated that
if some of the assertions and means used to destroy the
SST program were untruthful, it was all right, since
stopping the SST was the objective. John Gofman repeatedly compares the nuclear reactor in a power plant
with the atom bombs that fell on Japan—a specious and

scurrilous analogy. The calculated lack of validity and truth in his statements is acceptable to him. Authorities doubt the American public is fully aware of this widely used extremist tactic.

Time and time again environmental zealots' voices rise in a crescendo of protest that government hearings or orders are not open or made public. They speak of forcing business, corporate boards, and councils to allow them to monitor private decisions and programs. Ostensibly, they are going to insure that honesty and truth be a part of everyone else's activities, but they are not to be held to this same standard of truth themselves.

This explains why the environmental extremist has been described by many as mentally arrogant, elitist, and authoritarian. For instance, the author of the *Doomsday Syndrome* and editor of *Nature,* the world's most prestigious scientific journal, Dr. John Maddox, was ridiculed by the *Environmental Action Bulletin* for suggesting that engineers are capable of designing power facilities which will work safely. The *Environmental Action Bulletin* based its charge on the premise that Dr. Maddox is a physicist, not an engineer, and therefore unqualified to make such judgments about engineers. Yet, environmental extremists find it acceptable for their own nonprofessional and nonengineering associates to criticize engineers.

The environmental extremist shows the same curious disregard for economics. The welfare of his community and the nation's future as it relates to economic growth is irrelevant to him. There are significantly few black, chicano, or other minority members in the environmental movement. Our nation is busy providing more jobs to increase the standard of living for everyone. Most people wish to enjoy a standard of living comparable to that of the middle-class university professor or elected

official. Such aspirations are based on economic principles which must be understood and respected. Almost
without exception, a characteristic of the environmental
extremist is his refusal to think economically and his
contempt for middle-class society, precisely because this
is a society which thinks economically.

None of the environmentalists seems aware that production and trade built with entrepreneurial freedom are
the principal requisites for a social order which protects
individual freedom and preserves human dignity. This is
perhaps the most glaring deficiency in their arguments.
Gross profit to them is the same as net profit. Basic realisms are ignored, most commonly the ones concerning corporations. They choose to disregard the fact that
increased corporate taxes can result only in increased
costs passed on to the buyer as higher prices. They prefer to blame the businessman for inflation rather than
accept the fact that inflation is caused by ever-increasing deficit spending by government (with an assist from
the Federal Reserve Banks). Instead, they call for more
government spending and more government programs
for every ailment. They reject the need for additional
jobs, productivity, and development of natural resources
in a consumer-oriented society which can provide the
opportunities for everyone to enjoy an equal share of
America. They see the capitalistic utilities developing
the nation's energy supplies as the *enemy*. Energy, of
course, is the key to achieving many goals, yet energy-
development evokes a chorus of charges and obstructive
tactics. The extremist's goal is not clean economic energy production at all, nor resource management, nor
sensible solutions, but the death of free capitalism.

A case in point is that of Larry Williams, executive
secretary and spokesman for an environmental group in
the Northwest. Williams has spoken out in several sci-

entific and technological areas as an expert. He is not an engineer, scientist, technologist, or college graduate; in fact his background is sketchy. A two-year period was spent at Portland State University studying social science, which in no way qualifies him to speak as an expert on the biological effects of DDT or the genetic effects of nuclear radiation.

During a conference of industry, government, and civic leaders, designed to bring together those concerned about the environment, Williams asserted: "If present forest practices continue, Oregon and the rest of the Pacific Northwest will be a treeless prairie within forty years." The hope at the conference was that if the known extremists of the area were brought in touch with experts in the fields of agriculture, forestry, nuclear power, wildlife, and natural resources, an airing of mutual problems in open discussions would result in some enlightenment. This would surely enhance progress toward the common goal of environmental improvement. The "treeless prairie" statement provoked a lively discussion. Many at first accepted it as truthful. One knowledgeable person challenged the statement, however, and asked for facts supporting it. A recess allowed the director of the State Forest Service and the forestry chief of the Bureau of Land Management to be summoned. The discussion commenced, with Williams reluctantly repeating the statement that "Oregon would become a treeless prairie in forty years."

The forestry experts disagreed with Williams completely. Both experts brought results of completed work as well as on-going studies to support their statements. They presented data on numbers of trees being harvested, transplanted, acres available, and timber requirements of the future. Included were forecasts from many governmental and private forest resource agencies.

They discussed increased yields, improved methods of tree farming, and new techniques not yet accepted by the "forest worriers."

The presentation by these officials was a thoughtful and studied analysis of our actual and renewable forest resource and what this means to the United States. Contrary to what Williams had stated, in forty years, with recommended reforestation, there would be more lumber available, with larger stands of harvestable forests than presently exist. It was obvious to the group that Williams' statement was spurious. He had no supporting data or firsthand knowledge. But this had little effect on him or on those adamantly supporting him.

People who shoulder the responsibility for industry, government, and their community are challenged this way whenever possible by the hard core of irresponsible environmental extremists. The responsible leaders are the ones who must make the decisions for the future of the nation's economy and the welfare of the regions they represent. They have nothing to gain and everything to lose from frivolous or deceitful conduct. Unlike them, the extremists have nothing to lose. Williams could speak only subjectively, basing his statement on the interpretation of what others had told him. He had no educational investment or reputation to uphold. He was responsible to no one except the few members of his group, and their standards were not at all difficult to meet. He owed no responsibility to the many thousands of people in the region relying on sound and well-managed renewable forest resources. When his position was shown to be false, it had little or no effect on him. He shrugged it off as a stale joke.

The press shows its own curious disregard for the facts on many issues by printing what appears to be new or sensational revelations on environmental issues. It dutifully provides the environmental extremist coverage, while conveniently ignoring every recognized professional spokesman. Marge Davenport of the *Oregon Journal* is a typical example of journalistic treatment of nuclear power. Her opposition to nuclear power was obvious in a July 4, 1969, story intended to scarify readers: "Dr. E. J. Sternglass of the Department of Radiology and Division of Radiation Health, University of Pittsburgh, links increased United States fetal death rate to atomic fallout from the atomic test program. Mounting evidence... suggests... even relatively low-level doses from peacetime fallout may lead to detectable increases in death rates.... The AEC had previously reassured the public many times that there was no danger from radioactive fallout and that fallout was at safe levels."

This notion of Sternglass, and the data used for his absurd conclusions have been debunked by every scientific body that has taken a serious look at it. His statistical data were not only arithmetically wrong, but manipulated. There is no shred of valid evidence left to his "scientific" study when the data are cleaned up (this is discussed in detail later in the chapter on nuclear energy). This did not bother Davenport, and she has never published any sort of retraction or correction of the Sternglass report she printed. Roger Rapoport wrote in the same manner on December 18, 1969: "Two top AEC scientists warned of... an excess 64,000 deaths annually in America.... Drs. John Gofman and Arthur Tamplin...urged the federal government to make the standards at least ten times tougher."[5] Neither of these individuals was ever a top AEC scientist nor were they able to sustain these charges. They dropped them when it was shown that, by their own dubious calculations, if the standards were tightened by a factor of ten, they would still be accepting a death toll of 6,400 people per

year. No responsible scientist in the radiation research
field has ever been willing to settle for a figure other
than *zero,* or as close to it as possible, as being an acceptable number of deaths.

Many in the news media, from editors down to reporters, have no scientific training or knowledge and
should not be expected to interpret and report scientific
matters in depth. This does not excuse them from a responsibility for accepting standards and legally established professional societies as sounding boards and final
references for the authenticity of results and statements
they publish. Few TV and radio organizations have science writers regularly assigned. Jules Bergman of ABC
is a notable exception in television.

The public needs and desires to have the issues raised
and debated. But it also wants verified facts and responsible news reports rather than verbatim coverage of the
assorted environmental extremists, usually those with
the loudest voices. The debates are necessary to resolve
issues to the satisfaction of reasonable people, but not
to confuse the public, as was done in an editorial in the
Portland Oregonian. In attempting to clarify charges by
Drs. Gofman and Tamplin, the editorial led the public
to believe there is an equal split down the middle in the
scientific community; that the forces of Gofman and
Tamplin have squared off evenly against the forces of
the AEC, The National Council on Radiation Protection and Measurements, The American Nuclear Society, The Health Physics Society, et al, plus the
independent scientists working in the field of radiation.
In fact, only a handful of bona fide scientists in the field
of radiation effects ever listened seriously to the views of
Gofman and Tamplin. As reported in the press, this
handful of men allied with Gofman and Tamplin
against a scientific community in excess of 20,000 con-

stitutes an equal division. The editorial states: "The division among scientists and medical people over radiation safety levels is likely to widen as a result of a new report of the National Council on Radiation Protection and Measurements. Dr. Gofman, AEC scientist at the Lawrence Radiation Laboratory at Livermore, California, branded the report a farce. He and his associate, Arthur Tamplin, both of whom have used the radiation level issue in speeches in Oregon as a major argument against building nuclear power reactors, have insisted the standards are ten times too high [lax]."

This brings up another point that tends to confuse the public, that is, the difference between the educational and training backgrounds of a physician (M.D.) and a Ph.D. Both are referred to as "doctor" and both may be introduced as being from the faculty of a medical school. They may have totally different professional qualifications: a Ph.D. and a M.D. surely would. Often the Ph.D. will speak learnedly and freely of radiation or chemical effects on the human as if he were indeed a physician. Physicians specialize to such a degree today that one must scrutinize their backgrounds also, especially of those who speak on highly specialized subjects.

One physician specializing in neurology, Dr. Anthony Gallo, arbitrarily attributed birth defects of every kind to background radiation. His discussion was accompanied by color slides of serious and horrifying examples of birth defects as he appeared before legislative committees and lay groups. He ascribed these effects to the very low background radiation level of nature, as though he had discovered the cause after many years of failure by the scientific community to do so. He had not even taken time to review the literature concerning the two main aspects of his theory: 1. background-radiation level effects on the biological systems; and 2. radiation exposure levels required to induce birth defects. Had he done so, he would have learned that this subject has been intensely researched by worldwide groups and agencies for many years. There has never been a report submitted to a professional society which proved that background-radiation (or any source of low-level radiation) causes birth defects of the kind Dr. Anthony Gallo, M.D., alleged. On the contrary, all the scientific data and reports state the exact opposite, that the type of defects shown by Gallo are not associated in any way with low-level radiation injury and some only questionably with massive doses.

Few people are competent to speak on all sophisticated subjects from stratospheric loads of air pollutants, ocean currents, or famines, to radiation health physics, though many do so freely. The environmental extremist is aware of this and capitalizes on it, concentrating on political or emotional arguments to motivate the groups supporting him. Dr. E. J. Sternglass of the University of Pittsburgh, a Ph.D. in radiation physics, is a notorious example. Radiation physics is a difficult and exacting branch of science dealing with radiation effects on the structure of matter, generally non-living. This in no way qualifies Dr. Sternglass to speak authoritatively on the genetic and biological effects of radiation. He has shown his lack of proper background and understanding to do so many times. Others, like Dr. Sternglass, who are unqualified on a subject, are also willing to take broad liberties, most frequently at the level of press and television, and aggressively speak out. A group of such persons has preempted the bona fide experts in many fields and has delayed progress toward initiating proper solutions needed to solve environmental problems.

The reputable scientist or technologist with something valid to contribute has many channels available for submitting his findings or theories for evaluation in a constructive rather than a confusing manner. It is therefore necessary to examine closely what is said by the zealots in the environmental movement who have dedicated themselves to confusing the public by use of unsubstantiated assertions and scare tactics.

Government of the People

Many government agencies have become counterproductive under pressure from the environmentalists. While being paid high salaries to formulate and administer rules, officials allow groups of zealots to block necessary actions. The public must insist that these tax-paid officials regain control and get government working for the people once more. The environmentalist must no longer be allowed to hogtie established agencies and bulldoze officials upon whom the public depends.

Illustrative examples can be seen in the AEC's recent hearings on the Emergency Core Cooling System and the Appendix I regulations. These hearings in Bethesda, Maryland, dragged on for months and cost millions of dollars. The AEC has the authority and is charged by law to set these requirements. The tirades from attorneys representing environmental groups and the parade of witnesses lacking substantive information to improve the regulations were a grotesque parody of democracy in action. By taking a militant stand, employing attorneys, using archaic or seldom-used points of law along with scare tactics, extremists can usually halt or delay any project. Many zealots are tax-supported government employees or wives of people on state, federal, or local government payrolls, including many elected officials. Most, it seems, have academic connections. Professors or administrators of tax-supported facilities often pro-

vide the impetus, while the public action is carried out
by wives or students. They enjoy attending hearings and
legislative sessions, where they find a ready forum. This
is usually at a time of the day when the average citizen
is at work and cannot take the time these others can.

Group spokesmen identify themselves as the spouse
of Doctor "so and so," from the medical school or the
university, which seems to lend added stature to their
presence as well as their prouncements before legislators
and hearings officials. They preach conservation of natural resources, while they expend large amounts of tax
dollars. There is a surprisingly large number of groups
established to inject themselves into this quasi-official
role. Many have been able to dominate their counterparts in government, almost setting policy in some state
agencies and legislatures.

There are upward of 5,000 different environmental organizations in the United States, a large number of
which have taken up the cudgel of intimidation and obstruction, voicing irrational demands for environmental
protection. Some are:

> *The Natures Conspiracy*, Manchester, Maine
> *SOS (Save Our Streams)*, Massachusetts
> *The Michigan Environmental Council of Lenawee
> Time Limited*, of Montana
> *Joe's Place Table* and *Save Your Can Place*, Moron-
> go Valley, Calif.
> *The Good Earth Committee*, Illinois
> *STOP*, Independence, Iowa
> *Back More Sheep and Two Lane Highways
> Committee*, Morongo Valley, Calif.
> *Committee on Environmental Information*, St.
> Louis, Mo.
> *Washington Environmental Council*
> *Friends of the Earth*

The group selects a catchy acronym for a name, which describes some objective or goal. There are countless groups named *Pure, Clean, Now, Citizen Committees,* or *Environmental Councils* or *Coalitions* for every cause. They have sprung up in every state, seeking quasi-official status but having much more in name than they do in substance.

A review of the books in their libraries reveals the nature of their mentality and motivation. Most such books are paper tigers or bugaboos which quickly collapse when challenged with facts. More often they are the creations of those whose greed and ambitious instincts hope to exploit a ready market. Here are the titles of a few:

Our Plundered Planet
Our Poisoned Earth and Sky
Our Polluted Planet
Our Polluted World—Can Man Survive?
Timetable For Disaster
Agenda For Survival
Challenge For Survival
The Arthur Godfrey Environmental Reader—Man as an Endangered Species (sans Godfrey selling the 393 cc V-8, 4-door, 22-foot-long Plymouth)
Poisoned Power
Population Control Through Nuclear Pollution
The Careless Atom

There are seventy-two federal agencies in the Washington, D.C., area assigned major roles in the environmental field. Each has a staff and environmental policy. There are 338 environmental agencies or branches within international, national, and interstate organizations. Each also has its own environmental or ecological staff and policy. Finally, there are 450 state and territorial agencies also having their own staffs and policies for specific objectives. Many of these were originally organized to aid an official agency in a task mutually agreed on by the parties concerned. This number does not include the hundreds of local groups throughout the nation, each having a particular objective. By considering the amount of time and energy spent by these groups, plus publications, communications, etc., the tremendous additional costs pushed off on the taxpayer become evident. The environmental movement is a huge business today, requiring millions of dollars for countless lobbyists and staff executives; but it is totally unproductive as far as contributing to gross national product. It only consumes capital and provides no return. Already the joint efforts of the environmental groups have rendered a disservice to our nation unequaled by any other in our history. Here are a few examples:

1. Loss of trees and a beautiful forest from Tussock Moths, plus all ecological systems dependent on trees. $300,000,000.
2. Air emission control systems for sulfur and other by-products of power plant operation for Commonwealth Edison. In excess of $100 per kilowatt of plant capacity.
3. U.S. Plywood paper and pulp mill site preparation in Alaska prior to abandonment. $3,000,000.
4. One year's delay in the licensing of nuclear power plants at a total cost of six billion dollars.
5. The SST program cancellation. One billion dollars.

Needed quality projects delayed in face of a growing energy shortage becoming more and more critical:

1. Alaskan pipeline. Delayed for at least five years and at an additional cost of several hundreds of millions of dollars.

2. Offshore drilling for oil.
3. Refinery construction delay and cancellations.
4. Breeder reactor delay.

With regard to environmental objections to refineries, a December 1972 paper issued by the Department of Interior, Office of Oil and Gas, *Trends in Capacity and Utilization*,[6] lists ten refinery projects with a total of 1.1 million barrels per day crude distillation capacity, some of which are "blocked by or having difficulties with environmentalists' actions." These are:

Delaware: 150,000 barrels per day
Rhode Island: 65,000 barrels per day
Maine: 130,000 barrels per day
(fuels desulfurization)
New Jersey: 100,000 barrels per day
New York: 125,000 barrels per day
Maryland: 100,000 barrels per day

Five of the above have either been entirely blocked or seriously hampered by environmentalists' actions and represent a potential 570,000 barrels per day crude oil distillation capacity. In addition to the above specific proposals which have had siting problems on environmental grounds, it seems reasonable to assume that stricter environmental regulation and the threat of activist environmental objection has had a depressing effect on long-range refinery construction plans. Many refinery projects have probably died aborning and never gotten to the formal request-for-construction stage.

Unnecessary additional control devices have resulted in wasted natural resources:

1. Exhaust emission control devices for automobiles. Estimated increased use of gasoline by 50 to 60 per cent as well as cost for importing platinum, plus wasted expenditures of engineering costs and governmental administration.

2. Legally required environmental impact statements
   have become a nightmare of red tape and busy-
   work. Furthermore, on important projects the environmental statements have had little effect. The
   use of DDT as recommended by the Tussock
   Moth statement was rejected by Environmental
   Protection Agency, and the construction of the
   Alaskan pipeline was rejected by the courts.

Aside from any assumptions that environmental impact will or won't occur, the argument sidetracks the
energy issue. Consequently, the magnitude of the energy shortage is not understood by many. As will be seen,
tremendous quantities of energy, probably as electricity,
will be needed to combat the environmental degradation that offends us all. According to Robert Bendimer of
The *New York Times,* "We need more electric power to
do the very recycling of waste that is so desirable. We
need it to operate the vastly expanded sewage treatment
plants... for that immeasurable developed system of
mass transportation that our metropolitan areas must
have... for the herculean cleanup of the nation's lakes
and rivers, and not least, we need it if all who are just
emerging from dire poverty are to enjoy a standard of
living we have come to take for granted that many now
hold in scorn or pretend to."

The Atomic Industrial Forum sets forth some additional power requirements.[7] To place kilowatt-hour
(kwhr) figures into better perspective, note that in 1970
the average American household consumed 700 kwhr.
The following sample categories give some idea of mag-
nitudes:

Pollution Control. Several Pacific Northwest metal
smelters use more than 60 million kwhr per year each
for control of air and water pollution alone. That is
equivalent to the electrical consumption of 8,500 typical

households. In Chicago, Commonwealth Edison Corporation reports that eight out of thirteen area foundry and steel-making facilities have converted from polluting processes to electrical power. Recently, United States Steel and Republic Steel have both asked Commonwealth to supply more than two million kilowatts of additional power for electric furnaces and other purposes, thus more than doubling their total electric requirements. An electrostatic scrubber for a large industrial plant requires as much as 50,000 kilowatts of capacity.

A 1970 survey by the Bonneville Power Administration (BPA) showed that of the two million homes served by electricity in the Pacific Northwest 25 per cent were heated electrically. Based on an average unit consumption (for that region) of 12,000 kwhr annually, this totalled six billion kwhr per year for heating use only. The other 1.5 million Pacific Northwest homes were heated by oil (50 per cent), gas (18 per cent), and coal and wood (7 per cent). BPA estimates that their heating plants contributed 38,000 tons of particulate matter to air pollution last year. Northwestern utilities anticipate that power demands for home heating will more than triple by 1990, when 50 per cent of the projected 3.5 million homes in that region will be heated electrically.

Some large office buildings and industrial plants are installing high-temperature (1,600 degree) electric incinerators. One such installation, the Goder incinerator, requires a connected load of thirty-two kilowatts in order to process 400 pounds of waste per hour and to control air pollution. The efficient disposal of garbage and trash is calculated by some experts to require as much as two million kilowatts for the country as a whole. There may be some trade-offs if incinerators can be designed to produce rather than to consume power, but the control of air pollution caused by the burning of garbage and sewage will in turn require substantial amounts of electric energy.

Sewage treatment. Primary sewage treatment requires an input of 21 kwhr per year per person, according to a survey of Oregon and Washington State communities. Secondary treatment, which most American municipalities do not yet have, raises this to approximately 30 kwhr per year per person. The Federal Water Quality Administration calculates that in 1968 the United States consumed close to two billion kwhr for sewage treatment. Today the needs of an urban population of 165 million Americans require that this be more than doubled to 4.6 billion kwhr, or 28.1 kwhr per year per person.

Recycling. A conceptual design of a total recycling plant, commissioned by the Aluminum Association, envisages a facility that would take in garbage at one end and produce salable raw materials at the other. Designed to serve a city of 175,000 to 200,000 people, such a plant could consume nearly ten million kwhr per year. In 1969, some twenty million tons of scrap iron and steel were reclaimed in the United States, mostly by means of electric furnaces; and the total is even higher today. Metal industry sources say that to recycle one ton of scrap requires 500 kwhr of power, which would mean a 1969 consumption for this purpose of 10 billion kwhr. One Chicago plant, typical of its kind, uses nearly 4,000 kilowatts of electrical power to grind up junk automobiles into metal shreds for remelting.

Street lighting. General Electric reports that even with a highly efficient lamp, such as its 400-watt Lucalox, it takes 44,000 kwhr per year per mile properly to illuminate a four-lane street and 66,000 kwhr per year per mile for a six-lane highway. The 1,000-watt mercury clear lamps in common use today require approximately three times as many kilowatts per foot-candle as the Lucalox, according to General Electric.

Mass transportation. There are some 110 million registered motor vehicles in America, each traveling an average of 10,000 miles a year, for a total of more than one trillion miles. To convert a fraction of the mileage from internal combustion power to electric propulsion would take a great deal of energy. Chargeable batteries used in several experimental electric vehicles draw about one kwhr for each mile of travel. Bruce C. Netschert, a prominent energy consultant, has estimated that the ultimate conversion of this vast automobile fleet to electricity would require approximately 450 billion kwhr, or about a third of the total United States output today.

The 160 m.p.h. Metroliner railroad cars developed for the Northeast Corridor are designed for maximum acceleration and deceleration. Each Metroliner car has a peak energy demand of 2,500 horsepower, or 25,000 horsepower for a ten-car train. This is equivalent to an electrical load of nearly 15,000 kilowatts. Although the Metroliner does not draw peak loads continuously, it does require close to full power a good 50 per cent of the time, because the train automatically changes speed almost constantly as it negotiates the conventional roadbed. If the train operates 70 per cent of the time over the course of the year, its average power requirement could run to 45 million kwhr.

There are about 220,000 miles of railroad track in this country, and barely 1 per cent of this mileage is electrified. Power required to move loads over electrified lines can go as high as twenty kwhr per 1,000 gross ton miles of expedited traffic, according to General Electric's Transportation Systems Division. A rule of thumb

among railroaders when estimating power consumption
is one million kwhr per year per mile of electrified track.
The Washington, D.C., Metro subway system, now under construction, will require 500,000 kilowatts annually, which is equivalent to the output of a good-sized
generating station. The biggest urban electric utility in
terms of capacity is Consolidated Edison Company of
New York, and Con Ed's biggest single load factor is
mass transit, the city subways and commuter railroads.
Last year, Con Ed sold 2.8 billion kwhr (8.5 per cent of
its total) for mass transit use. Energy consultant Bruce
Netschert estimates that electric mass transport for our
twenty-five largest cities would require about twenty
million kilowatts of added electric power today—5 per
cent of the nation's total electric capacity.

One may ask, in face of such a serious shortage and
with all the problems to be solved to survive the energy
crisis, how a relatively few people could possibly bring
the entire nation to a virtual halt? The answer lies in
their zeal, tactics, and most of all experience in activism. They began as small, well-organized groups with
special causes and then exploded into the public eye
with Earth Day demonstrations in 1970. Many of the
Earth Day gatherings resulted in the same unsightly ac-
cumulations of litter and debris in the parks and streets
as the rubbish left by the earlier activists—to be cleaned
up by someone else.

However, the environmental extremists soon realized
they were creating serious problems for the labor force.
This seriously affected the future success of their ven-
tures, so an attempt was made to involve the unions
and reconcile their objectives. As an example, in mid-
January of 1972, the Sierra Club attempted to examine
in depth the case of electric power and its future demand at a two-day meeting in Vermont. It was supposed to help the club reach a national policy on energy

and electricity. As a result, the Sierra Club published a report that was to serve as the framework for an overall energy policy.

The meeting and the report both reflected some moderation in the group's attitude toward energy growth and no special opposition to nuclear power. The chairman of the committee was quoted in The *New York Times* as saying: "We've been considered irresponsible for too long. We are now at the point where we don't want to be in the position of arbitrarily blocking every new electric power plant that comes along."

The primary contribution of the conference was the expansion of the subject from alleged environmental effects of one plant to the broader and more complex area of energy in general, including its relation to the broader economic, social, and political issues. Most of the speakers or participants suggested a more comprehensive view of the subject than the conservationists had taken in the past. A leader of the black community in Washington, Mr. Julius Hobson, berated the environmentalists for middle-class arrogance in being more concerned about the environment than about basic social and economic policies. Mark Roberts, Harvard economist, emphasized the need for considering efficiency and cost "because we simply cannot afford to waste these resources in achieving environmental improvement." Perhaps the most incisive comment came from Frank Wallach, editor of the *UAW Washington Report:* "It is the height of life-style arrogance for people who summer at the seashore to deny city dwellers an air conditioner. I think a lot of electric gadgets are silly, but I am not impressed by the high-income purists who would deny the working class of America who make up 56 per cent of the employed population their option to household conveniences."[8]

The economic impact of environmental programs on

inflation over which the above spokesmen were concerned has become more significant recently. Economists, engineers, and business leaders have stated repeatedly that even if a strenuous government program of belt-tightening enabled us to manage inflation, the costs of environmental controls required by Congress for cleaning the air and water would initiate a further uncontrollable inflationary rise. Needed environmental improvements demand careful allocation of capital and an economy of forces. The added costs produced by the extremists' efforts will increase costs to the point that it is doubtful much equipment will ever be installed.

Some detail is provided by Richard B. Carroll, an industrial engineer and a specialist on air pollution problems: "In response chiefly to the demands of environmentalists, a plethora of environmental bills has been enacted by Congress in the past two years. Often prodded by demagogues, radicals, and self-appointed elitists, legislators have adopted harsh environmental emission restrictions without sufficient regard for what should be the primary criterion, namely environmental quality, i.e., the state of our air, water, and land.... Seldom, if ever, in all the information, misinformation, propaganda, and politicking on environmental questions, have the important associated issues of cost or of the developing energy crisis been considered, or explained adequately to the American people.... W. D. Ruckelshaus, at that time head of the EPA, has stated: 'I am not convinced that environmentalism is ruining our economy or posing a future threat to the progress and welfare of this nation. Such talk is nonsense.' The facts indicate otherwise. The steel industry, for instance, will have to invest nearly 3.5 billion dollars to meet proposed air and water pollution control standards—an amount almost equal to the industry's total earnings over the past five years.... To cite another example, eight out of fourteen zinc plants in the United States have shut down or announced shutdown, because they cannot comply with air emission restrictions. These and similar developments will have an obvious economic impact on employment, balance of payments, and perhaps our standard of living. That's hardly nonsense.... A case in point is the now-proven effectiveness of the tall stack as an aid in achieving satisfactory air quality.... Yet such legitimate technological considerations are invariably, and unwisely, discredited by our environmentalists and officials.... The developing fuel shortage and the consequent 'energy crisis' will have a profound effect on the American standard of living. The hell-bent environmentalists, once again, are not helping matters."[9]

Zealous environmentalists, when confronted with such realisms as those above, react by ignoring them and by escalating their demands which further strangle the company, the industry, or the agency of their focus. Their solution is to return to the days of our forefathers: the use of kerosene lamps, wood-burning space heaters, and fewer appliances and adopting a more primitive lifestyle—a regressive, unrealistic, and unacceptable alternative. Man's efforts have been directed to alleviating his drudgery. Maintaining the freedom of choice to do so is one of the most precious rights we have to protect. Cultural regression is ridiculous and unnecessary.

Environmentalist paralysis affects almost every branch of government. Some of the more outrageous cases include the AEC (Appendix I) hearings on environmental conditions around nuclear power facilities. Scientific issues have been hopelessly complicated by being thrown into the political and social arena, creating a special problem of subjecting technical issues to a public forum. Whenever science and politics meet head on, politics emerges triumphant.

Perhaps the most notorious of all is the case of DDT, although the federal government's position on laundry detergents is a close runner-up. The Environmental Protection Agency (EPA) was told in specific terms many times by leading scientists that a ban on DDT by the United States was unnecessary and unwarranted and would have an unfavorable worldwide impact. But the officials in charge ruled against DDT—and in favor of far more toxic poisons.

In an address during a symposium at Washington State University at Pullman, Washington, on March 27, 1973, Dr. Norman Borlaug said a food shortage almost became a world catastrophe in 1972. "After all, food is the first purpose of life." His plan was to set up a worldwide system of granaries and stockpile grain in them as insurance against famine. Dr. Borlaug talks of the enemies of agricultural chemicals and the fact that the American consumer has been spoiled by cheap foods, "...paying 15 to 17 per cent of his income in the thirty years I've been working," he said. In developing countries, people must spend 75 to 80 per cent of their income for food in good years, and all in the bad years. He called it folly to think that wheat and other agricultural crops could be bred to be resistant to all diseases. Chemicals are needed to improve food production, and "the biggest poison being poured into the environment today is the clamor against chemicals."[10]

In an address to the United Nations Food and Agriculture Organization in Rome, on November 8, 1971, Dr. Borlaug discussed the high-yield cereals he helped develop as the "Green Revolution."[11] "Criticism of the Green Revolution has become a popular pastime. Perhaps it reflects the feelings of some who had predicted famine and doom for the hungry nations and, consequently, cannot yet forgive the new strategy for being successful.... If agriculture is denied the use of chemical fertilizers and pesticides, for example, the world will be doomed, not by chemical poisoning, but from starvation.... No chemical has ever done as much as DDT to protect the health, economic and social benefits to the people of the developing nations.... More than 1,000 million [one billion!] people have been freed from the risk of malaria in the past twenty-five years, mostly thanks to DDT. This is an achievement unparalleled in the annals of public health. But even today, 329 million people are being protected from malaria through DDT spraying operations for malaria control or total eradication. The safety record of DDT to man is truly remarkable. In spite of prolonged exposure of considerable numbers, the only confirmed cases of injury have been the result of massive accidental or suicidal swallowing of DDT. There is no evidence in man that DDT is causing cancer or genetic change! If the use of pesticides in the United States were to be completely banned, crop losses would probably soar to 50 per cent, and food prices would increase four- to five-fold. Who then would provide the food needs of the low income groups? It behooves all mankind to increase the efficiency of agriculture throughout the world if we wish to alleviate human suffering, conserve wildlife, and improve recreational opportunities. For instance, unless the food production of East Africa is expanded to meet the region's growing food needs, the large animals in the game reserves and national parks of East Africa will be poached out of existence within the next three decades. Similarly, the elephant, tiger and peacock will perish from India because of population pressure. Unlike all other species, man can take stock of himself and project ahead to see the great difficulties that will be forthcoming."

In spite of the substantiated facts and justifications

presented by Dr. Borlaug and others supported by the National Academy of Sciences, the EPA banned the use of DDT, while some 500,000 acres of prime forest were being destroyed in Washington and Oregon by insect infestation (details of the Tussock Moth problem are presented in a later chapter). The taxpayer is being gouged while those who place the welfare of insects, birds, and fish over those of trees and people continue in their derangement to bulldoze public officials out of taking the necessary actions.

The quacks, pointing to *The Silent Spring*, a book of half-truths and nonsense, have pressured the politicians into blunder after blunder, leaving the taxpayer to soak up the costs in continued loss of natural resources. The forced removal of cyclamates, diethylstilbestrol (DES), swordfish, and tuna represent other instances of their destructive handiwork. For an eye-opening example, consider the tactics used and the results of Ralph Nader's campaign against cyclamates.

Cyclamates have been studied in depth since 1955, first by the Food Protection Committee of the National Research Council. Their reports showed that an acute toxic oral dose for mice is 10 to 12 grams per kilogram, and for rats 12 gm. per kilogram. This is an absurdly massive dose. No effects were observed from 1 per cent or less in the diet of laboratory animals. Five per cent in the diet of rats produced a mild diarrhea. Dogs fed sodium cyclamate for eleven months remained healthy. Human volunteers were given 5 grams per day for seven and one-half months with no toxic effects noted. The final report evaluated cyclamates as being relatively nontoxic at 5 gm. per day; 1 gm. per day is nontoxic. One gm. of sodium cyclamate equals 400 gm. of sucrose. With obesity as probably the most serious national health problem, and with the ill effects of sugar in dental health and diabetes, a strong case exists for the increased use of cyclamates and the decreased use of sugar.

Yet cyclamates were banned by use of an inappropriate regulation and on the basis of flimsy evidence. The link between cancer and cyclamates is highly improbable. Subsequent testing, involving much higher dosages, shows no evidence of carcinogenic qualities at all in cyclamates. Cyclamates can still be purchased in Canada and most of the world. This is because the fanatic consumer advocates and environmental extremists have no foothold as yet outside the United States. In face of such pressure, our government officials find it simpler, easier, and safer to sit tight, to conduct lengthy, expensive hearings and reviews, and finally, with feigned reluctance and often over the objections of their blue-ribbon committees, to ban useful materials from market. Once such issues are thrown into the political arena, they become hopelessly irrational.

Common sense and reason cannot be found in the workings of fanatic groups. They would do well to study and learn from Dr. Borlaug as well as Dr. H. E. Stokinger, especially his paper in *Science*, Vol. 174, 12 November, 1971, "Sanity in Research and Evaluation of Environmental Health."[12] "The ruinous concept of zero tolerance for pollutants must go! Man has never, before he was a man or ever after, survived in an unpolluted void. One has only on a sultry day to cast his eyes unto the terpene-laden haze of the hills, or on a humid day, to bring into view the fog born of condensation nuclei of many chemicals from the oceans to realize that this is true." Or, "...Of 18 major pollutants ...from all sources only eight were re-evaluated as potentially hazardous.... Respiratory irritants (particularly oxidants)

headed the list as pollutants of primary concern; yet
pesticides of all types, as well as teratogens and muta-
gens, as found in the three environmental sources, were
conspicuously absent from the list. Asthmagens were
not absent. What has the record shown since? (1.) DDT
and 2,4,5-T banned from further use, as were all uses of
organic mercurials as pesticides. Swordfish has been removed from sale, although people may still eat fish, just
as they have since before the time of Christ. (2.) Cyclamates have gone, and monosodium glutamate is on its
way out. NTA (nitrilotriacetic acid) the soap industry's
dream substitute for the polyphosphates that the industry itself banned from laundry detergents, was summarily prohibited on fragile and provocative evidence. (3.)
Detergent enzymes appear to be on their way out. Pota-
to chips may be next because of their increased solanin
content, caused by dehydration of hot fat. What next?
If man is prohibited from consuming foodstuffs because
of their content of natural toxins, where will it end?
Honey contains the potent grayanotoxins (given intra-
peritioneally, a dose lethal to 50 per cent of the animals
tested is approximately one milligram per kilogram). (4.)
German raisins have been found to be teratogenic. (5.)
While caffeine and tannin are tumorigenic, nutmeg,
parsley, and dill are highly toxic because of their myris-
ticin and apiole contents. Vitamin C has produced tu-
mors in mice." Dr. Stokinger lists seven
commandments as a means for achieving realistic evaluations of environmental pollution: (1.) Standards must
be based on scientific facts, realistically derived, and not
on political feasibility, expedience, emotion of the
moment, or unsupported information. (2.) All standards, guides, and limits as well as the criteria on which
they are based, must be completely documented. In
such documentation it must be made emphatically clear

on what basis a given standard rests. This must not only be done in a formal, written document, but in the press and other forms of news media as well, thus preventing the public from becoming unnecessarily or unduly alarmed. For example, in all the public announcements of the banning of DDT, it was never made clear that it was not for protecting human health, but for protecting such endangered species as the osprey, bald eagle, and other fowl. Similarly, in the confiscation of canned tuna in 1970, no effort was made to evaluate for the public the degree of hazard or the margin of safety in eating the fish. (3.) Avoid the establishment of unnecessarily severe standards. (4.) Determine realistic levels. (5.) Interpret the "Delaney clause" (banning carcinogens) with informed scientific judgment. (6.) Determine trends, not pro tempore monitoring. To take official action to ban distribution and consumption of industrial commodities on the basis of newly discovered environmental levels without the perspective afforded by comparison with past levels in the environment, is to put unbridled enthusiasm for environmental control ahead of common sense. "The most flagrant violations of this commandment," he writes, "are the previously noted recommendations that tuna and swordfish be confiscated or denied access to the family dining table. One moment's reflection would reveal that the concentration of mercury in the oceans has not changed perceptibly since the white men reached these shores, and that men have eaten these fish and lived and died without signs or symptoms of mercury poisoning." (7.) Delimit banning.

"Finally, it may be too much to hope that antipollutionists will not direct a blind eye and turn a deaf ear to the precepts I have put forth as necessary for proceeding rationally against problems with which we are all deeply concerned and involved. No matter what the immediate reception may be, antipollution efforts must ultimately take the direction indicated in these commandments, or we will be faced with an economic upheaval approaching disaster."

Almost none of Dr. Stokinger's common sense approaches to environmental health have been heeded.

Confusion about pesticides arises from not being aware of tremendous improvements in the sensitivity of chemical analyses. These highly sensitive methods, if interpreted by a poorly trained operator, will necessarily result in improper conclusions. One analytical procedure, called gas-liquid chromotography with electron capture, is so delicate (it detects chemicals in one or two parts per *billion*—in more cases, per *trillion*) that, in the hands of inexpert people, it may do more harm than good. Much has been made over alleged traces of DDT in the Antarctic penguins, amounts of the order of one or two parts per billion. The validity of these results is questionable. At the University of Wisconsin some soil samples that had been sealed since 1910 were tested recently for synthetic organochlorine pesticides by the latest, most delicate gas chromotographic procedure. Several pesticides were detected in thirty-two of the thirty-four samples. The only flaw, was that these pesticides not only were not used in 1910—they did not even exist until 1940.

Non-chemical methods for controlling insects responsible for crop and animal losses may eventually be developed, but they are far away. The control methods that are now being studied or used on different insects include improved biodegradable insecticides, natural predators, parasites and pathogens, resistant varieties, genetic sterility techniques, sex and food attractants, and hormonal interference.

Until such nonchemical means are proved effective, it

is senseless to propose such methods as serious means for food or fiber production. The hypothesis is being circulated, especially by Barry Commoner, that the production of synthetic fibers requires five times the energy as natural ones. No one has validated this statement and it is doubtful that it can be. Even if it were the case, the overriding point here is that Commoner and his cohorts oppose DDT and chemicals which are absolutely essential to most food and fiber production.

Population—Boom, Bust, or Fizzle

The enthusiasm of the environmental movement is reported to be on the decline. Warren Berry, writing in the *Los Angeles Times*, reported in October 1972, "in Texas and Pennsylvania, 60 per cent think the prime issue is stability; 30 per cent, prosperity; 11 per cent, the need for preserving the capitalistic system; 10 per cent, the local issues; 0 per cent appear to be worried about the environment. Ecology...has not caught on as the sequel to the dramatic civil rights campaign of the 1960s...the whole thrust of the fight has now been reversed. For the next year, it is safe to predict that ecology will be overshadowed by that new war cry, 'the Energy Crisis.' "[13]

Environmental extremists have accelerated this reversal through their unreasonable approach to almost every simple or complex problem of the environment. Too many of their arguments are fabricated or flimsy and directed toward an emotionally unstable United States of the late 1960s.

Outside of the United States, their alarming prognostications were viewed with disdain and suspicion. This was demonstrated at the United Nations-sponsored environmental conference in Stockholm in 1972. On

March 15, 1973, in a lecture on "Man on Earth: His
Environment" Dr. Frank Munk of Portland, Oregon,
called for a reassessment of priorities, both domestic
and international, to put the fight against pollution in
proper perspective. He said the environmental movement has included too much emotion and not enough
rational discussion. He said that environmentalists are
calling for a "planetary policy" against pollution. He cited a United Nations resolution, introduced by Brazil
and passed by a majority of United Nations members,
stating that economic development must take prece-
dence over environmental concerns. The leaders of undeveloped nations resent it when Americans who have a
high standard of living ask others to continue living an
impoverished existence.

In other words, would Barry Commoner give up his
United States citizenship and take up permanent resi-
dence in Bolivia? This is in no way intended to dis-
parage Bolivian life, but it is a valid question. Bolivian
livestyles and goals are markedly different from ours,
and these vital facts must be recognized by the "have"
nations. The Bolivian has an average annual per capita
gross national product of $199, a life span of 46.5 years,
and an infant mortality rate of 140 per 1,000 births.
(The United States rate is 19 per 1,000). Of the 45,309
deaths recorded in 1963, nearly half were of children
under the age of five. In that same year the reported
deaths for children under five was 194 per 1,000 births
and the birth rate was 42 per 1,000.[14] Bolivia is twice the
size of Texas with less than four million people. The
per capita density is 3.4 per square km, with over half
living in the high plateau region, the "Alto plano." The
environmental extremists would apply the "planetary
policy" to the underdeveloped nations like Bolivia and
add the charge that population density is the cause of

pollution. This is sheer nonsense. Where areas of high
pollution exist in undeveloped nations, they are caused
by a combination of cultural factors, tradition, and the
lack of capital for economic development, inadequate
supplies of energy and available resources. Yet the fanatics continue to subscribe to the idea that, in effect,
by removing people from the scene, everything will improve.

Cultural habits and traditions of some nations stimulate recycling and reuse of resources based on thrift or
common sense. Other societies reject these values. Serious discussions of strict pollution control of air and water, such as the release limits of sulfur or carbon
dioxide, nitrogen concentration of water from hydroelectric projects, auto emission controls, or wildlife conservation and soil erosion control, become impractical
when advanced in support of the "planetary policy" and
the "quality of life" arguments by environmental extremists using them to justify population and environmental controls.

Before capital can be available for such purposes in a
"have-not" nation, the Bolivian, for example, must first
increase his per capita income. Indians and Africans are
likely to continue poaching as long as the profit from
Bengal tiger skins or elephant ivories exceeds what they
earn from other employment. In this economic setting,
conservation and land-use planning with workable air
and water release limits is unrealistic. An agricultural
base must be developed first so meat and cereals are
available at reasonable prices. This may help discourage
the killing of wildlife including falcons or hawks now
captured to supplement the diet. In this same context
other programs such as tuberculosis eradication are
doomed to failure if the diet lacks essential body nu-
trients.

In building a productive agricultural supply system, a developing nation may need to provide water for irrigation, which causes a drop in water quality. Certain noxious harvest residuals must be burned, smoking the air; or to be more than marginally productive, fertilizer must be added to the soil. Its production and application may require relatively large quantities of energy. If these efforts are fruitful, resources to establish a marketing and distribution system must be provided which may also cause air pollution and the consumption of materials. DDT or other insecticides must be provided to save the investment of the "have-not" peasant. It is unthinkable that we should deny them the use of these modern useful techniques.

Bolivia is not a unique example. Many Americans have traveled and lived in other nations of the world and are aware that the vast majority of the world's population lives in this manner. They are not ready and will not accept the United States' brand of environmental extremism with all its ramifications, specifically population control, without a struggle.

Few, if any, have emigrated to Bolivia, Paraguay, the Sudan, Saudi Arabia, or Tanzania because of overcrowding in the United States. Some may have emigrated to other countries, notably to Great Britain, Australia, Israel, or Canada to escape economic or political systems. Some people leave the United States because of their dislike for the general decline in morality, or a rise in crime or tax rates, rather than overpopulation problems. But on the whole, far more people want to immigrate to this country than choose to leave.

In the meantime environmental extremists warn of a polluted civilization dying from lack of air, water, or land resources. The Zero Population Growth advocate at the same time warns of population increases of billions upon billions. The answer to the problem is, he says, the IUD (intrauterine device)— for the women of Guatemala and India.

The rules of the game should apply equally to all. The IUD (which has not been very successful), or other programs of birth control, the panacea supposedly for the undeveloped world, cannot bring a change in conditions. Only capital, available for industry to design and manufacture machines to replace man in the fields, can do this. Man is the capital in undeveloped nations. If manpower is not available to produce the crops, the nation will grow poorer, not richer. Without capital and tools, only a marginal or subsistence existence is possible. In China, 80 per cent of all the people work on the land, yet they must import food. The diligence of the available manpower to work, produce, and adopt new techniques is a function of the dynamics of culture and tradition. If the culture of India results in a poorly run government, if death from starvation (while cattle roam the streets) in face of a notoriously high birth rate is acceptable to them, it is the height of arrogance and naiveté to suggest we can inaugurate birth control and solve their problems for them.

That nations must first have agricultural self-sufficiency to make it possible for development is shown by Japan, which does not produce all its required foodstuffs. Japan first assured itself an adequate food supply through trade. Then it moved into an industrial development program designed to raise the standard of living. Its cultural background and traditions of thrift and hard work permitted Japan to respond to dynamic pressures in a way that India, Pakistan, and other undeveloped nations have not. Environmental problems accompanied the industrialization, but advancing technology has given Japan the means to correct them if she

chooses. Japan has been severely criticized by environmental extremists for not meeting necessary standards
in several areas that may be described as the "quality of
life" syndrome. This term may be used to cover any
number of illogical fears and crackpot concepts. The ill-
defined "quality of life" idea has provided population
control zealots a ready-made issue with which to state
their views—an issue too hazy or slippery to rebut. Often their prognostications stimulate the fearful into proposing poorly conceived schemes for land-use planning,
abortion on demand, family planning, statism in the
form of life-style control, euthanasia, infanticide, and
eugenics programs which could almost be lifted out of
Nazi Germany or Stalinist Russia. Paul Ehrlich, an en-
tomologist, is the leading proponent of population control in this context.

In this regard, Samuel McCracken, writing in the
May 1972 issue of *Commentary* states: "If Ehrlich's position can be described (with more simplicity than insight)
as a preference for a voluntary rather than a compulsory solution to the population problem, some of his colleagues, as he is fond of calling them, go further.
Martha K. Willing, for example, in *Beyond Conception*
doubts that people are responsible enough to avail
themselves of contraceptive services even if they were
provided free by the government. An enlightened public
policy, in her judgment, would view contraception and
abortion merely as tools to be administered as required
in pursuit of a well-directed program of population control. Thus, she proposed to make it a crime to have
more than two children, a prohibition she would enforce by the tattooing of the biparous, by compulsory
sterilization, and by compulsory abortion."[15]

Another of Ehrlich's colleagues, Edgar Cahsteen, ob-
viating the problem of "unwanted" conception in the

first place, proposed "inoculating males and females against fertility at puberty." Typically, they dictate restrictions for others not only in our country, but elsewhere. The specter of famine and subsequent disease and pestilence he projects are unpleasant to contemplate, and Ehrlich has convinced many young people and scientifically naive colleagues that the upward curve of population growth is ineluctable. But he has failed to convince the scientifically astute of the soundness of his theories. Most biologists have observed that populations fluctuate for various dynamic reasons; the increase in growth may slow and then level off. It may then start to decline, the slope of the curve continuing downward. If it works to the advantage of one's thesis, some investigators tend to employ the natural laws and growth rates but are reluctant to point out that the same rates may be applicable to the opposite slope of the curve as well. That is, the opposite of those factors which cause the line to ascend the graph can cause it to descend the same graph as well. For example, a straight line approach to projections made in 1920 would have resulted in an automobile population in the United States, by 1933, of one billion. Projections for such primary factors as population and energy usage are said to be variable to a limited extent, but the pat predictions of the population fatalists should never have been taken seriously.

During the period of 1967-1972, there appeared to be general acceptance of Ehrlich's notion that our population growth rates were on the upswing to such a point and at such a rate that drastic man-made innovations must be implemented. His studies of the insect had apparently unbalanced his thinking; nevertheless his point of view is widely disseminated in schools, legislatures, and in the media. Many speaking against the validity of this notion are denounced as stupid. However, the more astute and knowledgeable investigators in the field viewed the substance of the reports and the data with caution, for they were not supported by facts, or were distorted when taken into account.

It is useful to examine the birth and population growth rates of the United States because the alarmists charge that too many people live in our industrialized society and that the high consumption of resources has caused serious pollution problems. The picture is actually quite different from that painted by extremists. In early 1973, the Census Bureau forecasted a dramatic drop in high school-age youth in the United States by 1985, because of the sharp decline in the birth rate. It reported that the median age group of Americans had risen from 1971 to 1972. This reverses the downward trend which started in 1950. The number of young people from fourteen to seventeen is forecasted to drop from the 1972 figure of 16.4 million to 14.3 million in 1985. According to the Census Bureau, the population growth rate in 1972 was 0.78, less than half the peak rate of 1.83 in 1956. In 1945, it was 0.71. Even beyond these rates, the actual number of births dropped to 3,256,000 in 1972, a 9 per cent decline in one year.

A follow-up Census Bureau report of May 18, 1973, stated that for the first time in history, the rate at which American women have children declined in 1972 to a rate below the level necessary to sustain zero population growth. The total fertility rate—the number of births per 1,000 women aged fifteen to forty-four years during their lifetime—dropped to about 2,025 in 1972, below the level required for the population eventually to reach a zero growth status if there is no immigration. The fertility rate for the population to achieve zero growth is 2,100 births per 1,000 women during their lifetimes. The figures mean that the 322 million population high, predicted for the United States in the year 2000, has now been reduced by 22 million, and the predicted high is now placed at 300 million.

Britain has also seen a marked decline in her birth rate, to a present rate of 14.6 per 1,000. Like the U.S., it is approaching the zero population growth rate. Japan has already stabilized its rate and is now starting to show concern over manpower for the future. These are not the only nations with the declining birth rates. Denmark, Finland, Sweden, West Germany, Holland, Italy, Czechoslovakia, and Hungary already have declining populations.

The approach to population engineering by Ehrlich and Willing is palatable only to those they can alarm with the specter of disastrous overpopulation, which they have yet to define. Is it what one sees in Holland with 880 people per square mile? Or is it the United Kingdom with its 546 people per square mile? England is a prime example. Very little of England exists today as it was before man arrived on the scene. In England, as elsewhere, man has caused and will continue to cause the extinction of certain species (e.g., wolves). But the English, as bona fide environmentalists, have improved their world artificially. The loss of some species in no way precludes the creation of an esthetically pleasant, though cultivated, environment. Preservationists or extremists find this abhorrent. They are satisfied only with the impossible task of keeping everything exactly as is. England refutes the idea by example—it remains a pleasant place. Even in London many people live in a rural village environment, a cultivated setting. This is not accidental, but the result of artificially improving the natural situation to accommodate the species. Heavy population densities have not created the frightful scenes described by Ehrlich. If the United

States were populated at the same density as the United Kingdom, we could accommodate the entire world's population. Brazil and Bolivia together could do the same. This would leave the rest of the world free to serve as a granary for food production.

There is another more sinister ideology of population control suggested by ZPG advocates, in the name of environmental improvement or "quality of life." Norman Podhoretz tells of his participation in a conference of geneticists, biologists, medical men, writers, philosophers, and theologians to discuss the question of whether mongoloid infants should be permitted to live. Of course the organizers of the conference phrased the problem in considerably less brutal terms. Mr. Podhoretz expected that there would be very little disagreement on the main point. To his amazement, he discovered "a substantial body of sentiment...especially from the scientific community who [were] by no means willing to grant mongoloids an undisputed right to live....Mongoloids are defective, but so are many other kinds of people. Some are blind; some are deaf; some are halt; some are lame; and some have missing limbs; some are given to madness and some are the prey of other diseases. If mongoloids can be put to death, why not these, and if these, why not anyone who fails of absolute perfection?

"Martha Willing speaks of diabetics and dwarfs in exactly the spirit of that ethos. It is this which reveals that we are dealing not merely with an effort to control the size of the population, but with an effort to control its character; not merely with an effort to control the quality of the human 'stock' itself.

"The last time such an effort was made, of course, was by the Nazis, and so horrible were the consequences that many people assumed it would never be

tried again. Evidently however, it has taken only twenty-five years for the eugenic dream to return and now
that it is back, it is back in force, purged of its crackpot
racism, bolstered by an infinitely greater store of knowledge than was ever available to the Nazi scientists in
those primitive days before the discovery of DNA and
RNA, and the cracking of the genetic code: and armed
in the righteousness of a promise to eliminate all heredi-
tary disorders and to save the world at last from human
imperfection itself.

"If this is truly what we are faced with in the ideology
of population control, we all have reason to tremble.
'Use every man after his desert,' said Hamlet, 'and who
should 'scape whippin?' After this then: 'let only the perfect live, and who should 'scape killin?' Who that is, but
the framers of the definition of what perfection
means?"[16]

This discussion provides us with a basis for putting in
logical sequence the events of the past few years: starting with Rachel Carson's *Silent Spring*, Ralph Nader,
Paul Ehrlich, Barry Commoner, Mike Gravel and John
Gofman, and on to environmental extremists' relentless
striving to render the public fearful of what the future
holds and the need to reject in toto science and our social order. They proclaim that since people are the
cause of pollution, more people cause untenable degrees of pollution, and the environmental cleanup issue
becomes exacerbated by the population problem. The
zealots feel compelled to solve the problems through
brutality, including abortion, euthanasia, and limits of
growth.

Some statements of responsible officials confuse attempts to reach logical conclusions. William Ruckelshaus was interviewed by Martin Agronsky on the PBS
in March 1973. "The serious nature of the environ-

mental problems we both share will bring the USSR and the United States closer together." He implied that in having to work together on environmental matters we will somehow improve our relations. Anyone who has seen or read about how the Soviets handle their pollution problems knows that the Soviets have little regard for environmental protection, especially if it might jeopardize any segment of their production or economy. To suggest that we have a mutuality of existence with the Soviets on an environmental basis is absurd.

A Gallup poll of March 11, 1973, reported what has been in the minds of Americans for some time now, and it fits the consensus the author discovered in traveling to many parts of the United States during the past several years.

During the last three and one-half years of this period, I gained a keen awareness of the mood of the public, since I was the manager of a company whose sole concern was pollution control. This included new and exciting techniques developed to rid the environment of hazardous wastes through the use of special repositories and detoxification precedures. Some of the processes involved the use of special soils and subsurface materials, predetermined from detailed studies of the geological substructures, necessary to assure containment. In others we proposed using soil bacteria to degrade certain long-lasting chlorinated hydrocarbons, while in still others we planned using problem sources of carbonaceous wastes to enhance the degradation of other toxic materials. These included sewage, sludge, straw, manure, and other sources of wastes which can serve as food resources for bacteria and toxic materials. The process quietly disposes of hazardous materials using a natural process of degradation to accomplish the task. Advantages include the fact that within a relatively short span of time the soil is ready for reuse again. We planned to use high-temperature, high-pressure incinerators to cleave the molecule of certain toxic materials which do not burn. By cleaving the molecule the parts can be further degraded by conventional means.

Most people seemed enthusiastic about our proposed operation but were reluctant to believe that it was necessary to go to such extreme means and expense. Most felt that the problem was not that grave, that the extremists were saying anything to "scare the public into going along," and that very little of what they were saying was factual. Most felt it was not worth the added time and expense. Many suggested we were trying to make the problem sound more serious than it actually was to create public acceptance of our proposals. They did not realize that actually my most difficult problem was trying to convince governmental officials and their watch dogs that our proposals were sophisticated enough.

The Gallup poll of March 1973 mentioned above showed that only 14 per cent of the public felt that pollution was the most important problem we faced. It ranked below the high cost of living, drugs, crime and lawlessness, race relations, and unemployment.

What is needed is the proper blend of public willingness to support the government and industry with the economic means to clean up. It must be based on workable programs and not some emotion-charged plan-of-the-month, by instant self-appointed experts and newcomers to the field. Confusion must be eliminated with a presentation of the problems and with logical, realistic solutions. The quacks have been indulged too long at too great a cost. It is time to turn them out. We have had enough.

Chapter II
The Nuclear Controversy

Nowhere has the lack of common sense and judgment been more evident than in the activities of environmental extremists who oppose nuclear power, for the field of nuclear energy is "where the action is." Many environmental extremists cut their teeth in some area of the nuclear controversy, starting with the first nuclear weapons testing program in the early 1950s through the Pacific tests, and now into nuclear-electric power plants. Touching matters of science, technology, peace and antiwar activism, health, future population (genetics), energy supplies, pollution, and heat discharges, the subject is ready-made for scare tactics and demagogy.

The fact that the atom was born as a destructive force during war has given it an image apparently difficult to change. An analogy has been made that had gasoline been introduced to the United States during the Civil War, the automobile would have never made the scene in America. A much better analogy is the attitude toward hydrogen as a gas for fuel because of the *Hindenburg* explosion in 1937.

What are the issues and what are the facts concerning each? Although they overlap and smaller issues have been used, they can best be divided into two groups; the early issues and their spokesmen, and the later issues and their spokesmen.

The Early Issues

1. Low-level radiation; the news media; radiation protection standards; Gofman, Tamplin, Sternglass, et al.
2. Thermal effects; fogbanks; radioactive plumes; dead fish and Ed Newman.
3. Nuclear power plant insurance; Price-Anderson Act.
4. *Brookhaven Report* or "WASH 740."

The Later Issues

1. Uranium supplies; the LWR, HTGR, and the "Breeder."
2. Radioactive waste.
3. Emergency Core Cooling, the "Chinese Syndrome," and WASH 1250
4. Fusion CTR (controlled thermonuclear reactors)

One of the earliest reports to fall into the hands of antinuclear spokesmen and still used on occasion is an article published by Robert C. Fadely, a clinical psychologist listing himself as director of research of the Foundation for Environmental Research, Golden, Colorado, concerning a report he made on alleged cancer deaths in the state of Oregon from 1959 to 1964.[1] This article is still referred to throughout the nation. It alarms many people who wonder about the dangers of nuclear energy. These cancer deaths are supposed to be caused by the operation of the Hanford nuclear facility in Washington, on the Columbia River. Fadely attempts to show that the alleged increase in cancer and leukemia mortality is associated with the radioactive level of downstream water in the Columbia River; that it is higher as one goes farther upstream, closer to Hanford.

Fadely states his hypotheses in two parts. First, that malignant tumor rates of populations in counties bordering the Columbia correlate significantly with the (arbitrarily derived) degree of exposure based on his location on the river. He implies that radionuclides are injected into the Columbia by the Hanford operation, and that people along the path of the river water flow uniformly consume this water. The USPHS,[2] the Washington State Health Department, and the Oregon State Board of Health conducted studies to evaluate the problem, since it was raised by Fadely in this manner.

The exposure mechanisms along coastal counties are complex; no one considers the meteorological transport from sea to air of dissolved material possible. Fadely describes the cancer rate per 100,000 population in cities along the river and infers that at these sites cancer developed at a higher rate than at others. This is not the case. The total cancer rate per 100,000 population in the cities mentioned by the author in the years 1959 to 1963 was compared to the rates in New Orleans, Laredo, Texas, St. Paul, and Chattanooga. These rates are of the same order as the cities and coastal counties that Fadely described.

The author did not deal with the alleged contamination affecting the counties in Washington bordering the Columbia River just across from Oregon. A letter from Dr. Bernard Bucove, Washington State Director of Health, sharply criticized the findings as erroneous and unscientific, among other things. His letter takes issue with the thesis in general and challenges it on ten specific points. A similar letter backing up Dr. Bucove was also sent by Dr. Raymond Wilcox, the Oregon State Health Officer. Dr. Paul Kotin led a team of investigators from the National Cancer Institute through the en-

tire study and completely refuted the charges made by
Fadely.

It is appalling that Fadely confined his study to the
counties bordering the Columbia River and did not go
to other counties in central and southern Oregon for
similar comparisons. Had he done so, he would have
found that a similar increase such as he found occurs in
central and southern counties; there is also no consistent trend for the years 1940 to 1960, in the counties
mentioned by the author, that suggests a consistent increase in cancer mortality from the years prior to the
operation of Hanford up until the most recent six-year
period.

The USPHS concluded that there appeared to be no
demonstrated relationship between the location of an
individual developing cancer and his distance from
Hanford. The Washington State Department of Health
study for the period of 1959 to 1964 shows that Benton
and Franklin counties, which border directly on the
Hanford reservation and use Columbia River water,
rank third and fourth lowest in cancer mortality among
all thirty-nine counties in the state of Washington. The
Fadely article was published in the *Journal of Environmental Health*, the organ of the National Association of
Sanitarians, a group primarily concerned with environmental sanitation. This article apparently did not under-
go review by experts in the area of biostatistics,
epidemiology, and radiological effects, although such review is commonly a prerequisite to publication in reputable scientific journals. Final results of the study by the
USPHS have been concurred in by all the aforemen-
tioned agencies and are as follows: "Results of the study
reveal that in both states, mortality rates for all forms of
cancer combined have been consistently below those
mortality rates for the United States white population.

Both states have had consistent excess of leukemia mortality, but the excess was present before the Hanford operation started. No important mortality trends were observed in the individual counties in either state. No evidence was found that persons living down stream from the Hanford reservation along the Pacific Coast have had an excessive risk of deaths from cancer in general or from leukemia in particular, yet stories of misinformation disproved by all competent and responsible agencies continue to be used in hearings and meetings as factual data."

The Press

The real assault on the radiation protection standards first came through the press and the electronic news media. Alarm, sensation, and fright keynoted their stories during the early period of 1967 to 1969. With no well-known names involved, it was the press that presented the horrors of nuclear power as the possible end of the world as we know it and as the producer of disastrous effects on the environment from which there would be no return.

One example was an early Sternglass report, unabashedly published in the *New York Times* on July 24, 1969, entitled, *"Excerpts From The Death Of All Children."* The article is included later in this chapter where its falsehoods are detailed. Sensationalism was attached to anything associated with radioactivity. Example: a newspaper headline read, "Radioactive Waste Kills Man." The story beneath it was about a man who was run over and killed by a truck that happened to be carrying radioactive material. Example: a non-nuclear accident at the Surry Nuclear Power Plant killed two Virginia Electric and Power Company employees. While

the reactor was shut down for routine maintenance, two
technicians in an altogether different part of the plant
were burned by steam from a venting system (used by
all steam plants). Someone who described himself as an
environmentalist told the local newspaper that the
deaths were caused by a "runaway" reactor. The Associated Press, the *Washington Post*, and others carried the
story that radiation was involved. Too late to be carried
effectively to counter the story (twenty-one days later),
the final report emphasized that "no radiation or contamination was encountered or released during the
course of the steam system venting incident or as a result of it." The Richmond papers, Associated Press, and
the *Post* then ran the final article.[3]

At about the same time, NBC on its *Today* show reported a "crisis" in the Minneapolis area the weekend of
November 20, 1971. This was because of "radioactive"
water being released to the Mississippi River by the
Monticello Plant of the Northern States Power Company. The sensational report lost its glamor and newswor-
thiness when the press learned the facts, which were
quite different. The plant had been shut down for routine maintenance before the winter power peak, and it
was desirable to drain 500,000 gallons of water from its
dry well. On Friday 10,000 gallons of water were released, and even though the water was well below the
proposed stringent state standards (which were never
enacted due to a Supreme Court ruling), the story resulted in page-one headlines in the local press and drew
the attention of the national press and networks. On
Sunday, Northern States released 40,000 gallons of water from the fuel storage pool, which had never even
contained any fuel. This water had been recycled and
demineralized, and it contained less radioactivity than
the first 10,000 gallons had. By the end of the week, the

Minneapolis Star viewed the commotion as "much unwarranted fuss."[4]

Further impact was generated from the magazine articles and books which were published early in the game. These became the handbooks for the fanatics and antinuclear zealots and their news media sponsors. The press used every opportunity and technique to bring to readers any report alleging that nuclear energy was hazardous. The first to make a significant impact, *The Nukes Are In Hot Water,* appeared in *Sports Illustrated,* a not very scientific journal, on January 20, 1969.

It was an uneducated and coarse treatment of nuclear power written by senior editor Robert H. Boyle. He attacked the safety of nuclear power, pointed out the deadly thermal effects, and used the usual arguments of the "critical" nature of a reactor. He probably reached the largest audience of any article yet published. Because of its lack of balance and its inflammatory nature, many knowledgeable people tried to have *Sports Illustrated* review its information and spend some time studying the issue. It was not done. Mr. Boyle's report was left standing, to cause many thousands of Americans to question nuclear energy with false information.

In a critique of the article, Mr. Wadsworth Likely stated that Boyle's article was a masterpiece in using the English language to distort the actual picture and create an image of disaster.[5] Almost all effects of an undesirable nature were described. All possibilities were mentioned using the word "can" or "could." Boyle stated, "thermal pollution from a single nuclear plant can do all sorts of damage to the receiving waters." Mr. Boyle knew as well as anyone else that thermal pollution from any source can damage receiving waters. He showed no instance where a nuclear plant *had* discharged water in such a manner as to be guilty of thermal pollution. In fact, if all industries discharged their cooling water in the manner that nuclear power plants have designed their water discharges, thermal pollution would be rare. State and federal regulatory agencies have very carefully policed the thermal pollution problems for some time as far as new facilities coming on stream are concerned, and specifically in regard to nuclear plants.

Mr. Boyle further distorted the facts with such positive assertions as, "thermal pollution decreases the dissolved oxygen content, increases the toxicity of pollutants, increases the metabolic rate of fish and other organisms, changes their behavior or interferes with their reproduction cycles, and often kills them outright. A plant near a fish spawning nursery ground could be deadly. All fish or other organisms can be sucked up the intake pipe and given a fast trip through a condenser." He saddles the reader with the impression, not backed by facts, that nuclear power plants are unique in this regard and singularly exhaust hot water into streams, create pollution problems, and kill fish.

At about this same time, a sensationalized book, *The Careless Atom*, almost entirely false in substance, was published. It became one of the most widely read books among those interested in nuclear energy. Its author, Sheldon Novick, has no qualifications as a scientist or engineer in the nuclear field. Nuclear experts from the scientific community found little to approve and much to disprove.

Mr. Richard F. Lewis,[6] managing editor of *Science and Public Affairs,* the *Bulletin of Atomic Scientists,* stated: "Novick's implication that the AEC has only a perfunctory interest in nuclear safety and is allowing manufacturers to spread nuclear hazards across the land, is not likely to impress anyone who has followed the interminable and exhaustive hearings conducted by AEC examiners on applications of plants to be built and installed. In his eagerness to make a case for atomic carelessness, Novick in his field generally ends up a very dangerous fellow. Novick was even piped aboard the NBC *Today Show* on February 24, 1969, to discuss his book. NBC, with no specially assigned science editors to evaluate the qualifications of a 'scientist' such as Novick, showed little interest in ascertaining if such a person was qualified to treat a subject in any manner. In presenting *The Careless Atom* with Novick, the NBC *Today Show* treated viewers to a massive dose of misinformation and downgraded the significant potential benefits of the peaceful applications of nuclear energy. They helped undermine the public confidence through ignorance, since they did not understand the extensive and systematic provisions for safeguarding the public from any ill effects of peaceful nuclear power generating facilities."

Another book, *Perils Of The Peaceful Atom,* by Elizabeth Hogan and Richard Curtis, was published in July 1969. The book encouraged the public to stop all nuclear projects. The authors describe themselves as free lance writers; neither has any scientific or technical background. The authors' first article, "The Myth Of The Peaceful Atom," appeared in the March 6, 1969, issue of *Natural History.* Most of its eight pages dwelt on the Brookhaven Report, the Price-Anderson Act, and a theory on the concentration of radioactivity in the food chain. This article made no pretense of objectivity. Nuclear technology is called lethal; accumulated traces of radioactivity are described as a tidy package of poison. It states that the Texas City Disaster of 1947 was an appalling catastrophe and adds that it did not begin to approach the potential havoc that could be wreaked by a nuclear explosion in one of the plants now being constructed in several American cities. Of course the Texas City disaster had nothing to do with nuclear energy. The article received a lot of comment from nuclear scientists who generally described it as one-sided and sensational and completely devoid of fact. Unfortunately, this article has been reprinted and circulated throughout the country. The first generation of nuclear power opponents used it as a resource document.

Perils Of The Peaceful Atom is even more sensational and less objective than the 1969 article. The chapter titles, for instance, include: "The Goose That Laid the Radioactive Egg"; "Nuclear Roulette"; and "The Thousand Year Curse." The authors describe the Fermi reactor fuel incident as an event as close to Armageddon as this country has ever known. The book is described by Drs. James G. Beckerly and R. Norman Hilberry, eminent scientists, as a strictly biased, misleading, sensational, and political tract.

Following the publication of *Perils Of The Peaceful Atom*, Curtis began a speaking tour, visiting antipollution leagues and conservation society meetings and appearing on a number of radio talk shows in the Northeast. While he usually described himself and his coauthor as laymen in scientific areas, he spoke at length about the perils of nuclear energy and tried to answer even technical questions on the subject.

Throughout their careers as antinuclear proponents and in their writing, these authors reveal their technical ignorance. They do not understand fission or radiation measurement; they do not understand power reactors and how they generate power; and their technical shortcomings are apparent in every subject they touch upon. They discuss available uranium and fuel supplies of the future and other future energy resources, atomic submarines, atomic wastes, and thermal pollution.[7]

In the meantime, those who were countering the barrage of phony charges were obviously of a different
background in both educational expertise and experience. Some of the most outstanding, experienced, reputable nuclear scientists were trying to keep the record
straight about nuclear energy. Their views were rarely if
ever picked up by the newspapers and even more rarely
on national television. It was up to the Atomic Industrial Forum and the bona fide members of the scientific
nuclear community to do the best they could to get the
truth across. Here is a sample of the different points of
view that were being given but were not being publicized:

Dr. G. Hoyt Whipple,[8] professor of Radiological
Health at the University of Michigan: "The threat of
nuclear power is that public opinion, uninformed and
misinformed, will delay the acceptance of this form of
energy until we have wasted our reserves of fossil fuels
and fouled our world in fear of the imagined dangers of
radiation."

Dr. Edward Teller:[9] "One should insist that nuclear
reactors be installed as rapidly as possible, thereby reducing air pollution. I would not like to say anything
that may slow down the safe introduction of these reactors, and they indeed can be introduced safely."

Merril Eisenbud,[10] New York City's former EPA administrator: "A few individuals from the scientific community have capitalized on the general credibility of
scientists to obtain the ear of the public. The traditional
scientific method of preparing well-documented papers
for review by peers and publication in scientific journals
is being bypassed....Visibility is achieved by means of
the newspaper, the public meeting...these media are
excellent for the airing of views on public issues, but

public understanding of the issues might be better served if some way could be found to disassociate the scientist from special privilege when he speaks outside his field of specialization and when he bypasses the time-tested methods developed by scientists to assure the credibility of scientific information....And if responsible scientific voices will refrain from offering partial information in a form calculated to frighten, the people will understand the choices that are presented."

The Radiation Protection Standards

The first serious opposition to nuclear power development was an assault on the radiation protection standards used in medicine, industry, and academia. Understanding all aspects of the radiation hazard requires extensive study and specialized training. A discussion of these protection criteria is worthwhile to help in illustrating the intense care and thought that have been given the subject as well as the experience and research generated over many years which went into their development. Of special significance is the meticulous evaluation of this data by more bodies of scientific experts than ever examined any health hazard. These scientists represent national and international bodies working separately and jointly to bring all collective information together for final agreement.

The extremists are not recognized by the radiation community as thoughtful, analytical, or professional radiation specialists. This includes such newcomers as Drs. A. G. Tamplin and H. P. Metzger, as well as better known personages such as Drs. Gofman, Abrahamson, Pauling, Weil, et al. Many are relative newcomers to the field of radiation health and safety, thereby lacking the depth of experience and knowledge to make valid criticism. Some had preconceived notions and set out to interpret the literature by using other people's work to turn the results to their own purposes.

From personal conversations with both Tamplin and Metzger, the author knows that neither understood the biological effects nor radiation health and safety as translated in the official radiation protection standards. This is understandably frustrating to them and is perhaps the cause of their extreme reaction. For instance, units of radiation measurements are difficult for many, but it is necessary to understand them well to recognize the different hazards talked of so freely, and especially if one intends to play the role of a constructive critic. To understand them is to gain an understanding of why cancer and leukemia may be predictable products of high radiation exposure, but why, conversely, they can only be associated with very low exposure by theoretical and statistical extrapolation, which shows that the smaller the radiation dose, the less likelihood that radiation is in fact a prime cause.

Consider a totally different mechanism of injury: the cause and effect of propelling a man through the air at 75 m.p.h. against a solid concrete wall. He may suffer grave physical damage and probable death. The high velocity and force of impact will produce a predictable result. The same man walking at a speed of 1½ m.p.h., into the same concrete wall, may end up only leaning or resting against it and thereby suffer no detectable physical injury.

At lower and lower speeds, injury becomes less probable. The lack of velocity and force of impact are the two key factors. In this sense high radiation exposure levels may cause radiation injury such as cancer or leukemia, as does the combination of high velocity (75 m.p.h.) and force of impact produce physical injury; low-level radiation such as background or nuclear power plant levels is not likely to produce detectable radiation injury even as the slow-speed (1½ m.p.h.) impact is not likely to produce physical injury.

Most critics, and those who believe them, react to the attack on the radiation protection standards with a knee-jerk response, demanding more restrictions and reducing the numbers, without knowing what the numbers mean or how they were derived. The most often-cited numerical reduction has been by a factor of ten, with no rhyme or reason attached to it. It is the same rationale that a traffic safety council might apply in requiring that speeds be reduced from 10 m.p.h. to 1 m.p.h. in a school zone on the ground that reducing the speed from 30 to 10 m.p.h. had previously improved safety. Now the critics are calling for yet another reduction, which would amount to reducing the speed limit from 1 m.p.h. to .1 m.p.h., to guarantee absolute safety. Such a reduction is useless.

Radiation levels at nuclear plant boundaries are so low now that further reduction would have no significant effect, detectable or otherwise. If the present standards do not provide adequate protection against radiation, then according to an Environmental Protection Agency study, New York's Penn Central commuters should start driving to work. Anything to avoid Grand Central Station. In February 1971, Representative Melvin Price of Illinois wrote EPA Administrator William Ruckelshaus that he had heard reports that Grand Central exceeded the present levels of the federal guideline for population exposure to all sources of radiation, other than natural background and medical applications.[11] In April, Ruckelshaus wrote Price that the reports were indeed true. An EPA representative examined the station and estimated that if a person stood at the red-cap stand in the Vanderbilt Avenue Arcade for twenty-four hours a day, 365 days a year, he would receive an exposure of 525 mr; for a forty-hour week, fifty weeks a year, the exposure would be 120 mr. Continuous exposure in other locations in Grand Central were reported at 263 mr, 105 mr, and the lowest figure, 79 mr. The reason for the "high" exposure levels, Ruckelshaus explained, is the granite used in the building, which is also used in the Cloisters, and the United Nations building in New York, the Customs House in New London, and Grand Square in Mexico City. He also pointed out that the granite came from a quarry at Millstone Point, Connecticut, which is now the site of a nuclear power plant and that the quarry alone—before the plant began operating—registered about 20 mr. per year.

The scientific community is concerned about "background" radiation and has studied it intensively. It will continue to demand a great deal of study because it is interesting, and there are areas where information about it is useful; but the most study has been on the practical aspects of radiation health and safety as it applies to radiation workers and to the public at large.

Time is the second component of radiation effects on a biological system. None of the opponents of the present radiation standards cares to discuss or take into account the time factor which is as important as the level of radiation. An exposure sufficient to produce cancer or leukemia in a one-day period may not produce the illness if divided into thirty separate small daily doses. Furthermore, if the exposure adequate to produce cancer or leukemia in one day is spread over 300 days or 3,000 days or 30,000 days then the effects become less and less significant, in each instance diminishing with the increase in time. In this regard, the radiation levels close to nuclear power plants are so low that there is no adequate way to compare them to hazardous situations except that the exposure of pregnant women to X-rays (during medical examinations) has resulted in an increase in incidence of leukemia in the exposed children. However, the doses at which this effect has been seen are such that a woman living on the property line of a nuclear plant would have to remain pregnant for four hundred years in order to accumulate the same radiation exposure as that from the X-ray series. The critics of radiation protection standards conveniently ignore these "real-life situations" which help to explain the magnitude of the issue. Yet, the very low doses which Tamplin, Gofman, and their proponents are alarmed over, even though insignificant, become absurdly more insignificant with time.

Critics also speak of radiation effects as being cumulative, as if not reversible. The healing and repair of burn damage is not equivalent, but it is a good analogy. If left to repair away from further radiation exposure, a body may heal almost entirely, and many of the genetic effects from high doses will be repaired as well. In general, radiation injury repair occurs, and with time the injury may be reduced to almost zero. The small residual effect remaining is nothing when compared to the biological effects of such "hazards" as sunlight, eating different foods, sleep variations, and other environmental factors.

On reviewing the history of radiation protection and effects, one finds mountains of data published over the past seventy-five years, which have been subjected to sharp criticism by scientists working on radiation effects and protection as their life's work, and who live by these standards. It is not a field that was only recently discovered and developed as a playground or pasture by the likes of Metzger and Tamplin.

Radiation health and safety have created a new field of "Health Physics," a field which requires a background and considerable knowledge of chemistry, physics, biology, and medicine. It deals with different types of radiation, units of measurement, measuring devices, and fundamental medical and genetic effects. Understanding relative dosages, intensity, and long-term effects at low levels requires intensive study of these subjects. A statement such as "no radiation is better than any radiation" is a difficult and possibly erroneous concept. As an example, a chest X-ray may deliver a measurable dose of radiation, and there is awareness that the body is absorbing all of it. But if tuberculosis or lung cancer is detected, the radiation dose is insignificant compared to the life-saving information obtained from the X-ray picture. This is an illustration of "benefit versus risk." The benefits of the detection of a lung disease versus an undetectable radiation risk make it irrational not to utilize such a valuable diagnostic tool. The same benefit-versus-risk formula is applicable to anything done by man. In the case of nuclear power, the benefits so totally and overwhelmingly outweigh risks that it is more than irrational not to utilize this source of energy; it is lunacy.

Chronologically it began when Wilhelm Conrad Roentgen discovered X-rays in 1895, Henri Becquerel discovered radioactivity (uranium) in 1896, and Marie Sklodowska Curie discovered radium in 1898. Their discoveries had new properties which they enthusiastically sought to learn more about. The radiation properties which they could not see but could detect with photographic plates were unique to be sure. Roentgen found he could use his "X-rays" for seeing bone through flesh. Early experimenters discovered that the skin of their hands reddened (erythema) and its degree could be directly related to the time they allowed their hands to be exposed to the newly discovered energy. The damage from radiation is produced by the ionization of the atom or molecule in body tissues instead of by heat. As a matter of comparison, a lethal exposure of gamma radiation may raise the body temperature by only 0.01 degrees C.

Those who discovered radioactivity and their colleagues learned that protection was necessary for the user's hands, which became injured if the materials were handled too much. This was characterized by the graded erythema, mentioned above, related to the time or constancy of exposure to an X-ray beam. A chronological order of the main events in the evolution of radiation protection and measurements follows:

1902   "If a standardized photographic plate is not darkened in seven minutes, one is not in a harmful radiation area."

1915   "If there is a thickness of lead thick enough to prevent darkening of a standard film then the radiation hazard is of no significance."

1925   "The operator of a radiation device is safe if in a thirty day period he receives 1/100th of an erythema dose." (This amounted to about 200 milliroentgen per day.)

1928   The International Committee on Radiation Protection was created.

1929   A national organization was created; the National Committee on Radiation Protection.

1931   An ICRP (International Committee on Radiation Protection) report suggested "A tolerable Maximum Permissible Dose of 200 milliroentgen per day."

1934   The ICRP established 0.2 Roentgen per day as the tolerance dose in tissue.

1936   The United States Advisory Commission on
       Radiation Protection advised "100 milliroent-
       gen per day in air as the recommended Max-
       imum Permissible Dose." There was no
       reason other than to accommodate higher
       energies of X-ray machines being used more
       and more. This was done to reduce the dose
       to bone marrow.

1940   The radiation protection program directors
       of the Manhattan Project adopted 100 milli-
       roentgen per day as its Maximum Permissible
       Dose.

1946   The Manhattan Project reduced its Maxi-
       mum Permissible Dose to 300 milliroentgen
       per week.

1949   The NCRP adopted 0.3 rem or 300 rem
       (roentgen equivalent man) per week as its
       Maximum Permissible Dose.

1950   The ICRP adopted the 300 mr per week as
       the recommended Maximum Permissible
       Dose based on the increased use of X-ray
       and nuclear materials. This amounted to a
       maximum total dose of fifteen roentgen per
       year.

1951   The 100 mr per week was justified as a prop-
       er Maximum Permissible Dose and the provi-
       so added "a total accumulated dose for the
       year could not exceed 5x (N-18) roentgen per
       year." N and 18 both in years. The term rem
       had now started to come in more and by the
       time of the next report it was used exclusive-
       ly. It more adequately related to actual dos-
       age, for it is a unit of biological dose.

1959   The Federal Radiation Council was estab-
       lished.

1959 to 1971 A chronology of main events from 1959 to 1971 is overshadowed by the tremendous activity in every phase of radiation health and safety. At both the national and international levels, intensive review of new and existing data was accelerating. This activity resulted in the publication of three documents:

1971 The National Committee on Radiation Protection and Measurements issued NCRP Report Number 39 on Basic Radiation Protection Criteria. This was the result of the review and evaluation of all of the research and biological experience accumulated during the period 1958 to 1971. The 135-page document updates the information that had been published in the earlier reports. It retained the 100 rem per week and 5 x (N-18) since overwhelming data showed this to be appropriate safe maximum permissible dose. (The formulation of the 5 x (N-18) equation applies only to operators or radiation workers. This is referred to as the occupational exposure rather than the population exposure, described later. The 5 rem yearly dose was arrived at by evaluation of many applicable factors. The NCRP report included them in all exhaustive analysis and investigations.

1972 The National Academy of Sciences, National Research Council published its report of the Advisory Committee on the Biological Effects of Ionizing Radiations, on the Effects on Populations of Exposure to Low Levels of Ionizing Radiation. In summary it reinforced in great depth the NCRP Report Number 39.

1973   The United Nations Scientific Committee on the Effects of Atomic Radiation report was published and in effect reinforced the Radiation Standards in more detail than did all the reports published to date.

National and international bodies conduct their reviews and evaluations in a thoughtful and emotion-free atmosphere of professional deliberation. In the United States, the National Committee on Radiation Protection and Measurements consists of sixty-four leading and recognized scientists from every area of radiation research and representing many different professional societies. It is monitored by separate radiation protection agencies, including several in the federal government. The EPA, DOD, FDA, JCAE, and NASA all have radiation protection groups that participate in the establishment of protection guidelines. The AEC establishes no radiation standards but, rather, adopts those set by the NCRP or other official standard-setting bodies. The NCRP has a Collaborating Group of Organizations concerned with units, measurements, quantities, or protection, with which it maintains liaison. These are:

American Academy of Dermatology
American Association of Physicists in Medicine
American College of Radiology
American Dental Association
American Industrial Hygiene Association
American Insurance Association
American Medical Association
American Nuclear Society
American Public Health Association
American Radium Society
American Roentgen Ray Society

American Society of Radiologic Technologists
American Veterinary Medical Association
Association of University Radiologists
Atomic Industrial Forum
Genetics Society of America
Health Physics Society
Industrial Medical Association
National Bureau of Standards
National Electrical Manufacturers Association
Radiation Research Society
Radiological Society of North America
Society of Nuclear Medicine
United States Air Force
United States Army
United States Atomic Energy Commission
United States Navy
United States Public Health Service

All of these bodies, plus the ICRP (International Committee on Radiation Protection), IAEA (International Atomic Energy Agency), and UNSCEAR (United Nations Scientific Committee on the Effects of Atomic Radiation) concur in the health and safety standards now in use in the United States. Those who challenge the radiation protection criteria are deceiving the public when they assert that nothing is known on this subject or that the guidelines are not properly arrived at. These same critics have been unwilling either to submit their findings which they claim to have or to accept the evaluations of the NCRP or other official bodies.

So important is the necessity to demonstrate the comprehensive study of radiation that a copy of the Table of Contents from NCRP Number 39 is presented.[12] Some of the subjects have been excluded from this presentation to conserve space, but the majority of the material is given. As for biological effects, it illustrates that nothing is overlooked.

BASIC RADIATION PROTECTION CRITERIA. NCRP REPORT NUMBER 39 CONTENTS (extracted)

PART I—BACKGROUND AND SUPPORTING MATERIAL

Chapter 1—Radiation and Man

Attitudes Toward Natural Radiation
Radiation as a Resource for Man
Basic Approaches to Radiation Protection
Outline of Radiation Effects

Chapter 2—Radiation Exposure Conditions That May Require Consideration.

Kinds of Radiation Exposure
Natural Radiation
Radiation from Medical Procedures
Radiations Applied in Research on Human Subjects
Occupational Irradiation
Man-made Environmental Radiation
Radiation Control
Access Controls for Controlled Areas
Areas Immediately Adjacent to a Controlled Area
Categories of Individuals Controlled
Individuals Occupationally Exposed
The General Public

Chapter 3—Basic Biological Factors

Framework of Biological Studies
Age
Protracted Exposure; Fractionation
Protracted Exposure; Dose Rate
Repair
Organism Sensitivity
Cell Sensitivity
Effects of Low and High LET Radiations
Relative Biological Effectiveness (RBE)
External Irradiation of the Whole Body
Dose From Incorporated Radioactive Nuclides

A 5 rem per year occupational limit evolved following years of research and medical histories. It is based on the best evidence of radiation effects on mammalian cells. Experiments with radiation exposures have shown that the total dose required to sensitize all mammalian cells given in fractional doses for the longest number of days, so as not to produce an acute radiation syndrome effect, is approximately 165 rems administered over a thirty-seven day period. If the total dose or the length of time is varied, the mammalian cell sensitivity syndrome cannot be observed consistently.

The first safeguard provided by the standards prohibits occupational exposure under age eighteen (except
from background and medical radiation). The usual
working age of a radiation employee is age eighteen to
sixty years, resulting in a forty-two year working span.
Five rems per year amounts to a total of 210 rems. By
extending the fractionation time from 37 days to 16,000
days (42 years) and reducing the exposure rate from 37
days to 0.01 rem or less in 37 days, detectable effects are
reduced to potentially zero, either grossly or microscopically. An additional proviso in the radiation protection
standards allows no more than 3 rems accumulated exposure in any thirteen consecutive weeks which, if it
were to occur, allows that worker only 2 rems exposure
for the next thirty-nine weeks. This assures worker safety by allowing only a low daily exposure rate and prevents the obtaining of the total yearly exposure in a
shorter time. The 5 rem limit applies to the critical organs as well; this includes the blood-forming organs,
gonads, and lenses of the eye. This is restrictive in the
minimal sense and not permissive; i.e., 5 rems to the
whole body or critical organ and not 5 rems to both. A
worker must wear radiation measuring devices as part of
the law governing his employment.

The gonad is discussed most frequently as a critical
organ, especially by the scare artists. The total population pool is considered in the standards, but radiation
workers will be discussed first, for they represent the
principal target group. The great concern over genetic
effects started with the work by Mueller in 1926. By
1955 there was a good understanding as well as an acute
awareness of the genetic effects of radiation. The National Academy of Science—National Council on Radiation Protection Reports on Genetic Considerations
stated that in the opinion of the body of qualified genet-

icists, a total exposure of 50 rems to age thirty years was acceptable for the occupational worker. This opinion assumed that genetic damage was directly proportional to the total accumulated exposure. This was an overly conservative approach in view of recent knowledge, but the standards have not been relaxed.

The occupational exposure of 5 x (N-18), or 5 rems x (30-18) = 5 x 12 = 60 rems, is comparable with the 50 rems from the NAS–NRC study. Considering even the extremely unlikely case in which a worker is exposed from ages eighteen to age thirty to a total of 50 rems, the impact of this exposure would be lessened because:

1. his exposure is gradual, and at the time he fathers his first children he would have received much less than the 50 rems total, and

2. his wife would not have been exposed at all, and this effectively reduces the impact by half.

At the same time, the number of radiation workers in relation to the total population is very small and therefore has very little effect on the collective genetic material. It is important to recognize that a condition of employment as a radiation worker depends on whether or not the spouse is also involved in the radiation industry. If so, employment is deferred, and the spouse must seek nonradiation employment.

There are three other major factors, among many that differentiate a person occupationally exposed from a person in a group of the population at large, as provided in NCRP Report Number 39:

"1. The radiation worker accepts some small degree of risk, which is balanced against benefits to him, based on competent technical appraisal. By contrast, the member of the population has radiation exposure imposed on him above the background level. Theoretically he can exert influence as a member of the population to

control the additions. The benefits, if any, accrue to society, not specifically to the individual. A natural consequence is that the exposure risk to persons in the
general population should be markedly lower than to
occupationally exposed persons.

"2. There is a conscious selection of occupationally
exposed individuals. Minors are excluded. Exposure is
limited to adults between age eighteen and normal re-
tirement age. Pre-employment medical examination to
exclude those with abnormal blood cell patterns or other characteristics that might be confused with radiation
effects is feasible and proper. Periodic examinations may
detect beginning reversible anomalies due to irradiation.
It is possible to exclude fertile women from radiation
tasks to avoid irradiation of fetuses. It is possible to as-
sign specific tasks preferentially to people beyond repro-
ductive age to reduce total genetic risk. By contrast,
exposure of the population at large influences persons
of all ages, including the sensitive embryonic stages,
children whose uptake of radioactive material may be
high at a time of fairly high radiosensitivity and people
in all states of health. A conservative approach dictates
that exposure for the public be less than for radiation
workers because the range of ages and possible individual deleterious response is much wider.

"3. The number of persons exposed is a prime factor
in genetic considerations, and where all individual exposures are low, the principal residual risk is the integrated
effect on the population's gene pool. Under these circumstances, the relevant exposure index of genetic effects is some measure such as the genetically significant
dose (GSD) of the population. It is unnecessary to measure individual exposures, provided that group averages
can be reliably ascertained. For example, while it is
deemed appropriate for male radiation workers to accept

an average of 5 rems per year, such a dose equivalent for the entire population would be judged improper by geneticists. Thus, the conventional occupational limit implicitly involves a limit on the percentage of radiation workers in the total population. Achievable limits for population exposure do not introduce limitations to occupational exposure in the foreseeable expansion of radiation use."

The NCRP used the accumulated radiation exposure research and medical history for a long period of time, from 1900 to 1955. This data showed that 100 mr per day or 25 to 30 rems per year and even higher limits which were allowed by the international community for the same period produced no detectable bodily injury to those exposed at these levels.

The next standard for radiation protection applies to specific exposure limits for individual members of the public; not occupationally exposed:

"The limit for the critical organs (or the whole body as well) of an individual not occupationally exposed shall be 0.5 rem in any one year, in addition to natural radiation plus medical and dental exposure." "This amounts to one-tenth of the maximum permissible occupational dose. For instance, if one, two, or several of a group wish to visit a nuclear facility or a radiation-controlled area, they must be furnished radiation measuring devices or be logged in and out of the facility and controlled, as if they were radiation workers; or a radiation monitoring system must be present to show they received not more than 0.5 rem during any one year. If they exceed this or visit other facilities, they are in violation of this protection limit and denied further access. They represent a very small portion of the population as a whole."

The last set of radiation protection criteria applies to

the "average" population exposure limit. This is assuming that each member of the population receives this exposure from man-made sources. The exposure to the gonads (and other critical organs and whole body) of the United States population from all sources of radiation (other than natural radiation and radiation from healing arts) shall not exceed a yearly average of 0.17 rem (170 mrem) per person. This equals one-third of the 0.5 rem whole body exposure of the individual member of the public at large discussed above and one-thirtieth of the occupational exposure limit. This means that for a group (village or community), living near a nuclear facility, all other criteria are preempted by the average population exposure limit of 0.17 rem per year. NCRP report Number 39 adds the following comments: "No specific evidence can be established that would seem to warrant further reduction of average or individual dose limits for members of the public at this time. The low dose and low dose rate of radiation exposure of the population still provides adequate safety factors. The idealized objective of having public exposure, in addition to that from natural radiation, as close to zero as is reasonably possible, of course, remains. In this connection, it must be pointed out again that although these limits do not include the contributions of radiation from the healing arts, there is a clear intention to encourage their reduction to the lowest practical levels."

In reference to the gonadal exposure consideration, the NCRP comments as follows: "Either formulation is somewhat more restrictive than the NAS-BEAR [National Academy of Science-Biological Effects of Atomic Radiation] recommendation of 1956 [above, 50 rem gonadal exposure] in spite of the fact that radiation research since then indicates that genetic damage is probably less than calculated, the continuation of this conservative position is justified by the residual uncertainties in translating data from animal to man, and by the demonstrated practicability of the limit."

This last opinion is derived from one of the most massive and prestigious animal experiments ever conducted by man, the genetic effects research program being conducted by Drs. Russell and Russell at the Oak Ridge National Laboratory. One experiment alone used 50,000 mice; gonads of each were microscopically examined in detail. Many other thousands are being used to develop additional data to that already evaluated. In October 1969 during a seminar on nuclear energy at Burlington, Vermont,[13] Dr. W. L. Russell discussed the recent findings about the genetic effects of low-level radiation: "We would now predict that the risks are about one-sixth of what they were before we found these discoveries. The permissible doses have not been raised since we made the discovery. The conclusion, I think, is that we are now using a permissible dose that appears to have only one-sixth as much genetic risk as we thought at the time when that dose was fixed."

No effects from these low exposures and rates have ever been detected in adult populations of both human beings and animals, though a very careful examination for them has been continuously made over the years. In Hiroshima and Nagasaki no effects have been found at doses below approximately 25,000 to 50,000 millirems. In closely observed animal populations, no effects have ever been found at or below dose rates of several thousand millirems per day given over their entire life span. Several experiments on large populations of animals given exposures of approximately 1,000 millirems per day actually *increased* the life span of the animals.

Based on the massive amounts of data collected on the millions of worker man-hours for over seventy years used for establishing present standards, it is still impossible to attribute any additional cancer cases from very low exposures, except by empirical association or by theoretical and statistical extrapolation downward. This downward extrapolation injects conservative and "safe-side" errors in every case where a conflict arises and at the same time excludes the repair of tissue and cells. This repair is well documented and recognized, but it is *not* used by the scientific community to raise the permissible radiation levels. The author is not proposing they do so, but only points out that these important new findings and "safe-side" errors in radiation health and safety standards should be known by the public and given credit by the critics.

The present data can only show an increase in cancer or leukemia of one case per one million deaths per year. By the time one reaches the age of fifty-five, the chance of this causing his death has been lost in the noise and static of other more probable causes of death, and by age sixty, is totally lost, having no significance. For a comparison, examine the following tables of death chance probabilities and United States population dose:

Chart I: Chance of Serious Injury or Death Per Year

Auto accident (disability)	1	chance in	100
Cancer, all types and causes	1	" "	700
Auto death	1	" "	4,000
Fire death	1	" "	25,000
The "Pill" death	1	" "	25,000
Drowning	1	" "	30,000
Electrocution	1	" "	200,000
Reactor Emanations at site boundary (5 to 10 mrem/yr)	Less than 1	" "	1,000,000
Average for population within 50 miles of reactor	Less than 1	" "	10,000,000

Chart II: United States Population Exposure, Year 1970

	AVE. DOSE millirem/yr.
Natural Background	100-150
Diagnostic X-ray	50-150
The "Standards"	170
Weapons Testing	3
Jet travel, watches, color TV, etc.	1
Nuclear power plants	less than .001
Radiation risk x average dose x	
200,000,000 people	less than 1 death per year.

* V. P. Bond, M.D., "Radiation Standards, Particularly as Related to Nuclear Power Plants." Presented to Council for the Advancement of Science Writing, Eighth Annual Briefing on New Horizons in Science, November 16, 1970.

Other interesting and valuable data are now being generated by many researchers, especially in the field of genetics, including the Russells of Oak Ridge National Laboratory. They deal with the proposition that genetic damage to the gene or chromosome from any agent, including radiation, is reparable. A precise repair process that can be relied on to occur has been described.

Genetic damage (chromatid-type) generally occurs as the DNA molecule replicates. Such injury may occur during meiosis (germ cell cycling), which covers the prophase, metaphase, anaphase and finally the telaphase. DNA replication occurs during the late G-1 (Gap-1) and S-1 phase or the initial DNA synthesizing step in cycling and is usually completed by the time the prophase is finished. The cell then enters the G-2 (Gap-2) or second resting phase which may also vary, depending on the demands placed on the cycling system by the organism for completion of maturation. The important point is that DNA production and replication have most likely been completed prior to the start of the anaphase, and the G-1 (first resting phase) is short. Then if the metaphase and anaphase follow soon and the G-2 (second resting phase) is long, repair of damaged material can be completed. When the final signal is given to end the second resting phase, the telaphase is then completed after the genetic material has been repaired.

In the human female, all the germ cells (primordial germ tissue) become primary oocytes shortly after birth, probably within seven days. This means they have completed the prophase and the S-1 phase. Then heterotypic division is completed without a prolonged resting phase, and they enter G-2, a long resting phase (from seven days after birth to puberty) where they stay until called upon to ovulate between puberty and menopause. This gives any damaged DNA or genetic material a tremendous span of time to repair itself.

The male germ cells, on the other hand, remain as primordial germ cells in the germinal epithelium of the testicle until puberty. Then spermatogenesis begins as a continual process. A primary germ cell completes the entire meiotic cycle in about sixteen days, a short period. If the genetic material of a male germ cell is damaged after DNA synthesis, it has a short time to repair and thus is far more vulnerable to irreparable damage. The female germ cell with a very long time (seven days after birth to age twelve or thirteen to repair any injury) is considered more resistant, and there is really not much the liberated woman can do about it.

Gofman and Tamplin

The first assault made by the extremists on the nuclear community occurred in September 1969 during a nuclear science symposium in Burlington, Vermont.[14] The first charges were made by Dr. A. G. Tamplin, Ph.D., who had been employed rather recently at the Lawrence Radiation Laboratory. He was brought to the laboratory by Dr. John Gofman as his assistant. Speaking to the assembled group, Tamplin assailed the radiation standards as follows: "The present levels of radiation protection guidelines have been set by a group of competent scientific individuals who have weighed this situation carefully. You should be able to present a number and defend it before a scientific community, because right now no one knows what are the effects of three R's in thirty years, which is what the 170 mr per year works up to." His scientific naiveté is revealed by observing how his position changed during the next weeks.

Tamplin's next public statement on the radiation standards and low-level limits came at a symposium held at the University of Minnesota. It is apparent he had been further educated during the interim, but his initial presentation during the day required that he make a fast retraction that night, when it was pointed out by reactor experts in the audience that he had used the wrong figures and was off by a factor of one million.[15] During his initial presentation he started by saying, "*If* the 137 Cesium concentration in air were maintained at the MPC [maximum permissible concentration] for just one day, a child consuming one liter of milk per day would get a whole-body dose of 7 rad as a consequence of just one day's deposition. If the MPC in air were maintained for one year, the dose would be 2,555 rad, 5,110 times higher than the 0.5 guidelines of the AEC and 15,000 times the radiation protection guidelines of the Federal Radiation Council." At the evening session, Dr. Tamplin admitted that his assumed release rate was *a million times* higher than what is actually released. "If it is, I don't know what this meeting is all about." In other words, there is no hazard worth discussing.

Dr. Merril Eisenbud rebutted Tamplin anyway, to put the genetic risks of low-level radiation in perspective:[16] "It should be noted that it is well established that temperatures can cause genetic mutations, and it has been suggested that as much as 50 per cent of the mutations that occur normally in contemporary man might be due to the increase in testicular temperature caused by the male practice of wearing trousers. Although this observation appeared in the literature in 1957 (Gonad Temperature and Spontaneous Mutation-rate in Man, *Nature* 180: 1433-1434), I am unaware of any subsequent popular movement to prescribe kilts in place of the more mutagenic habit of dress of the American male."

Other comparative examples on the subject of low-level and background radiation are becoming better known. For example, moving from the seacoast to a higher altitude like Denver adds 100 milliroengten per year because of exposure to more cosmic rays, originating from the sun; living in a wooden house adds about 50 mr; living in a brick house adds 100. A concrete house adds 70. Every chest X-ray adds 35 to 100. Flying across the United States and back in a jet adds 5 mr, again due to the high altitude and cosmic rays. Compare these numbers with what happens if one were to sit at the edge of a reactor site for a whole year: one would receive a total exposure of no more than 5 mr, the same as flying across the country and back once.

Tamplin changed his attack in a dramatic manner in December 1969 in Oregon when he stated that the AEC's radiation guidelines could result in 17,000 additional cancer deaths a year and in even worse genetic effects.[17] H. J. Dunster of the United Kingdom Radiation Board and International Commission on Radiation Protection was on the same panel. He challenged Tamplin's calculation, pointing out that it is physically impossible for the United States population as a whole to receive the 170 mr exposure. Tamplin repeated: "Our calculations are based upon the whole population getting it." Dunster replied: "If I may say so, that's stupid. If you have the capability of giving 170 mr to every member of the population, without exceeding 170 mr to any exposed group, you are a magician....The figure of 17,000 [deaths] is quite simply wrong, I have done the same arithmetic with the same information, and the figure I arrive at is somewhere between 0 and 60." The National Council and International Commission on Radiological Protection found Tamplin's data and calculations had no significance.

In March 1970, Dr. John Gofman, Tamplin's superior at the Lawrence Radiation Laboratory, joined the attack with Tamplin.[18] Gofman alleged that the ICRP agreed with him, but it had not, and the ICRP was quick to make that known. Gofman had now raised the total number of deaths from 17,000 to 32,000, or almost double the original number. This was all based on the same data. He referred to the AEC's radiation protection standards as a "cruel" joke on an unsuspecting public. He defended his figure of 32,000 cases, the origin of which he never explained, as "a very conservative estimate." He said the AEC position was: "We don't have to prove it's safe—you've got to provide the corpses to prove it's unsafe." It was at this meeting that Gofman was asked whether he and Tamplin had done any original research, or if they had merely reinterpreted old data that the standard-setting bodies had been familiar with for many years. His answer: "Sure I'm using others' data." This is hardly a responsible or rational way to take over as the "protector" of American public radiation health and safety.

In April 1970, Dr. V. P. Bond, M.D., associate director of life sciences and chemistry at the prestigious Brookhaven National Laboratory, using the same type

of calculations that Gofman and Tamplin used, concluded that their statements have been "enormously exaggerated" and "scare-laden."[19] Gofman and Tamplin
had implied that radiation from reactors could result in
up to 32,000 cancer deaths annually. Instead, the operation of such nuclear plants now and in the foreseeable
future (year 2000) would not contribute even one additional cancer fatality per year. In fact, if a person could
live at the very site boundary of a nuclear power plant
full-time for one million years, he would probably not
receive cancer from the plant radiation. Dr. Bond said
there are many reasons for this great discrepancy.
"Gofman and Tamplin's risk estimates are in excess, by
a factor of at least ten, of the already conservative estimates recently made by a task group of the ICRP. In
addition, Tamplin and Gofman assume that everyone in
the United States is exposed to an average of 170 mrems
a year; but even if all existing nuclear power plants were
operating at maximum release limits, the average population exposure would be approximately 0.01 mrem per
year, which is a factor of 17,000 less than the Tamplin-
Gofman assumption. Moreover," Bond added, "today's
power reactors actually operate at about 1 per cent or
less of the allowable release rates, another reduction by
a factor of 100. Altogether, these factors mean that the
number of 32,000 hypothetical deaths a year should actually be 0.08 per year as an upper limit."

Dr. Bond commented further on Gofman's theory:
"Gofman's data have been reviewed by the world's
many radiation standard-setting bodies, and they have
not seen fit to change their recommendations. In no
case has an effect been found at low doses." And that
fact does not represent "a tremendous void in our
knowledge, but it is an indication that any effect is so
small that it cannot be detected. In fact, some cases in-

dicate zero effect." He also pointed out that in several studies, animals exposed to low doses have lived longer than non-irradiated control animals. "I do not know any scientist that agrees with his [Gofman's] approaches or results. Dr. Gofman's own colleagues say that he is completely mistaken. He refers to some of my experiments, but only an initial paper, not the later ones in which we point out why our data can't be used in the manner that Dr. Gofman used them. Personally, as a scientist," he said, "from my extensive studies on the effects of radiation, I believe there has not been one added case of leukemia or cancer from nuclear power plants."

Dr. Charles Mays of the University of Utah also was disturbed by Gofman's and Tamplin's misuse of others' data and wrote to the JCAE staff:[20] "It is with dismay I have learned that Drs. Tamplin and Gofman have not corrected their manuscript which relates to our work, although they knew well in advance that their manuscript contained 71 numerical errors (yes, seventy-one!), and that it deliberately omitted that part of our data which failed to support the linear hypotheses. Drs. Gofman and Tamplin had the necessary data and could have corrected their manuscript. But they did not. Their manuscript, now printed in your hearings, still contains 71 numerical errors. It still contains only highly selected data. Quite frequently they may have disregarded pertinent data in their other analyses."

Dr. Joshua Lederberg, the Nobel Prize-winning geneticist at Stanford University School of Medicine, has made even more explicit his differences with the Gofman-Tamplin charges against radiation standards (though they often cite him as a supporter).[21] In a lengthy article in the *Washington Post* of May 2, 1971, entitled "Radiation Debate Is Off-Base," Lederberg describes the battle over the 170 mrem standard as an unfortunately misplaced issue. The AEC has produced new figures that throw a completely different light on the problem. It claims that the United States population today is exposed to an average radiation level of less than .001 millirads per year from nuclear power plants. This is so inconsequential compared to background that it would be impossible to determine by direct measurement.

Gofman and Tamplin have testified at nuclear hearings and compare the reactor size and activity to Hiroshima and Nagasaki. Why would two legitimate scientists choose such a frightful analogy when there is nothing analogous in the comparison? The reason is that the atomic bomb analogy has a high alarm factor they use to scare their listeners. Nuclear reactor size is rated in watts—usually in megawatts (millions of watts). The reactor has no nuclear explosive capability; and there is no way the nuclear material can be formed into a critical mass in such a way as to explode like a bomb, because the concentration of 235 U in a power reactor is not sufficiently rich. To be made into a nuclear explosive device, it would have to be enriched with a higher percentage of 235 U. In the unlikely case of a meltdown of some fuel element (no nuclear power reactor has ever melted), the other materials present in the reactor vessel would "poison" the system to the extent that even if in proper quantity and configuration, there would be no way for it to explode. These other materials include the fuel-cladding material, boron shim, safety rods, and water, all of which would quickly reduce the 235 U to an insignificant per cent of the total.

A letter was signed by twenty-nine of the nation's most prominent nuclear scientists and sent to the chairman of the Joint Committee on Atomic Energy reconfirming their confidence in the official Federal Radiation Guidelines.[22] It was a unanimous statement of disagreement with the theories of Gofman and Tamplin. The letter was an obvious rebuttal to the Gofman-Tamplin theory that current radiation standards are less than conservatively safe. Portions of the letter are reproduced to show what was thought of these two critics by recognized scientists in the field:

"We are increasingly concerned at the prominence given to the alarmist views of a tiny minority of experts on the effects of radiation in the general population. Such material as is necessary is obtained in the publications of the Federal Radiation Council (FRC), the National Council on Radiation Protection and Measurements (NCRP), and the International Commission on Radiological Protection (ICRP). These reports show evidence of the great competence of these bodies and their concern for public health. In setting the current radiation standards, the ICRP in 1958 considered the then available evidence relating to somatic and genetic damage induced in human beings by radiation. Whenever data were contradictory or obscure, the commission consciously and consistently took the more conservative (safer) interpretation. They concluded the risk to the general population due to the development of the nuclear power industry within these safety standards 'to be not unacceptable' and indeed very small, compared to the risks we subject ourselves to in our everyday lives. At the present time the vast majority of experts in the field of human response to ionizing radiation who have been involved in setting current radiation standards are convinced that these standards are based upon the best scientific evidence available and the deepest concern for public health."

This letter was signed by twenty-nine of the outstanding scientists and radiation researchers in the nation and sent to Representative Chet Holifield, chairman of the JCAE.

Finally, by March 1971, in an effort to gain more impact and alarm more listeners, Gofman increased his radiation effects theory and stated there would be 104,000 deaths a year, or double what he had said before and four times the original figures, all based on the same data. It met with little acceptance because all his data as well as Tamplin's had been totally rejected as spurious by all professional bodies and commissions.

Dale E. Wretlind, a knowledgable, respected spokesman of the nuclear industry, offered an analogy for the Gofman-Tamplin radiation controversy:[23] "What they are doing is like guessing how many deaths from drowning there would be if the entire country were under ten feet of water, and then on the basis of that, trying to scare you if you happen to be standing on a damp floor."

Dr. Edward Teller, quoted by Gofman and Tamplin on occasion as supporting their position, put them in proper perspective in October 1970.[24] He said: "Reactors are very much more safe than Tamplin and incomparably more safe than Gofman. Under normal circumstances you can tell what a reactor will do." Teller said that hazards from low-level radiation from power plants are "practically nil and have been incredibly exaggerated and there is a zero probability that a reactor could explode. No other pollutant has been so carefully regulated, so super-cautiously regulated as radiation."

Sternglass

Running neck and neck with Gofman and Tamplin for headlines and television spots at that time was Dr.

E. J. Sternglass of the University of Pittsburgh. He told an absurd series of tales which have left his reputation as a scientist in a shambles. It is best described by the Berwick, Pennsylvania, *Enterprise*, in an editorial headline: "We were all taken in." The editor wrote: "There was a story in the *Enterprise*, along with most other papers, last week—that we wish we had tossed into the wastebasket. No one complained about it—but after we ran the AP item, we heard comment that this Dr. Ernest Sternglass isn't infallible by any means. Fact is, after we checked into it—we found that a tremendous number of scientists and scientific groups have no time whatever for his ideas on radiation. It is unfortunate that, at times, headline hunters can succeed in their 'hunting' by giving out stories on the sensational side. Now here's Sternglass, whose title is director of the Radiology Physics Laboratory at the University of Pittsburgh Medical School. He made the news wires and, as a result, got publicity in most papers. Looking at it in retrospect—and after doing some checking—we would say the wire (and the paper, including ours) were taken in by giving him publicity. [The editorial then listed eight rebuttals of the Sternglass theory.] So, so much for Dr. Sternglass. We regret that our paper was among those over the nation which ran the release about him."

The *New York Times* was not as astute. On July 29, 1969, it published "Excerpts From *The Death Of All Children*," by Sternglass. It apparently made no effort to accredit the facts of the report. If it had, it would not have printed the material. Portions of the article are extracted as follows: "...long-lived strontium 90 necessarily released into the world's rapidly circulating atmosphere could lead to the death of all Russian infants born in the next generation, thus ending the existence of the Russian people, together with that of all

mankind. The anticipated *genetic* effect of *strontium 90*
has become evident from an increase in the incidence
of infant mortality along the path of the fallout cloud
from the first atomic test in New Mexico in 1945, and
from a detailed correlation of state-by-state infant mortality excesses with yearly changes of strontium 90 levels
in milk. The specter of fallout has of course loomed before in the national anxiety over nuclear explosions. But
the result of these studies comprises the strontium 90
and infant mortality. From our examinations of the infant mortality changes from a computer-fitted base line
for 1935-1950, for various states in which the Public
Health Services reported monthly on the strontium 90
concentrations in the milk since 1957, there emerges a
close correspondence between average strontium 90 levels and infant mortality changes. Wherever the strontium 90 levels rose to high value over a four-year
period, as in Georgia, a large, parallel, year-by-year rise
in infant mortality also took place, while in areas where
there was little strontium 90 in the milk, as in Texas,
the infant mortality remained at a correspondingly lower value. Other states such as Illinois, Missouri, New
York, and Utah also show a rise, peaking in the same
1962-1964 period at levels between these extreme cases,
each according to their local annual rainfall and strontium 90 concentrations in their milk. For the United
States as a whole, we found a detailed correspondence
between and among: (1) the excess infant mortality relative to the 1935-1950 base line; (2) the total strontium 90
produced by nuclear weapons; (3) the strontium 90 thus
produced actually reaching the ground; and (4) the
four-year average concentration in United States milk
from 1955, the year after the first large H-bomb test;
and 1964, the year when strontium 90 concentrations
began to level off and started to decline once again.

Since increases of some 20 to 30 per cent excess infant mortality were observed from a thousand to fifteen hundred miles downwind in Arkansas, Alabama and Louisiana, where mortality rates were between 3 and 4.5 per hundred live births, the detonation of a single, small tactical-size nuclear weapon on the ground in the Western United States appears to have led to one out of one-hundred children born subsequently, dying before reaching the age of one year."

Only the most scientifically naive clodpole would present such data in a serious attempt to link fallout from the Alamogordo and Nevada test series to infant mortality in the first instance and with infant mortality 1,000 to 1,500 miles distant in the second. The AEC, USPHS, and all the state health agencies were closely involved in monitoring the tests using both instrumental and biological means. No one ever observed radiation levels of any significance associated with these tests as far away as Georgia which could cause infant mortality even if the isotopes involved were high energy and rapidly assimilated ones such as 131 I or 137 Cs. But Sternglass speaks repeatedly of 90 Sr. which: 1. is a bone-seeker; 2. is involved in a time-consuming food-chain assimilation process; and 3. has never been associated with infant mortality, but with bone absorption and on a long-term basis. The foolish assumptions he made, along with the statistics he prepared to support them, have since been shown to be too shabby for even his ally and colleague Tamplin to swallow.

Dr. Leonard Sagan, M.D., associate director, Palo Alto Medical Clinic, Palo Alto, California, was the first to shred the Sternglass report.[25] After the first publication by the *New York Times* (never corrected or retracted), Sternglass expanded his thesis by estimating that the magnitude of these effects was such that approximately

400,000 infant deaths could be attributed to this cause. Although the manuscript in which this thesis was elaborated was rejected by both the journals *Science* and *Nature*, the views of Sternglass reached a wide audience through publication in *Esquire* magazine and the public news media. Dr. Sagan listed the fallacies in Sternglass' work: 1. errors in methology. a. Sternglass relied on samples of data that are so small they are statistically insignificant. In his testimony on March 20, he admitted that the sparsity of data made it "difficult to draw absolutely firm conclusions." b. Sternglass failed to test each of his major correlations for their statistical significance. c. Sternglass ignored the lack of controls and limitations in his data. For instance, he disregarded changes in the definition of fetal death, differences in state requirements for reporting fetal deaths, and changes in the coding of such deaths. d. Sternglass assumed a priori that one segment of a curve may be used to predict with assurance the shape of the next segment. He stated that "there is some degree of arbitrariness inherent in using any given period as a base-line, and it is therefore important to find other data that is not subject to the same criticism." e. Sternglass assumed a priori that a trend in one set of data may be used to establish a trend in another causally *unrelated* set of data. He correlated congenital malformation deaths with the incidence of nuclear fallout by using a reference base for malformation deaths predicated on the number of *accidental* deaths. He did not, however, show that the number of accidental deaths was in any way related to that of malformation deaths. He abandoned any pretense that accidental deaths can be used to establish the trend for congenital malformation deaths. Even the man in the street knows that accidents are not diseases, and certainly an epidemologist would reject out of hand Sternglass' statement that "this is about as good a control as you can get."

2. Failure to take into account certain pertinent considerations, including radiation dose. a. Sternglass consistently failed to take into account many factors known to influence infant mortality rates—e.g., socioeconomic status, medical care, maternal age, race, and nutrition. b. His failure to consider cigarette consumption demonstrates a flagrant disregard for objective inquiry. c. He failed to take into account the effect of age on the incidence of disease. d. He failed to take into account differences in radiation levels.

3. Inconsistencies. Sternglass maintained on the one hand that the twenty-kiloton Alamogordo blast caused the death of one child in every 100 born in the downwind areas. Yet, he also said that the 200 *megatons* of nuclear testing up to 1963 caused only one excess death per 100 born in the entire United States. Dr. William Bibb, an AEC physician, remarked: "If in your first argument you had twenty-kilotons killing one in one hundred, how come, when we scale up by a factor of 10,000 to 200 megatons, we haven't already killed off all the babies in those Southeastern states?" b. He changed his time delays for the appearance of radiation effects. In Albany-Troy he showed a clear correlation 6 to 8 years after the arrival of the fallout. Then in the next paragraph, "Again peaks of leukemia incidence were clearly present some 4 to 6 years later." c. He has varied without explanation three key variables—time delays, number of years for establishing an "average norm" and the actual years used for establishing this average. By this methodology it is possible to "prove" practically anything one desires.

4. Selective use of data. Dr. Sagan showed how Sternglass misused facts; made mathematical errors in

his calculations; revealed his inadequate understanding of basic radiological concepts; and disregarded the general body of knowledge about radiobiology. As to his lack of knowledge of radiobiology, Sternglass stated that 90 Sr, via fallout, was responsible for 400,000 infant deaths. In doing this, Sternglass was forced to the conclusion that prolonged doses of radiation are more harmful than intense bursts of radiation. Such is exactly contrary to everything that is known about prolongation of dose which in every known circumstance is less harmful if prolonged because of the repair mechanisms discussed earlier, which need time to operate.

Of all fission products present to any degree in fallout, 90 Sr is considered relatively harmless with respect to genetic defects since strontium, like calcium, concentrates in the skeleton where its short beta rays will not affect the gonads. For congenital malformations, Sternglass accidentally steps to firmer ground since in animal studies congenital malformations are indeed the most prominent effect of in-utero radiation exposure. However, he trips himself up since the dose of radiation required to produce such effects in animals are enormous; the usual dose employed in such animal studies being 200 rads, e.g., more than 20,000 times greater and probably closer to 100,000 times greater than that received by any in-utero fetus in Utah. In any case, the amounts required to do what Sternglass alleged was done would have tripped the automatic radiation alarm monitoring network clear across the nation and on around the world at the time of the detonation. Sternglass could have obtained all this information had he taken time to first read United Nations document number 14 (A/6314).

Regardless of this he persists today in his assertions, even though he continues to be rejected by every scientific group on every charge. The Atomic Industrial Forum published a compilation of reviews of the scare theories of Sternglass.[26] First from the Health Physics Society: "On the third such occasion since 1968, Sternglass has, at an annual meeting of the Health Physics Society, presented a paper in which he associates an increase in infant mortality with low levels of radiation exposure. The material contained in his paper has also been presented publicly at other occasions in various parts of the country. His allegations, made in several forms, have in each instance been analyzed by scientists, physicians, and biostatisticians in the federal government, in individual states that have been involved in his reports, and by qualified scientists in other countries. Without exception these agencies and scientists have concluded that Dr. Sternglass' arguments are not substantiated by the data he presents. The USPHS, the EPA, the States of New York, Pennsylvania, Michigan, and Illinois have issued formal reports in rebuttal of Sternglass' arguments. We, the president and past presidents of the Health Physics Society, do not agree with the claim of Dr. Sternglass that he has shown that radiation exposure from nuclear power operations has resulted in an increase in infant mortality." This was signed by Dade W. Moeller, Harvard School of Public Health (the current president), and it was also signed by the fourteen past presidents of the Health Physics Society.

The Michigan Health Department made the following comment on a Sternglass allegation that the Big Rock Point nuclear power plant in Michigan had caused an increase in infant mortality in nearby counties: "Sternglass' papers have not been based on scientific tests, but rather on a statistical data evaluation of infant mortality rates and reactor plant emissions, selecting

and rejecting figures to arrive at an apparently biased
conclusion. In his statistics, Sternglass lists ten counties
on a chart called 'Adjacent Counties.' What they are
adjacent to is unknown, because if it refers to the Big
Rock Point plant, he is using Crawford, Kalkaska, Ben-
zie and Grand Traverse counties, all of which have a
buffer county between them and the power plant. But
only by using Grand Traverse county, forty-five miles
from the plant and approximately 180 degrees from the
direction of the prevailing winds, is he able to make his
point of a rise in the infant mortality during 1966-1967.
Sternglass' conclusion that the reactor plant has influence over the ten counties is certainly questionable
when the two closest counties show no effect, and he is
forced to use counties far to the south to buoy his figures. The 'three independent tests' (with which Sternglass claimed to have verified his data) were not tests at
all, but other papers written by Sternglass using the
same irresponsible method of interpreting and selecting
figures to fit his conclusions. Based on the material used
by Sternglass, there is no logical reason to conclude
that there is a connection between infant mortality and
radioactive effluent from Big Rock Point Reactor."

According to *Science*, October 10, 1969, "One of
Sternglass' most provocative bits of evidence is a map
purporting to show that there was 'excess' infant mortality in a band of southern states that he describes as
'downwind' of the first 'Trinity' nuclear test at Alamogordo, New Mexico, in 1945. Sternglass contends that
the fallout drifted eastward from New Mexico and that
by 1950 there was substantial excess infant mortality in
those southern states over which it had drifted. He calculated the excess mortality by comparing 1950 figures
with the trend for a base period of 1940-1945. But
Edythalena Tompkins and Morton L. Brown, of HEW's

Bureau of Radiological Health, have recalculated the rates and have discovered that 1950 is the only year that gives Sternglass his result. If 1947, 48, 49 or 51 are used, a different pattern of states with 'excess' deaths emerges. Similarly, if the base period is changed to 1935-1945 to coincide more nearly with the base period used in other discussions, then there seems to be no effect. To top it off, the AEC contends that the fallout cloud from Alamogordo did not even go eastward. On this point, Sternglass appears on shaky ground. His authority for saying that the cloud went eastward is a popular book written by a *Time* correspondent, but a perusal of that book reveals that it has part of the cloud drifting in several different directions—none of them eastward."

Dr. Edward Teller: "In many cases, the fallacious nature of Sternglass' handling of data is explicitly demonstrated; it is hard for me to see how a man like Sternglass who claims to be a scientist can fail to respond to arguments contained in this paper and still maintain that his case has scientific merit."

A new generation of propagandists has entered the scene: the Union of Concerned Scientists, whose chief spokesman has been Dr. Henry Kendall. Ralph Nader acts as coach. Their initial maneuver was to request a preliminary injunction in a Washington District Court which would force the AEC to withdraw operating licenses for twenty nuclear plants. Kendall told the twenty-five attendees at a news conference that the twenty plants were named because they are free of litigation of one kind or another. Kendall stated that these plants produce only 3 to 4 percent of the nation's electric capacity. He said the loss of this 3 per cent was insignificant, but admitted that he had not conducted a study of the individual service areas. The most casual study would have shown him that the loss of 3 to 4 per cent of our energy capacity would have a crippling effect on the nation's economy. The loss of the nuclear energy plants would represent an impossible burden for the utilities to carry. The Midwest and New England would be hit hardest. Costs would run in excess of $40 million annually just on one plant of the Consumers Power Company. In New England there would have been zero reserves in 1973, a deficit of 461 Mwe in 1974, and a deficit of 967 Mwe in 1975.

The Nader moratorium announcement was held as a news conference. The rhetoric and charges expressed at the Washington meeting were familiar to newsmen and industry representatives. It seemed to have been conducted at least in part for publicity, and it was shrewdly handled. Selected reporters were carefully briefed in advance to the point that the first AP story ran an hour before the press conference started.

The Birmingham, Alabama, News wrote: "Nader has built a career out of the calculated overstatement and assumed expertise outside his own field of competence. Now it is up to the courts to judge whether this zeal will throw the entire nation off an already perilously close schedule for meeting tomorrow's energy needs. If Nader is successful, he will damage the nation far more economically than he could hope to gain in protecting the public's safety. We hope the court will take the gravity of this matter into the proper consideration."

The Tampa, Florida, Tribune wrote: "Power shortages are not confined to Florida; they are a serious national problem. But this means nothing to Ralph Nader and Friends of the Earth, an environmental organization. What information does Nader have that the plants are dangerous? Absolutely none. Nader, the acclaimed conscience of the consumer and environmentalists, is shooting from the hip. Nader ought to be more concerned with proposing methods to save and produce energy than to reduce what's available. The attack on nuclear power is an act of irresponsibility."

A few days later, two more giants of nuclear science, Barry Commoner and Margaret Mead, were successful in delaying for a while the breeder reactor (LMFBR) through a unanimous, three-judge ruling of a federal appeals court. The ruling dealt with the potential impact on the environment of the LMFBR, which informed people hope eventually will solve the national energy crisis. The Scientists' Institute for Public Information argued that since such reactors breed plutonium, the system should be studied more before the construction program starts. The AEC had already issued an Environmental Impact Statement on the demonstration plant at Oak Ridge, Tennessee, but this had no impact on Commoner or Mead.

Thermal Effects

Waste heat from nuclear power plants (as well as others) not used to create electricity has to be disposed of, since it is difficult to use in a practical way. It is possible to dispose of it to the environment so that the effects are entirely acceptable and negligible. Presently no one method is used, for each plant with its environment presents a unique system, and all physical and biological effects must be considered.

Thermal issues can best be appreciated by using 1,000 megawatt electrical light-water reactor plants as an example. They produce 180 billion BTU's of excess heat to be disposed of daily. In terms of hot water (heated up 10 degrees F.) this equals eighteen billion pounds or two billion gallons or 300 million cubic feet per day. In agricultural terms it amounts to 6,500 acre-feet a day of water being heated 10 degrees. To cool these amounts of hot water requires evaporation into the atmosphere where cooling occurs. Plant improvements will reduce the problem, but only by a factor of two at best; therefore, the hot water problem must be dealt with as long as electricity is produced with heat engines. Using the 1,000 megawatt electrical plant as an example, in 1968 the total installed capacity in the United States was the equivalent of 290 1000-MW plants—a 290,000 MW electrical capacity. Most forecasts predict there will be 600,000 megawatts electrical by 1980.[27]

Though the methods for cooling will vary, the once-through system, where water from a stream or a bay is circulated through the condensing system, cools the condenser water, and is discharged, is being replaced by cooling towers, lakes, etc. Any environmental effect depends on temperature rise of the water and its method of disposal into the receiving bay or stream. State and federal regulations governing water quality have been established. In general, these do not permit water to leave a facility more than a specified number of degrees hotter, or none at all, than when it entered, depending on the entering temperature. There are also conditions on the amount of water one can take from a bay compared with flow rates and volumes. To stay within these water quality regulations is possible, but it costs money. Other methods for cooling water are towers and ponds.

The cooling tower, as an alternate method of cooling hot water generated from condensers of nuclear power plants, is costly and contributes nothing to the environment. A 400-foot high cooling tower, which recirculates 750,000 gallons per minute of water in a closed system, currently costs about $14 million to construct and $200,000 a year to maintain.

Currently, of 91 per cent of fossil fuel plants in operation, 77 per cent use once-through cooling, 4 per cent use cooling ponds, and 19 per cent use towers. The once-through system presents the greatest problem, although much more experience with the once-through system is available.

The public objection to date has been based on the fate of fish in hot water. With proper plant design to allow staying within water quality limits, effects are absent or extremely small. The public debate on how large the effects are, if present, or whether the effects are important or not, will be resolved best by long-term experiments. To meet needed power requirements we are not permitted to wait for long-term experiments. As a result, most power plants having problems with a once-through cooling system are planning towers. Towers may cause some local minor problems, but none of significance. Good engineering, careful thermal design, and use of available information will result in minimal environmental effects. These are insignificant compared to actual effects from seasonal climatic changes.

A vast amount of information is available on this issue. Most of the critics who complain of thermal effects would lead us to believe that no studies at all on heat transfer to large bodies of water or use of cooling towers have been done, which is simply not true. These same critics have also rediscovered the wheel on this issue. Questions remain, but none are of extreme importance in regard to the construction of nuclear power plants. Protection of water quality and reduction of environmental effects are assured if the proper system is developed.

The agricultural use of the hot water, or the use of the hot water to warm a portion of the sea or bay to increase the production of food crops or animals, is probably the single most exciting feature of the thermal

effects "problem." Professor Daniel Merriman studied
the thermal effects of the Connecticut Yankee nuclear
plant on the river system used to cool it. He reports:
"The operation of the plant does not seem to have significantly affected the small, but relatively stable catch
of resident fishes. At the mouth of the Salmon River,
about a mile below the mouth of the plant's discharge
canal, however, the catch rate showed an increase in
1969; this may be correlated with the presence of the
warm-water plume nearby. Indeed, a number of fishermen now prefer to fish near the mouth of the canal."
He adds the thermal effects "have had no significant
deleterious effect on the biology of the river and may
even prove to be beneficial in one way or another."

On the contrary and unscientific side, NBC-TV carried a Sunday afternoon environment series, "In Which
We Live," with Edwin Newman in June 1970. In one
segment he concentrated on thermal effects and began
with this statement: "The gloomiest forecast we know of
about the future of our water resources is that by the
end of the decade our rivers may have reached the boiling point; three decades more, and they may evaporate.
This vision of cataclysm is based on the assumption that
we will continue to discharge heat into our rivers at the
rate we are doing it now. One of the causes of this thermal pollution is the spread of nuclear power plants
across the land." This prediction can only have credibility at the nuthouse.

Local fishermen at San Clemente, California, prefer
fishing near the water discharge area near a power plant
because they catch more fish, and in England they are
looking optimistically at the hot water as a resource. A
beneficial use of cooling water from a nuclear power
plant has been reported in Bridgewater, England—the
"farming" of shrimp at three times the normal produc-

tion. In water near the Hinkley Point power station, seven degrees warmer than nearby Bristol channel, shrimp are reaching maturity in eighteen months instead of the normal three to five years.

Work is now going on at several universities on the use of hot water in agricultural projects. Oregon State University has an active research program underway, and Israel has employed many of the favorable aspects of warm water for some time. A practical solution to the problem of huge quantities of hot water, as much as 750,000 gallons per minute, which are a by-product of large nuclear power plants and other industrial operations, is being demonstrated near Eugene, Oregon. Conventional methods of removing the heat from the water are, of course, more expensive. The water at 103 degrees F. in the Eugene project makes beneficial use of the heat and the water to protect orchards from frost damage and to irrigate crops. The same system could be applied to nuclear power plants and other industries in most areas of the United States.

Another project is a proposal to irrigate semi-arid land in eastern Oregon and Washington. The present $1 million, three-year program, sponsored by the Eugene Water & Electric Board (EWEB), a municipal utility, was designed and is being managed by the Hanford Engineering Services Division of Automation Industries, Inc. A demonstration irrigation system, using hot water from condensers of a Weyerhauser Company paper mill near Eugene, lies along the McKenzie River, which is rated by sportsmen as one of the top four trout streams in Oregon. The water, ranging in temperatures from 90 to 147 degrees F., travels from the paper mill through nearly three miles of pipeline to irrigate crops and orchards, then filters through the soil and returns to the McKenzie at normal temperature.

The effects on a local economy of a nuclear power plant supplying thermal water for irrigation are vast. EWEB, in a written study of its existing project, estimated joint development of irrigation with nuclear power in the Willamette Valley of Oregon would provide an additional $25 million annually in farm income plus another $85 million in related economic development a year.

Multipling by twenty the number of nuclear power plants now proposed for Oregon, Washington, and Idaho to the year 1984, and measuring all related areas of business development, economists come up with an estimated $10 billion annual injection into the economy of the Pacific Northwest, simply by using the thermal "pollution" intelligently. Economic factors considered in the analysis include increased employment, urban development, higher agricultural yields, an expanded food-processing industry, recreational facilities, and related generation of more tax dollars.

There are now 4.7 million acres in the Umatilla Basin of Washington and Oregon which are being dry-farmed on a crop rotation basis. Wheat yields of 36 bushels are obtained without irrigation. If irrigated, this could be raised to 135 bushels per acre or could be used for planting of multiple crops and orchards.

Price-Anderson

The Price-Anderson Act, an amendment to the Atomic Energy Act, covers five points. It:

1. Limits liability (but is not a waiver of liability or a disclaimer). Congress said: "We will provide $500 million of insurance above whatever the private insurance industry can provide to protect or to pay those persons who may be injured."

2. Provides indemnity for anyone injured by the operation of a university or teaching reactor up to $500 million in excess of $250 thousand.
3. Authorizes the AEC to provide an indemnity agreement to its contractors engaged in hazardous projects, in which it says, "we will insure the liability for the nuclear energy hazard if any of your activities in our behalf cause injury to anyone."
4. Provides that the AEC will indemnify the operators of the nuclear ship *Savannah* with a $100 million limit on it anywhere in the world. (This once beautiful vessel is now dismantled.)
5. Provides an excess provision over and above private insurance. This provision is causing the controversy today.[29]

The act provides that every reactor operator, over a nominal size, shall buy all available private insurance. The $500 million of Price-Anderson covers above this maximum amount of private insurance. When Price-Anderson was enacted in 1957, the insurance industry agreed to provide liability coverage up to $60 million for each nuclear power plant, even though there was little operating experience. In the thirteen years since then, the insurance pools have reduced their premiums, provided refunds of up to 97 per cent of the premium after ten years, and increased the amount of private liability insurance from $60 million to $82 million, and perhaps to $110 million by 1975. As the private insurance increases, the government's indemnification decreases correspondingly to keep the total coverage at $560 million. Therefore, based on the original commitment of $60 million of private liability insurance plus $500 million Price-Anderson, there is $560 million available to pay indemnity to anyone injured by nuclear energy. The act further provides that if private insurance becomes available, the $500 million is reduced accordingly. Since $82 million private liability now exists, liability under Price-Anderson has been reduced to $478 million.

Price-Anderson is being opposed in the light of today's knowledge, but Price-Anderson was enacted in 1957, when much less was known. Most people connected nuclear power at that time with Nagasaki and Hiroshima. Certainly many people feared that a power reactor would explode. Utilities were being asked to spend millions for nuclear power plants not knowing with certainty that they would pay off. The manufacturers, the insurance industry, and the directors of the utilities were all risking their capital when they embarked on this venture. If loss ensued, they would be open to stockholder suits. Under these conditions it was reasonable for Congress to indemnify persons injured up to $500 million over the available amount if an incident should occur. This is clearly as much in the interest of the injured person as it is in the interest of the utility. The overriding fact is that this additional indemnity was not a subsidy to the power industry. Every utility pays for Price-Anderson at the rate of $30 per Mwt. The operator of a three-unit plant, each 1,000 Mwt (or about 3,000 Mwt) will pay $270,000 per year for the indemnity in excess of private insurance of $82 million. That amounts to considerably more than the insurance industry will retain after the operation of the Industry Credit Rating Plan. Instead of a subsidy, it is now a profitable business for the government. Several countries in the free world have done the same. The Paris and Vienna Conventions are subsidizing a similar program on an international basis, as does the Brussels Convention, on the liability of operators of nuclear ships. Canada has just enacted a similar law, but the Canadians are much more optimistic (or perhaps realistic) on the maximum possible damage. Their limit is $75 million. Since Price-Anderson was passed before any nuclear power plants were built, based upon the knowledge of fifteen years ago, some utilities now feel it is of no help, and several would continue to build without it.

But the continuation or repeal of the Price-Anderson Act is irrelevant to any legitimate environmental concern about nuclear-electric generation. The decision to go forward with nuclear power should be made as though that law were not on the books. No rational person could regard the Price-Anderson Act as a justification for proceeding with a nuclear-electric station if there were a serious risk of an accident causing harm to persons in the vicinity; the strong support for nuclear-electric power over the years in Congress, in the commission, in the engineering profession, and in industry rests on the judgment of the most knowledgeable and competent people that the probability of a reactor accident of any consequence is, as they say, vanishingly small. When it was concluded that the nation should meet the growing demand for electricity with nuclear-generating plants, then the act became the most logical measure.

The opposition to the act is that "industry doesn't really believe" that the risk is so small, or it wouldn't have asked for passage of the act in the first place. The test of the industry's conviction about the extent of the risk then becomes its willingness to see Price-Anderson repealed. This is a nice rhetorical flourish, but it rests on an egregious misconception, namely, that industry has made a massive investment in nuclear electric power just because Price-Anderson provides liability coverage. There are two critical points, then, since the probability of a serious nuclear incident is negligible: 1. it becomes rational to use nuclear fuel as a means of meeting the public's requirements for electricity. However, because a major incident is not absolutely inconceivable, but because the probability approaches zero (or of that order) though not absolute zero, 2. it becomes rational to establish the system of public protection embodied in the act.

This poses a question generally evaded by the advocate of repeal. Considering the specific provision of the act, no purpose would be served by repeal, since the act provides that in significant cases, persons injured by an offsite nuclear discharge will be able: 1. to recover without proving negligence; 2. to make a recovery expeditiously; and, 3. to get compensation in spite of inadequate state statutes of limitation. The government, then, has supplemented this insurance beyond the resources of most industrial companies and provided more if it proves necessary. The indemnity provision is an important feature of the Price-Anderson Act, repeal of which is one of the least relevant and least useful measures which could be advanced in the name of a good cause—improving the environment.

The spectacular safety record of the nuclear industry is the important statistic. *To date, no member of the public has ever been injured from a nuclear energy hazard in connection with a power or university reactor.* No other industry has such an enviable safety record. There have been nine transportation incidents and seven nontransportation incidents for a total of sixteen. Five of the transportation incidents involved property damage caused by contamination, the most costly of which involved a $3,519 payment for loss and the expense of investigation. The average loss and expense for these five transportation incidents was $1,706. The sixth incident involved minor uranium contamination of a small portion of a warehouse and truck weighing station. No loss payment was made. The seventh involved alleged bodily injury from a shipment of a small quantity of depleted uranium delivered to a wrong address. Investigation determined that the injury, if any, was covered by the conventional liability insurance. The remaining two incidents each involved bodily injury alleged by a worker in the transportation industry.

Two of the nontransportation incidents involved encapsulated radioactive isotope sources which leaked, causing contamination of property of third parties. The loss and expense for each was about $1,350. One reported incident involved possible radiation exposure to children who had stolen a radium source. Radium and Radon are not within the scope of the Atomic Energy Act, so this was not covered by nuclear insurance. A fourth incident involved possible exposure to employees of a contractor modifying milling machines. Depleted uranium chips were found in the machine. There was no exposure to any of the men working on the machine. The expense of the investigation was $47. A fifth incident arose from a criticality accident in July 1964 at a facility processing enriched uranium in solution. A worker at the facility died as a result of the accident. A third party claim, made against persons within the definition of insured under the facility policy, was settled.

A sixth claim involved an employee of an independent contractor retained by a facility (not a power reactor). The employee of the contractor alleged that he suffered radiation injury to chromosomes while at the nuclear facility, which in turn caused his child to be born with birth defects. The claim, which had no basis in fact, was successfully defended and the litigation terminated with judgment entered for the defendant (the facility). The remaining reported nontransportation incident involves a claim made by a worker at an oil well

site who alleges that he sustained bodily injury from exposure to a small quantity of radioactive isotope used at
the site.

Another problem has arisen recently involving what is
regarded as an essential provision of fire insurance policies. This point has been misinterpreted in connection
with homeowners' policies, but the same provision essentially applies to *all* forms of property insurance. It is
referred to as nuclear exclusion. In their latest book,
Poisoned Power, Gofman and Tamplin say: "If one is de-
sirous of knowing about environmental hazards, there
exists one unusually reliable source of unbiased information. This is the insurance industry." They present
nuclear plant liability procedures as a vote of "no confidence" in nuclear power by the insurance industry—totally disregarding the recent announcement by the Insurance Information Institute which praised the
"extraordinary safety record of the nuclear power reactor industry."

In a press conference on February 22, 1970, Gofman
said: "The second point every Minnesotan ought to look
at is his homeowner's insurance policy, and he'll find in
well over 90 per cent of the policies a little clause that
says: 'In the event of nuclear accident, in the event of
radioactivity contamination, this policy is null and void.'
What did the private insurance industry say to itself
when they saw nuclear electricity coming on the scene?
They said: 'We don't know the risk of an accident' so
true to their very effective function, which is to make
money, the private insurance industry took the necessary steps to protect themselves, namely, by putting this
exclusion clause in the policy. I would say that the day
the private insurance companies take that exclusion
clause out of their policies, and the day the Price-Anderson Act is repealed, I'm going to have a massive

jump in confidence that nuclear plants are safe. Until that day, I go along with the insurance industry. If they say it's too risky to insure, I say it's too risky to risk your life on."

Dr. Gofman's statement that the insurance industry is "an unusually reliable source of unbiased information" is probably correct. However, every other conclusion he draws from the exclusion is false, and he does not even quote the exclusion correctly. Section 168-a of the New York Insurance Law reads, in part: "Insurers issuing the standard fire insurance policy pursuant to section 168 are hereby authorized to affix thereto or include therein a written statement that the policy does not cover loss or damage caused by nuclear reaction or nuclear radiation or radioactive contamination, all whether directly or indirectly resulting from an insured peril under said policy." Therefore, in New York, the Nuclear Clause reads: "The word 'fire' in this policy is not intended to and does not embrace nuclear reaction or nuclear radiation or radioactive contamination, all whether controlled or uncontrolled, and loss by nuclear reaction or nuclear radiation or radioactive contamination is not intended to be and is not insured against by this policy, whether such loss be direct or indirect, proximate or remote, or be in whole or in part caused by, contributed to, or aggravated by 'fire' or any other perils insured against by this policy, however, subject to the foregoing and all provisions of this policy, direct loss by 'fire' resulting from nuclear reaction or radiation or radioactive contamination is insured against by this policy."

Nuclear Exclusion: "This policy does not insure against loss by nuclear reaction or nuclear radiation or radioactive contamination, all whether controlled or uncontrolled, or due to any act or condition incident to any of the foregoing, whether such loss be direct or indirect, proximate or remote, or be in whole or in part caused by, contributed to, or aggravated by any of the perils insured against by this policy; and nuclear reaction, or nuclear radiation, or radioactive contamination, all whether controlled, is not 'explosion' or 'smoke.' This clause applies to all perils insured against hereunder except the perils of fire and lightning, which are otherwise provided for in the Nuclear Clause contained above."

Any connection between these clauses and the operation of power reactors is almost coincidental, and the existence of these provisions is not an expression of "no confidence" in the nuclear power industry.

To understand this exclusion, one must examine the whole pattern of insurance underwriting as it relates to "catastrophes." This refers to earthquakes, wind, and nuclear incidents particularly, although it also applies to fire and explosion. The company must determine how much it can place at risk, subject to loss from a catastrophe. It does this by recording its total earthquake exposure, separately, for Los Angeles, San Francisco, Seattle or any other Pacific Coast location with earthquakes and limits the amount of insurance written to keep its earthquake losses below the maximum to exposure from one catastrophe. It also must maintain similar records for hurricane territories. In the petrochemical and nuclear field, there are similar problems.

Nuclear exclusion was a matter of primary concern when the exclusions were adopted because nuclear explosives were being tested in the atmosphere. The possibility of widespread contamination from atmospheric testing and the venting of underground shots—both our own and Russia's—existed. China and France still must be contended with, as do the flights of bombers carrying nuclear bombs. In this connection, the European insurance industry promptly adopted a complete nuclear exclusion after the Palomares incident. Prior to that, the property values exposed to a single loss in Europe had not seemed great enough to cause them to take this action throughout the industry. Related to this is the fact that the insurance industry was asked to place at risk for the power reactor itself (property and liability) the maximum amount that it was willing to place on any one risk, and to do that, it had to limit totals to the then $120 million, now $166 million, on property and liability coverage in the reactor itself. In event of radioactivity release from a reactor, payment is made under the liability cover until it is exhausted, and then Price-Anderson pays. Under the "Extraordinary Nuclear Occurrence" provisions, in event of any widespread contamination, there is no necessity for the homeowner to prove anything except that his house has been contaminated by the reactor, and *the private insurance coverage or Price-Anderson pays him.* With no cost to the homeowner (he would pay if his insurance policy provided the protection), he would be collecting the same amount of loss from the same companies or Price-Anderson indemnity that he would under his own direct policies. To repeat, the nuclear exclusion is in no sense a vote of "no confidence" in the nuclear power industry. To the contrary, the amounts for which insurance is extended constitute a vote of real confidence.

It would be well to comment briefly on the operation of the industry Credit Rating Plan for the liability coverage. So far, claims have been nominal. After a period of ten years, about 97 per cent of those premiums paid have been returned. In addition to losses and loss expense the remainder is used for expenses which include premiums, taxes, agents' or brokers' commissions, company expenses including engineering, and approximately

10 per cent retained by the companies as a pure insurance charge for exposing their assets to loss in excess of the amount in the industry Credit Rating Plan fund, which is now about $17 million. As a result, in July 1970, $634,122.17 of the $943,724.04 paid in 1960 was returned. For the fourth consecutive year the two nuclear energy liability insurance pools refunded a substantial amount of the annual premium of the nation's nuclear power industry because of its "extraordinary" safety record.

On July 9, 1970, an announcement was made in New York that underscored the extraordinary safety record of the nuclear power reactor industry. The two American nuclear liability insurance pools which insure every privately operated nuclear power reactor in the United States announced substantial premium refunds to insureds. It reflected the virtually loss-free experience of the nuclear power reactor industry. To that date no loss had been paid nor had any liability claim been made due to the operation of a reactor. In addition to power reactors, the pools afford nuclear liability insurance to all of the privately operated test and research reactors in the United States and virtually all of the smaller reactors operated by universities. Nuclear fuel fabrication, reprocessing of spent fuel, and nuclear research and development activities are also insured by the pools. Mr. Joseph Marrone, general manager of NELIA, stated: "The effort made by industry and the AEC to make the nuclear industry safe strongly suggests that a similarly strong and talented effort to achieve safety could bring our society substantial benefits if applied in other areas. The success of the safety effort in the nuclear reactor industry warrants emulation."

The record carried over into 1971, when $1,017,609 was refunded, and again in 1972, when the refund amounted to $1,167,152. It was accompanied by another statement which "expressed continued optimism regarding the liability coverage afforded atomic energy installations. There has never been a claim arising from the operation of a nuclear reactor."

The attack on the insurance industry, along with the government-operated Price-Anderson Act paid for by nuclear operators, and the exclusion clause, does not stand up to these facts. Faced with the spectacular safety record of the nuclear industry, the environmental extremists have generally had to drop their charges against Price-Anderson, and the insurance issue is relatively quiet. Perhaps even Dr. Gofman will see the light some day.

Brookhaven Report

In 1955, the Joint Committee on Atomic Energy (JCAE) of the Congress asked the AEC for a study on the need for third-party liability insurance in connection with the operation of nuclear power plants. Up to then only relative estimates had been made of the theoretical consequences of accidents that could be imagined for such facilities. In May 1956, the AEC presented to the JCAE some estimates of damage from "conceptual" accidents and promised more information by the Brookhaven National Laboratory on a study covering: 1. what the possible consequences of major accidents might be, and 2. what the likelihood of occurrence of such major reactor accidents might be. This report, also designated as WASH-740, was used primarily in preparing the Price-Anderson Act, but has been used as a separate issue of fact by environmental extremists. It needs discussion and explanation in clear factual terms, always keeping in mind that it deals with purely hypothetical or "what if" situations.

A number of decisions and assumptions were required in conducting the study described in the Brookhaven Report. First, it was necessary to describe the term "catastrophic accident." The report stated that under no conceivable circumstances could accidental nuclear explosions in power reactors cause significant direct public damage beyond the boundaries of the exclusion areas around such installations. It also stated that gross malfunctioning in power reactors could not possibly lead to a devastating explosion similar to those produced by nuclear bombs. Therefore, catastrophic accidents could only be interpreted as hypothetical events presenting two possible questions: 1. the probability that accidents might take place, leading to extensive damage through release of fission products, and 2. the magnitude of the hypothetical damage from such large releases. The lack of data or history of such accidents was simply because there had never been any such catastrophic accidents at nuclear power plants. Likewise, there have been no cases of injury to the public as a result of a release of fission products from a nuclear reactor. No other comparable field of endeavor has ever in the history of the human race achieved such a record of safety.

The review of the probability of large accidents was therefore pursued in two other ways. 1. A review was made of the features of reactor design and operation that affect the possibility of accidents to see what might be learned from these. 2. Estimates of the probability were solicited from scientists and engineers prominent in the nuclear field. The list of reactor safety features is formidable. Radioactive fission products generated during operations are confined within a succession of physical barriers, all of which would have to fail simultaneously in an indescribable series of incredible events, for a major accident to occur:

1. The fission products would have to escape from the solid fuel elements where they are part of the solid structure.
2. Thus the elements would first have to melt or evaporate.
3. The fission products would then have to escape the cladding that surrounds the fuel which gives it structural rigidity and protection.

The fission products would then have to escape from the primary reactor vessel and piping which are excessively sturdy and substantial. These barriers are inherent built-in features of nuclear reactors; that is, they are present for operational reasons. The safety that they provide is inherent safety. In addition, other features of reactor design increase safety still further. The most important and impressive of these is the containment structure that surrounds the reactor and is designed to retain its contents despite anything that might conceivably happen within.

The concept of containment is so startling that when the first containment structure was introduced some years ago as a requirement for a test facility, it was regarded largely as a curiosity, a gilding of the lily, an unneccessarily extreme act of devotion to the goal of safety. These containment structures, most unusual engineering concepts, are large in size because they must completely surround large facilities, yet highly leakproof and capable of containing gas pressures without failure. They have become so familiar that they are taken for granted. This is unjust, because the containment structure enveloping a nuclear reactor is almost a revolution in the engineering of absolute safety unmatched in any other area.

To produce a large accident hypothetically, it must be assumed that somehow an accident involving two major failures in concert has started and that no safety features have been effective at all. Fission products must be assumed to have escaped, in succession, passing each of the barriers engineered to confine them as listed above. Furthermore, a number of additional redundant secondary or back-up safety systems required for every modern nuclear reactor would also have, incredibly, to fail. These include such engineered safeguards as core spray systems, coolant injection systems (extremists have charged that one of these, the ECCS emergency core cooling system, is unreliable; this is discussed below), containment spray systems, and similar systems for controlling the pressure in the containment, and containment air cleanup systems. All of these would have to fail, as all of the successive physical barriers. This adds up to less than 1:100 billion accident probability.

These protective features are so impressive that it was concluded that the probability of a large accident which would submit the public to hazards from fission products is extraordinarily improbable (now estimated, as noted, at less than 1:100 billion). In spite of this conclusion, the JCAE *required* estimates of the magnitude of effects of the "hypothetically incredible" accident. An analysis was therefore made of the consequences of accidents in which *no safety features were present in any form.* Since no realistic method of dispersing fission products was known, it was assumed that by some "unknown process" an "instantaneous" dispersion of the power reactor occurred (a ridiculous assumption). Calculations were then made of the distribution and deposition of fission products as a function of time. In 1957, much of the physical and chemical information basic to an analysis of the distribution and deposition of the fission products was unknown. Many simplifying assumptions were arbitrarily made as needed, purposely chosen to be conservative, so that damage estimates would be at the upper limits. Better data on fission product release mechanisms now available prove that the calculations led to gross overestimates, as was intended. The final report made the following statement: "We are not aware of such a study undertaken for any other industry.... If such a study were to be made with the same free rein to the imagination, we might be startled to learn what catastrophic accidents in other industries could be in contrast with the actual experience in those industries."

To estimate a corresponding hypothetical accident in the area of the commercial air transport of passengers, we might dream up an accident involving a collision of all the aircraft simultaneously stacked up over Kennedy, La Guardia, and Newark airports, all the debris falling into Shea Stadium during a Sunday doubleheader. The Brookhaven Report is not used by environmental extremists for what it contains or says, but as a scare document using the results of a "hypothetically incredible" incident. They would better use their time preparing for another "Krakatoa."

Light Water, Gas-Cooled, and Breeder Reactors

On June 4, 1971, President Nixon announced that "our best hope today for meeting the nation's growing demand for economical clean energy lies with the fast breeder reactor." He then increased the federal support of both breeder research and the construction of a commercial-size breeder demonstration plant by 1980. This commitment to the breeder capitalizes on a new, complex, and sophisticated technology. An understanding of the basic principles is helpful in appreciating the breeder's importance.

The fast breeder reactor approaches both the perpetual motion machine and the alchemist's dream. It complements present-generation light-water reactor plants and adds two major benefits: 1. a potential to reduce the cost of power generation, and 2. the contribution to an improved environment. By the year 2000 electric power consumption is projected to be several times greater than it is today. If the fast breeder is developed to commercial readiness within a reasonable period, about half of the power generated in the year 2000 will be produced by nuclear energy.

One type of breeder reactor, called the liquid metal fast breeder reactor (LMFBR), is economical because it uses leftover by-products from today's conventional light-water reactors (LWR) as fuel. It also produces more breeder fuel than it consumes by transmutation of uranium into plutonium at a faster rate than plutonium is consumed. Most uranium-fueled light-water reactors on today's nuclear power scene produce some plutonium. The LWR has captured a large percentage of new-generation investments. Their acceptance has been enhanced by the favorable economics of today's plants, which are outperforming fossil-fueled plants in most parts of the country. Lelan F. Sillin, president of Northeast Utilities, reported in April 1973 on the Millstone Unit 1,[30] "The cost of electricity it produced in 1972 was about 8.5 mills per kwhr. In our fossil plants the comparable costs were about 11 mills per kwhr. Furthermore, the Millstone Unit had generated in excess of seven billion kwhr of electricity prior to the shutdown and for a large new generating unit, it had performed well during the first twenty-one months of its operation."

Connecticut Yankee is in its sixth year of operation and is the lowest-cost producer of base-load electric power in New England, about 5.4 mills per kwhr. Its plant availability during its first five years was 81 per cent, high for any type of generating station.

Commonwealth Edison, which operates about 20 per cent of the nuclear capacity in the nation, shows that from September 1972 to February 1973 its nuclear power plants significantly outperformed even its newest coal plants.[31] Commonwealth's four largest fossil plants averaged 74 per cent availability and its four largest nuclear plants averaged 72 per cent. This does not include the company's oldest and smallest nuclear plant, Dresden 1, which had an availability record of 95 per cent. During the calendar year of 1972 the fuel, operation, and maintenance cost of Commonwealth's oil and gas-fired peaking units were 15.1 mills per kwhr; for its base-load fossil plants, 6.3 mills per kwhr; and for its nuclear plants, 2.4 mills per kwhr.

There are two types of light-water-cooled power reactors: pressurized water reactors and boiling water reactors. In the pressurized water reactor, the cooling water (primary coolant) is kept under sufficient pressure to prevent boiling in the reactor vessel. On leaving the vessel, the water passes through a heat exchanger in which it gives up its heat to a separate flow of water (secondary coolant), thereby converting the latter to steam. Then it flows back to the reactor in a new cycle. In a boiling-water reactor, the cooling water is allowed to boil in the reactor vessel, generating steam in the primary system. This steam can be used to drive the turbine, then is condensed, and the condensate is returned to the reactor vessel. It should be emphasized that in both systems the reactor's cooling water circulates within a closed circuit and is completely isolated from its

130

Pressurized water reactor (PWR)

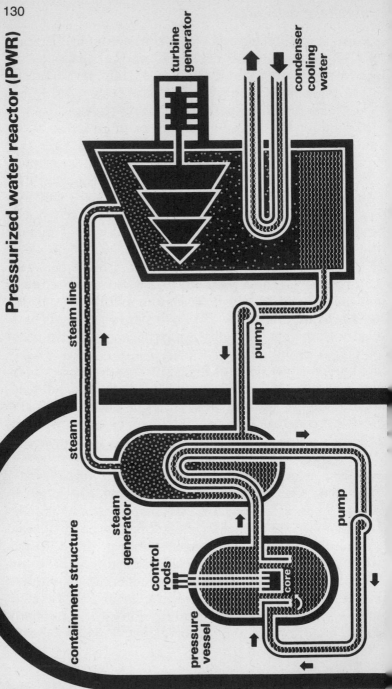

turbine generator

condenser cooling water

steam line

steam

pump

containment structure

steam generator

control rods

pump

pressure vessel

core

Boiling water reactor (BWR)

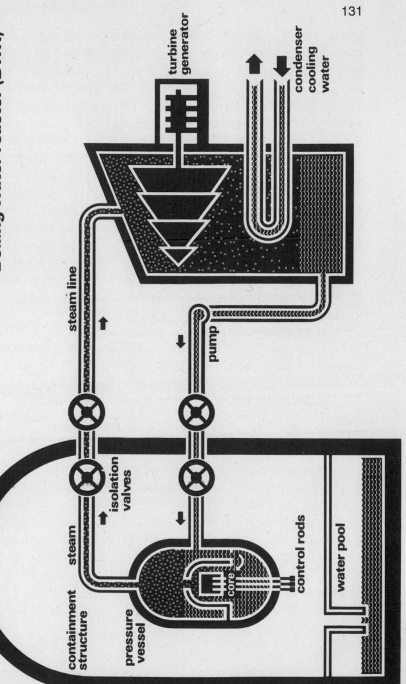

original source (river, lake, or ocean). The only water that flows in and out of the plant is the water used to cool the turbine's condensers. This water does not flow through the reactor. Its function is merely to carry unusable heat away from the plant. The LWRs are not obsolete or on the verge of being replaced. They have proved to be highly efficient, much more than originally anticipated, and with further experience will improve greatly. They are "light-water" reactors because they use regular water (HOH) in the reactor core as opposed to some experimental reactors which use "heavy water" (HOD—D meaning deuterium, an isotope of hydrogen) in the core.

The safety record of LWRs is the strongest statement in their favor. Some extremists charge otherwise, describing them as dangerous. David Brower, founder and president of Friends of the Earth, is one of the most vocal and active opponents of nuclear power. He has lashed out at the AEC as "...being more concerned with the safety of an estimated $40 billion commitment to the development of atomic energy than it is with protecting the public from the worst pollutant on earth." In his monthly publication, *Not Man Apart,* he wrote: "Rattlesnakes are harmless unless, of course, they bite." Brower has joined with other environmental organizations in petitioning the Joint Committee on Atomic Energy to include environmentalists in the two groups set up to administer the fast breeder reactor project. The petitioning organizations include Environmental Action, National Intervenors, Natural Resources Defense Council, Scientists' Institute for Public Information, and Ralph Nader's Project for Corporate Responsibility. In a later issue of his letter, in a piece titled "The Sun is a Splendid Nuclear Reactor But You Wouldn't Want to

Live There," Brower says that because of the possibility
of accidents, "your genes and those of everyone you
love or will someday love are at stake." A form letter,
soliciting donations, is included with each mailing.

LWR accident probability is now calculated at one in
one hundred billion. Nevertheless, a recurring statement about a relatively high probability of a major nuclear power accident has made the rounds. It stems in
part from misquoting an AEC report on reactor safety,
which was prepared for the JCAE. In a *Science* article
of January 26, 1973, Robert Gillete wrote:[34] "The report
estimates that the chances for a nuclear power plant
suffering a serious accident and a consequent release of
radioactivity may, for a given reactor in a given year, be
as great as one in a thousand. Coupling this estimate
with the AEC's projection that about one hundred reactors will be operating in the United States by 1980, and
one thousand by the end of the century, the report indicates that one such accident each year may become a
virtual certainty."

The interpretation is generally that the probability of
a serious accident is about one in a thousand, "serious"
generally implying a catastrophic accident. The fact is
that the AEC report says that a truly *major* accident,
one releasing five million curies of radioactivity, has a
probability of about one in one hundred billion each
year. The one in a thousand estimate relates to a fairly
minor accident releasing one to ten curies. This amount
is described as "comparable to the annual releases of radioactivity in liquid effluents from LWRs." The *Science*
article did include the one in one hundred billion odds,
but several paragraphs later, and reporters basing a story
on the article have uniformly been omitting the greater
number. The passage in its entirety reads: "For a thou-

sand operating nuclear power plants (the approximate number expected by the year 2000) having the characteristics assumed directly or indirectly in the study, the chance of an accident leading to the release of about five million curies of activity is about one in one hundred billion each year (10^{-14} probability/year x 10^3 reactor years of operation per calendar year = 10^{-11} combined probability per year for all reactors). However, for an accident leading to the release of 1 to 10 curies, the chance is about once a year from one of the one thousand operating reactors (10^{-3} probability per year x 10^3 reactor years of operation per calendar year = 1 per year)." On the following page the AEC expressed the risks in terms of fatalities. It said that even after a "pile-up" of pessimistic assumptions, "for a dense urban population of fifty persons per acre, the total risk to the nearby population was found to be 9 x 10^{-5} fatalities per year, or about 0.003 deaths during a thirty-year reactor lifetime." Another way of expressing this figure, the AEC said, would be a "chance for one fatality from about 370 contemporary 1,000 MWe plants during their minimal service life of thirty years." Even these numbers, the report emphasizes, "involve a number of upper limit assumptions which surely lead to overstating the risks that would be encountered in practice by a larger factor."

In a more recent amplification of the accident probabilities, Dr. Herbert Kouts, Atomic Energy Commission director of reactor safety, stated: "the odds on a major catastrophe at a nuclear power plant were given in [an MIT] study as 'once in one billion to once in ten billion years' for a given reactor." The catastrophic accident refers to an incident which might cause 10,000 fatalities. To put this into perspective, with the 1,000 reactors expected to be operating by the year 2000, odds would be once in a million to once in ten million years.

The probability of a less severe accident, Dr. Kouts reported, is "once in a million to once in ten million years for any given reactor." The less severe accident can be compared to an airline crash where some 100 fatalities could be expected. Considering the 1,000 reactors expected to be in operation by the year 2000, the odds would be once in one thousand to once in ten thousand years.

In a recently published book, *Your World, My World: A Book for Young Environmentalists,* the Environmental Protection Agency states: "Nuclear power can generate electricity in almost unlimited amounts without using up scarce supplies of fossil fuels," and on safety, "in nearly twenty years of nuclear development, no member of the public has been injured by the operation of a commercial nuclear power plant."

In February 1971, the midwestern chapters of the Sierra Club submitted to the national board of directors a report that called for "qualified approval of nuclear power. For most situations, nuclear power plants appear to offer the best source of electrical power for the immediate future with a minimum of environmental damage. The Sierra Club should not oppose nuclear power plants in principle."

In October 1970, the *New England Sierran* contained a two-page analysis of the energy crisis and its environmental ramifications.[35] It states: "Common sense tells us that [power plant emission] is of no danger whatsoever. . . . One would have to pack one-half of the population of this country within one mile of the [Dresden plant] for one year to detect one or two cases of leukemia due to radiation over the 6,000 cases which would normally occur in the unexposed other one-hundred million people." The article concludes: "The choice: overwhelmingly in favor of nuclear power."

LWRs consume enriched uranium fuel, which may become more expensive in the future; therefore, the breeder must be developed. It produces more fissionable fuel than it consumes, by 1. using waste fuel components from LWRs to fuel itself; 2. producing power, and 3. producing more fuel than it uses, which in turn can be used to run other LWRs or breeders. Therefore, breeders and LWRs will work together, sustaining each other with a shared fuel cycle and reducing the cost of electric power. They complement each other in another important way. The lower fuel cost of the breeder is ideal for base-load operation, while the greater loading flexibility of the LWR enables it to respond to variations in load. The LWR is fueled with nonfissionable but fertile 238 U, slightly enriched (2 to 5 per cent) with the fissionable isotope of uranium, 235 U, the only fissionable material found in nature. A LWR produces heat through fission, the process by which slow or thermal neutrons strike and split 235 U (or fissile plutonium atoms if they are present), causing them to release energy and more neutrons to continue the reaction. Other neutrons classed as "fast" are not as readily used in this reaction and are usually lost or wasted. Uranium in its natural state contains about .7 of 1 per cent of 235 U. The rest is nonfissile but "fertile" 238 U, fertile because it can capture the otherwise wasted "fast" neutrons and produce plutonium, a fissile fuel. 235 U is concentrated to 2 to 5 per cent by gaseous diffusion, an expensive process. A method using a centrifuge is gradually being improved in the European countries and Israel, but does not produce the purity of 235 U obtained in gaseous diffusion. Gaseous diffusion depletes the bulk of the natural uranium by removing the 235 U, leaving only 238 U. Since the LWR does not use depleted 238 U, it is simply stockpiled. At the present time it has no practical use except in a breeder.

The Atomic Energy Commission has now consigned all the enriched uranium it can produce from the gaseous diffusion plants it operates. This requires the future completion and use of gas centrifuges in the enrichment process. In testimony before the Joint Committee on Atomic Energy on February 21, 1973, and March 5, 1974, F. Baranowski described the AEC pilot centrifuge plant due to start up in 1975, which will have a capacity "appreciably greater" than the 25,000 separative work units per year of the Dutch or German plants. Newer centrifuge designs promise a significant gain in economics. Mass production techniques will be demonstrated with an integrated prototype manufacturing line at both Torrance, California, and Oak Ridge, Tennessee.

The economics of the centrifuge process are promising, but offer no significant capital cost differences compared to gaseous diffusion. The Garrett Corporation, the prime contractor for the AEC on centrifuges for over a decade, has operated centrifuges for eight years without failure. Newer designs have been in operation without failure for two years. The obvious advantages of the centrifuge process are lower operating costs and reduced plant size, allowing enrichment facilities to be located closer to power plants and, in fact, as parts of large power parks. Plant size can be increased on demand and can be owned and operated by the user companies.

Several European nations, Israel, South Africa, and Australia, to name a few, are planning gas centrifuge facilities for 235 U production. The enriched isotope will be sold or traded rather than the ore, thereby providing these producers the price advantage of value-added processing.

Diffusion depletes the bulk of the natural uranium by removing the 235 U, leaving only 238 U. Since the

LWR does not use depleted 238 U, it is simply stockpiled. At the present time it has no practical use except in a breeder or limited military applications.

Another energy source is made available with the High-temperature Gas-cooled Reactor (HTGR) referred to by many as the second generation of power reactors to follow and replace LWRs. There are fewer of them in operation, but they represent concepts and possess features which make them more efficient and attractive in several ways. Developed and built by the General Atomics Division of the Gulf Oil Corporation, they are now being proposed in more applications and models.

HTGRs have a higher thermal efficiency (39 per cent) and discharge heat quantities comparable to the most efficient fossil units, somewhat less than the LWR of comparable size. The HTGR's gaseous coolant system, combined with the installed fission-product trapping devices, results in lower radioactive gaseous discharges.

Helium gas is used as a reactor coolant while graphite serves as the moderator and core structural material. The fuel is a mixture of enriched uranium and thorium, used in the form of carbide particles individually clad with ceramic coatings. Helium makes it possible to achieve high operating temperatures and it also remains in the same phase, making complete loss of coolant a physical impossibility. Helium is specifically desirable because it is chemically inert, absorbs essentially no neutrons, contributes no reactivity to the system, and is readily available in the tonnages required to meet large-scale HTGR requirements.

Graphite used as the moderator and core structural material presents a low neutron capture cross section, excellent thermal conductivity, mechanical strength at temperatures beyond the HTGR range, high specific heat, and ease of fabrication. There is no metal in the HTGR core. All structural elements within the active core and reflector region are graphite, which gains strength in an inert environment as the temperature is increased to about 4,500°F and maintains usable strength up to much higher temperatures. It does not melt, and essentially no sublimation occurs below 6,500°F. The fuel, in the form of coated uranium and thorium particles (melting point about 4,450 F), is coated with pyrolytic carbon to retain fission products and is then incorporated into the graphite fuel/moderator elements.

The reactor and the entire primary coolant system are contained within a massive prestressed concrete reactor vessel, which provides significant inherent safety advantages. It also has the practical advantage of being built and assembled at the site instead of having to be transported from a factory to the plant.

The HTGR program is based on the thorium fuel cycle. The thorium cycle with uranium 233 recycle is highly economic, provided that a growing HTGR economy allows for a sufficient throughput for the reprocessing and refabrication facilities. This is the standard cycle, though various fuel cycles can be used with HTGRs. Thorium used in combination with highly enriched uranium, has two highly desireable features. First uranium 233, bred from thorium 232 during reactor operations, has the highest neutron yield per fissile loss of any fissile material in a thermal neutron environment. Since a significant fraction of the total energy output of HTGRs derive from the fission of bred 233 U, higher conversion ratios can be achieved than are possible in nuclear power systems that operate with the low enrichment uranium cycle. Secondly, the use of thorium, which is available in abundance and at low cost,

High temperature gas-cooled reactor (HTGR)

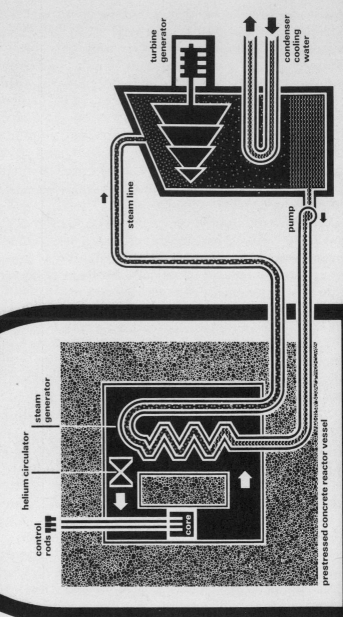

containment structure

control rods

helium circulator

steam generator

core

prestressed concrete reactor vessel

steam line

pump

turbine generator

condenser cooling water

helps conserve uranium resources. It is on this latter point that the HTGR is perhaps most attractive. Because of its inherent efficiency and its utilization of thorium, R. H. Brogli and K. R. Schultz, staff physicists of the General Atomic Company, described thorium use in a Gas-Cooled Fast Reactor (GCFR), producing uranium 233 in a thorium blanket, with several uranium 233 fueled HTGRs forming a symbiotic GCFR/HTGR system. This is discussed briefly under the breeder programs.

As 235 U fissions in a reactor, a certain percentage of the released neutrons are captured by the "fertile" 238 U, and by the process of transmutation, 239 Pu is created. The nuclear process thereby revolves around neutrons. About every ten atoms of fissile 235 U consumed in a LWR create six atoms of 239 Pu, providing for a LWR breeding ratio of 0.6, since during fissioning the LWR uses only the "slow" or thermal neutrons and the high-energy neutrons are wasted or lost.

The interaction characteristics of fast neutrons with 238 U produce fourteen atoms of 239 Pu for every ten atoms of uranium fissioned, a breeding ratio of 1.4. Fast-breeder fuel is enriched with about 14 per cent fissile 239 Pu, one of the by-products of LWRs. The remainder of the core is made of depleted "fertile" 238 U. This entire core is then surrounded by another blanket of depleted "fertile" 238 U. During the breeder chain reaction, while some neutrons are fissioning 239 Pu atoms and releasing heat energy, other neutrons are being captured by 238 U atoms. These 238 U atoms are thus converted into more new 239 Pu atoms. All nuclear reactors generate a certain amount of fissile 239 Pu during the release of energy through neutron absorption in 238 U. Although 238 U is fissionable by high-energy neutrons, this fission reaction has different physical characteristics than the 235 U fission and contributes very little energy output in a reactor. The important difference, then, in the two reactors is the "plutonium conversion ratio": 0.6 for the LWR and 1.4 for the breeder. A ratio of one is required to be a self-sustaining breeder.

The 239 Pu produced by LWRs, the unfissioned 235 U, and fission products are periodically removed from the fuel at a reprocessing plant. There are two products left from the LWR fuel cycle, depleted 238 U left over from the gaseous diffusion plant, and 239 Pu recovered during fuel reprocessing. The breeder employs them both, creating highly favorable economics for nuclear power generation. Both the breeder and the LWR use 238 U as the bulk of their fuel components, but in the breeder it is more highly enriched, in either 235 U or 239 Pu. Much of the latter initially will come from the growing stockpiles of 239 Pu being extracted as a by-product of today's conventional LWRs. This interdependence between the reactors of today and those of tomorrow is basic to the rationale of the breeder.

Another advantage of fast-breeder economics, besides a high breeding ratio, is "high burn-up," a key to the breeder's potential for low overall power generation cost as measured in mills per kwhr.[36] By sustaining itself on bred plutonium and producing excess plutonium for sale, the breeder fuel cycle cost will be .4 to .7 mills per kwhr compared to 1.1 mills per kwhr for the LWR. Recovered plutonium, when fabricated as a fuel for a conventional LWR, will be worth about $9 per gram. That same plutonium used to fuel a fast breeder will be worth about $14. The extra value is from the physical characteristics of plutonium which make it a better fuel for a breeder than for a light-water reactor. The time it takes a breeder to produce enough fuel to replenish its own plutonium needs and those of one other reactor like it is called doubling time and varies depending on how it is done. Simple doubling time, achieved by storing the bred plutonium, requires about sixteen years; compound doubling time, achieved by putting the bred plutonium to work immediately to breed more plutonium, is calculated to take twelve years. There is a third formula, system doubling time, the period required to double the amount of plutonium in the entire fuel-cycle system, not just the reactor, but also fabrication, reprocessing and storage sites, requiring possibly nineteen years by simple doubling time and just under fourteen years by compound doubling. All these projections are based on today's reactor and fuels technology. Advanced breeder reactors may reduce doubling times to seven to ten years.

Fuel management schemes can improve these figures significantly. It should be noted that minimum doubling time does not necessarily produce minimum fuel-cycle costs. For example, design may attain a shorter doubling time by simply adding more blanket elements. However, a point is reached where the incremental costs of the blanket elements are greater than the value of the incremental increases in plutonium production. The design must be optimized, taking into account capital costs, fuel costs, and power generation costs, as well as doubling time.

The fast breeder will conserve the world's energy resources by stretching available, reasonably priced uranium reserves from less than a century to thousands of years. The breeder's second desirable attribute lies in its relatively slight environmental impact, although it differs only in amount or degree, not in kind. To consider resource conservation first, while a conventional reactor uses only 1 to 2 per cent of the energy available in uranium, the breeder will use 60 per cent or more. Over

144

Liquid metal fast breeder reactor (LMFBR)

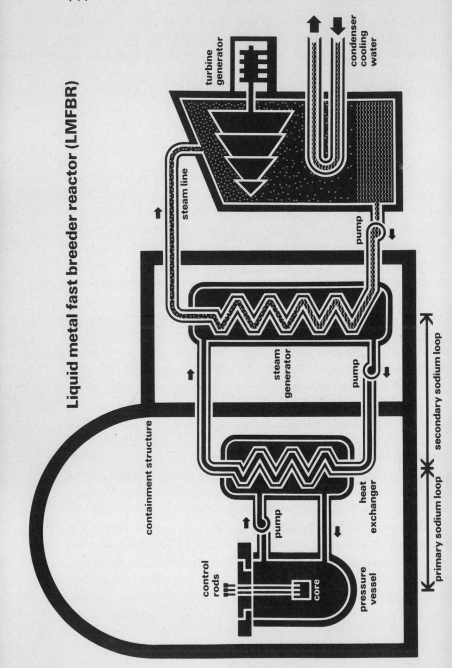

turbine generator

condenser cooling water

steam line

pump

steam generator

pump

secondary sodium loop

containment structure

heat exchanger

primary sodium loop

control rods

pump

core

pressure vessel

the next fifty years, use of the breeder could reduce by 1.2 million tons the amount of uranium consumed. This is the energy equivalent of about three billion tons of coal. If the breeder is introduced in the mid-1980s, the gross savings in United States electric energy cost to the year 2020 are estimated by government economists at well over $200 billion.

The breeder's biggest environmental advantage over LWRs and most present-day fossil-fueled generators is its greater thermal efficiency, reducing the thermal impact on cooling water sources. Water is not needed to cool the breeder reactor itself but, like any steam power plant, requires coolant water to condense steam. The breeder operates at higher temperatures and steam pressures than the LWR, at a thermal efficiency of 39 per cent or better and on a par with the most modern fossil-fueled plants. This compares with about 32 per cent for LWRs and a current national average for all fossil-fuel plants of 33 per cent. The breeder will dissipate about 4,800 Btu's of heat for each kwhr generated, compared to 6,600 Btu's per kwhr for a conventional reactor. Of prime importance, like today's nuclear power reactors, the breeder will not add products of combustion to the atmosphere.

Three types of pollutants result from routine operation of fast breeder reactors: waste heat, radioactive effluents, and radioactive wastes. A fast breeder operating with a thermal efficiency of 41 per cent would convey 1440 Mw of heat to condenser cooling water, about the same as modern fossil-fired plants. In terms of fission product production, LWRs generate about 25 per cent more radioactive fission products than fast breeder reactors of comparable electric generation capacity because of their lower thermal efficiency.

There are differences in the activation products formed by the neutron irradiation of reactor coolants in LMFBRs and LWRs. For the most part, the activation products in LWRs are composed of gases which have very short half-lives and decay rapidly. The main activation product in a LMFBR is the sodium coolant. The principal radioactive isotope of sodium has a half-life of fifteen hours, limiting access to the primary system for a week or ten days after reactor shutdown. Amount of high-level wastes from LMFBRs is small. In one demonstration plant of 500 Mwe, it is estimated to be less than ten cubic feet per year. Solid waste disposal at the plant site is similar to that for all nuclear plants and involves packaging waste materials in a form that is safe for shipment to a government waste management site. Liquid wastes generated in the reactor building from cleaning and decontamination of the primary system are collected, stored, monitored, and packaged for off-site shipment, using solidification to reduce the cost of disposal. Gaseous waste, released as planned, would be less than .1 to 1 per cent of the exposure from natural background radiation. Normally the gases are collected by a low-temperature system and bottled for shipment to a management site for storage and decay. Only a few cubic feet per year are expected to be generated.

The safety does not differ significantly between the LMFBR and LWRs. Both have conservative design margins, inherent safety design features, multiple barriers to fission products, adequate protective systems to prevent accidents, and engineered safety features to mitigate the consequences of accidents. The sodium-cooled fast breeder reactor has unique advantages due to the excellent cooling properties of sodium and its low vapor pressure.

A LMFBR operates at low pressure, well below the boiling point of sodium. As a result there is negligible stored energy in the coolant and no loss of primary core cooling or potential for pressurization, and the sodium provides good heat transfer even at very low flow. Sodium also has an affinity for fission products which tends to inhibit fission-product problems. Here are the reasons so much emphasis is being placed on the development of the LMFBR in both the United States and Europe as the energy source of the future: 1. savings on power-generating costs; 2. establishment of a premium market for plutonium generated in LWRs; 3. protection of today's investment in LWRs; and 4. an abundant supply of low-cost electricity. The LMFBR breeder reactor can achieve these economic goals while protecting the environment better than any alternate method of generating electric power currently available. Its potential environmental benefits include: 1. conservation of natural resources; 2. lack of air pollutants; and 3. reduced thermal pollution. Yet, despite these facts and the fact that an environmental impact statement has been prepared for the LMFBR, Barry Commoner and Margaret Mead have obtained an injunction to stop the breeder program (the injunction was later set aside).

The principles of fast breeders have been known for as long as man has tried to use nuclear energy in reactors. It was a small breeder, the AEC's now-decommissioned Experimental Breeder Reactor No. 1 (EBR-1) in Idaho, that generated the world's first electricity from nuclear energy in 1951. Since that time the United States and several other countries have experimented with a variety of materials to extract heat from a breeder core. These included steam, helium gas, molten uranium, thorium salts, and liquid metals. Virtually every country pursuing the breeder concept is now concentrating on liquid metals, specifically molten sodium as the preferred coolant, although work continues on alternate and back-up coolant systems.

In the United States these other experiments include one fast breeder, the gas-cooled fast breeder being developed by Gulf General Atomics with AEC and utility support, and two so-called thermal breeders, the Molten Salt Breeder, under study at Oak Ridge National Laboratory, and the LW breeder reactor, being investigated under Admiral H. G. Rickover's direction with AEC funds at the Bettis Atomic Power Laboratory operated by Westinghouse. The priority program adopted by both the AEC and United States industry is the LMFBR, using molten sodium as a breeder coolant.

The three announced United States manufacturers of LMFBRs are pursuing two different core-containment concepts. General Electric proposes the pool-type system, in which a large tank filled with sodium encloses all major components, the reactor vessel, sodium pumps, and intermediate heat exchangers. Westinghouse and Atomics International are developing the loop-type system in which, much like present-day pressurized water reactors, the reactor vessel is filled with coolant (sodium) and the liquid metal is circulated by pumps through heat exchangers mounted outside the reactor vessel. Both systems employ two sodium heat-transfer loops to isolate the radioactive sodium from the steam-generation equipment.

The impression is often given that the fast breeder is new and only now a coming thing, but prototype and test reactors have operated for years in the United States and abroad. This country now has three experimental fast reactors, none of which is really intended to breed; the Enrico Fermi plant near Detroit, a privately owned sixty-one-megawatt facility that first went on-line in 1963 and was then the world's largest operational fast reactor; the AEC's 16.5 Mw EBR-2 at the National Reactor Testing station in Idaho; and the internationally sponsored SEFOR (Southwest Experimental Fast Oxide Reactor) near Fayetteville, Arkansas, which was operated by General Electric solely to confirm LMFBR safety characteristics. Ground has been broken for a $100 million AEC breeder experiment, the Fast Flux Test Facility (FFTF) at Hanford, Washington, which Westinghouse will operate. In this reactor, fuel components will be irradiation-tested in an intense and highly instrumented neutron environment.

Roughly $500 million is being spent annually (about 25 per cent of it in the United States) the world over for breeder research. For fiscal year 1972, the AEC asked Congress for $103 million for LMFBR reseach and development, up $18 million from the previous year. To this, President Nixon added $27 million. In addition, the AEC recently sought full appropriation of $50 million previously authorized as the government's cash contribution toward the first large-scale demonstration plant, and President Nixon doubled this request to $100 million. The AEC also expects to contribute services and fuel-charge waivers worth $30 million toward this first plant. All three LMFBR contenders have submitted proposals for 300 to 500 megawatt demonstration plants to AEC and their utility supporter.

The big question is, how many such demonstration plants can or should the government and industry build, considering that the first one will cost between $400 and $500 million? The impression has also been created that other countries are ahead in the breeder race. While physical plant progress supports this view, not all national development schemes take the same approach. (The United States, for example, is concentrating on component development before it turns to large reactor construction.) It is unlikely that anyone will produce a large commercial LMFBR before 1980, a target the United States would be hard-pressed to meet under its present funding and rates and data schedule.

Priority has been given to achieving fuel performance objectives. The fuel should achieve close to 100,000 MWD/T (megawatt days per ton) or about 12 per cent burn-up of the uranium and plutonium in the fuel. This is about three times the burn-up of LWR fuel.

With regard to the importance plutonium will have as a fuel and its importance to the future, some background on it as an element and a resource is interesting. Plutonium (Pu), element number 94, was discovered in 1940 by Glenn T. Seaborg, Arthur C. Wahl, and Joseph W. Kennedy at the University of California. There are fifteen isotopes of plutonium whose half-lives range from twenty minutes to seventy-six million years and whose atomic weights range from 232 to 246. 239 Pu is worth about $7,416 per kilogram.

One breeder reactor can be refueled exclusively with the plutonium produced each year by about four reactors of the same size. New reactors require more fuel initially, three to four times the annual replacement requirement. The recycling of plutonium in the fuel of nuclear reactors will significantly affect future needs for uranium raw material and separation capacity. Plutonium exists as a metal, an alloy, or in a number of chemical compounds.[37] It has some unique properties—239 Pu and 241 Pu are the most abundant fissionable isotopes recovered from spent nuclear fuel from LWRs. Alpha particle emission absorbed into the crystal structure of a plutonium compound makes 239 Pu metal warm to the touch, and 238 metal too hot to hold in the hand without protection. This 238 Pu intensity makes a valuable source of heat for use in thermoelectric generators, heart pacers, and other prospective applications requiring a concentrated and reliable source of heat.

238 Pu thermoelectric generators are used in a number of space missions, both manned and unmanned.

Like most other heavy metals (including eleven which are more toxic, eight which are equally toxic, and many slightly less toxic), plutonium emits alpha particles which have little penetrating power (less than 4 cm. in air, and less than 50 microns in body tissue). Because of this low penetrating power, the particles dissipate their energy close to the point of deposition in the body; for this reason, alpha particles are assigned a high RBE (relative biological effectiveness value). Plutonium, like most other materials, can enter the body in three ways: inhalation or absorption through the lungs; ingestion and absorption through the gastrointestinal tract; or by absorption through the skin. Like many metals, plutonium is a bone-seeker and may be deposited in the skeleton. Radiation protection standards discussed earlier are based on the toxicity of plutonium intake as well as for uranium, radium, americium, neptunium, etc. Protection of persons outside plutonium processing facilities is accomplished in accordance with the population exposure criteria of the official radiation standards, which require special processing and monitoring of all wastes, plus engineering design which protects against natural phenomena or hypothetical accident situations.

One of the major recent assaults on nuclear power stems from the suggestion by antinuclear spokesmen that plutonium is subject to hijacking for bomb construction and subsequent blackmail. This strange equation hinges upon large quantities of 239 Pu being in unguarded locations known to hijackers, its seizure and fabrication into an explosive device, followed by capitulation by authorities to blackmail. If this is indeed a valid proposition, and such great risks will be taken to obtain a nuclear weapon, why have no raids or attempts to steal conventional nuclear weapons been made? Hundreds are stored, shipped, and transported routinely with no history of hijacking. It would be much simpler because these weapons are already fabricated and tested, and more importantly, they are available. The response from antinuclear spokesmen usually deals with the protection the Armed Forces provide for the security and safe handling of these devices. If this is the argument, it reinforces the proposition that plutonium can also be handled with equal facility. Next, the companion argument that 239 Pu is so highly toxic as to be unique is just not so. As stated above, a host of heavy metals are assigned equal or greater levels of toxicity by the International Radiation Protection Committee, the National Committee on Radiation Protection, and the United Nations Scientific Committee on Atomic Radiation. An additional comment in this regard is made in the section on radioactive waste. Altogether the 239 Pu fear is lacking in substance and when examined scientifically and rationally, evaporates like other superstitions.

Molten-salt reactors are a type of breeder that use liquid fuel: solutions of uranium and thorium flourides in lithium, zirconium, and beryllium flourides. They operate at high temperature and low pressure and have excellent nuclear characteristics. They offer promise as breeders of fissionable material and as producers of low-cost electricity in large central power stations. A molten-salt reactor experiment (MSRE) has been conducted by the Oak Ridge National Laboratory to demonstrate that the desirable features of the molten-salt concept can be embodied in a practical reactor which could be constructed, operated, and maintained with safety and reliability. The fuel is a mixture of molten lithium, beryllium, and zirconium flouride salts, which is a solvent for uranium or thorium and uranium flourides. The fuel is pumped through several hundred channels in a graphite core where the fissioning occurs, heating the fuel to 1,225 degrees F. The fuel is fluid at reactor temperatures, thereby eliminating extra costs associated with fabrication, handling, and reprocessing of solid fuel elements. The fuel can be reprocessed continuously in a side stream for removal of fission products, and new fissionable material can be added while the reactor is in operation. Molten-salt reactors can operate at high temperatures and produce high pressure super-heated steam to achieve thermal efficiencies in the heat-power cycle equal to the best fossil fuel plants.

The most important aspect of the MSRE is its ability to utilize thorium as a fuel. Resources of thorium are tremendous and will continue in abundant supply. Thorium as a nuclear fuel poses no environmental problems more severe than those of uranium. United States reserves are about 23 per cent of acknowledged world reserves, mainly in thorite deposits of Idaho and Montana and in monazite beach sands of the southeastern United States, and are enormous relative to the present production. Thorium will continue its minor, supplementary role relative to uranium nuclear fuels. It can expand United States and world resources of fissionable material. As a source of fissionable material, thorium was placed under the control of the AEC by the AEC Act of 1946, and a license is required for most transactions in thorium-bearing materials.

Radioactive Waste Management

The problem of radioactive waste management is one of the most widely discussed later nuclear issues. As the nuclear industry increases its role in meeting the nation's energy requirements, the quantity of radioactive waste, though small, is amplified. It is an issue which can quickly be blown out of perspective. The history of radioactive waste storage and management reveals that the problems are minor in regard to public health and are rather easily managed from a technological point of view.

Stories have been written frequently of the disastrous occurrences at Hanford, Washington. Periodically a news reporter with nothing to do, or at the suggestion of his boss to "stir the pot," makes a trip to the Hanford facility. He first·rereads all of the previously published reports on the liquid waste stored there and the "leaks" that have occurred. In 1971, A. Robert Smith, Washington, D.C., correspondent of the *Oregonian*, wrote a feature article headlined "Public Unaware, Hanford Waste 'Frightful Problem.' "

Smith writes: "Surely enough to eliminate human life from much of the continent if it ever got lost into the air or water, [it is] the terrifying residue of a quarter century of manufacturing plutonium for atomic bombs and nuclear-armed missiles. This waste dump...will threaten mankind, and in the meantime no one is sure what is to be done with the stuff." Smith is particularly upset because the persons who have "known about it and those who have been informed found no reason to make a public issue of it." This is an untenable situation for a scrambling newsman; the pot must boil. It may produce a by-line and build the watchdog image of the paper.

It has been no secret that leaks occur, but geological conditions at the site prevent hazards from developing by isolating the material from the ground water. These facts are too tame for such observers as Smith. The area has been thoroughly and continuously monitored, indicating these wastes were absorbed in the soil within ten feet of the bottom of the tanks, or about 200 feet above the ground-water supply. The AEC plans eventually to solidify all these wastes, but though the waste is only of an intermediate level of activity, there is a lot of it, and solidification is costly.

Smith was also alarmed by an incident that occurred on the Hanford Reservation when ducks alighted in a holding pond, even though it was screened and noise guns were used to scare off waterfowl. Hanford officials estimated that one pound of flesh from a duck would give a person 1 per cent of the maximum permissible intake of two microcuries of 90 Sr. Smith did not know what this meant. He describes isotopes as killers, and plutonium as the chief killer. In the words of Ralph Waldo Emerson: "Fear always springs from ignorance."

Ralph Nader was next. On July 4, 1973, he wrote about a leak that occurred in June 1973. Nader insinuated a dark conspiracy and illicit activities on the part of the AEC. He stated that the AEC had no positive knowledge and noted that they were in the dark on the situation, when in fact, as mentioned above, Hanford is one of the most carefully monitored areas of the world.

Nader erroneously stated: "No technically or economically acceptable method for long-term waste disposal is yet available. Moreover, no scientist holds out much hope that these wastes can be detoxified, certainly not in the next several generations.... Serious genetic damage, various kinds of cancers, and depending on the massiveness of the dose, fairly sudden fatalities can occur from exposure to these virulent wastes. For the most part, the potential longer range damage of this silent violence to present and future generations lulls people into a false sense of security. By the time the risks materialize into their human tragedies, it will be too late to do much about them." This is nonsense.

The best solution for the public is to look at the record. In spite of all shrill cries for someone to do something, and dire warnings of a frightful and terrible catastrophe, there has been no significant adverse ecological effect shown from the Hanford waste situation. Nader describes the terrible consequences of the radioactive materials if dispersed into the environment. As a matter of fact, he reported in the same column the release of 115,000 gallons, and Smith reported the release of 227,400 gallons, but there have been no demonstrated effects. Where are the catastrophic effects they predict?

Los Angeles must have been quiet during July of 1973, so the *Los Angeles Times* sent reporter Lee Dye to Hanford to do another story on the waste. He headlined the story, "Mishandled Nuclear Waste Poses Disaster Threat." He writes: "Radioactive waste is threatening to contaminate areas of the United States, endangering thousands. The AEC, custodian of the deadly byproducts, has taken risks. On many occasions, disaster has been avoided partly because luck has been with the AEC." This reporter is ignorant in the first place and several years late in the second. He also uses such terms as deadly, dangerous, cancer-causing, suffering and says of plutonium, "a speck can be dangerous." Not a very helpful scientific quantification. But, "time is running out," says Dye. Trying to outdo earlier scare items, he quotes an unnamed AEC consultant: "We're sitting on a time bomb." There is no way he can justify this analogy. The only conclusion is that he neither understands the situation nor is qualified to write about it.

Dye uses the same photograph that Smith used in his article in 1971 and the same general story line about Enrico Fermi achieving the first self-sustaining chain-reaction in 1942 in the University of Chicago's Flagg Stadium. He then goes into the wartime Manhattan

Project and in the body of the report copies the useless routine that Smith and others have already published. He includes a statement which is a disclaimer to his own study: "Fortunately, the clay soil beneath the tank held the liquid within the first few feet. Thus, it never entered the water table about 200 feet below the tank or ultimately the Columbia River." There is also a layer of basalt beneath the Hanford reservation, one of the thickest in the world, in excess of 7,500 feet. The AEC is conducting studies of this rock as a possible future permanent disposal site.

If there is a hazard connected with the Hanford waste storage situation, it is one quite different from the radioactive one. It is the awful example of governmental rigidity that the problem presents. The AEC on one hand will not permit the slightest deviation in the private or industrial sector from the radiation protection standards, and none should be expected. Moreover, the AEC enforces strict standards for radioactive waste disposal. As a former member of a nuclear-based company and as a state radiation control director dealing with the AEC, I know the AEC has held a whip-hand and maintained a paternalistic attitude unequaled by any other agency. The suggestion of any problem with the disposal of wastes would always bring a fast and thorough investigation. On the other hand, the AEC's position on its own massive self-operated nuclear waste disposal operations was not an item for discussion anywhere with anyone. This double standard of regulation and performance is government at its most exasperating. The necessary action is to abolish this double standard and require the AEC to do what the private sector does, or vice versa, whichever is in the public interest.

Stories of mischievous reporters looking for a headline will continue to appear as long as Hanford continues to exist. They will all have the same old stale photographs, coot and duck story, plutonium trench situation, and will be well punctuated with the usual scare words, *deadly, disaster, time bomb, cancer, genetics, killer,* and always the ever-present *"can"* or *"could"* rather than what *has,* or *does,* or *will happen.*

The fact remains that no significant impact to any ecological system has occurred, and the only damage done has been to the budget of the Hanford Operation. As a point of explanation, the wastes there are of a lower level than those generated in the nuclear power program, but of a much greater volume. Most are in liquid form. Tankage and maintenance, then, are the Hanford problem, and these have been costly. "Hotter" wastes from the nuclear power program will be small in volume and stored or disposed of in a different manner.

The most significant are the high-level wastes, characterized by intense, penetrating radiation and high temperatures. A portion of the radioactive nuclides contained in these wastes decays slowly and must be isolated for many thousands of years. Providing safe long-term storage for these wastes is a significant part of the nuclear power program. There is presently little waste of this type. Only one commercial fuel reprocessing plant is in operation, with one more nearing completion. Construction may start on another, and at least one additional plant is being designed.

During the past fifteen years, programs and studies have been directed toward completing the nuclear power cycle to include fuel reprocessing. The last required building blocks are: 1. A completely safe inerting storage and shipment program of high-level wastes; and 2. A permanent repository for the storage of such wastes to isolate them from the biosphere.

Some have questioned whether such extreme steps are necessary because on-site storage of fuel reprocessing wastes has been, to date, an acceptable interim solution. The actions now being taken are to assure that high-level liquid waste from nuclear power plants will never become a hazard. Acceptable methods of solidifying high-level liquid wastes will provide for safe shipment and storage. The AEC has already conducted a salt mine demonstration project which would enclose the fuel cycle. The AEC also has established a policy requiring the fuel reprocessors to solidify liquid waste within five years and transfer it to federal repositories within ten years. The salt mine demonstration was intended to be the first federal repository.

A site in the salt beds of central Kansas, at Lyons, was explored as a follow-up to an experiment carried out in the same mine by the Oak Ridge National Laboratory from 1965 to 1967. It demonstrated the effects of heat and radiation on salt with highly satisfactory results. An intensive geological and hydrological program to confirm the safety and suitability of the site was carried out and resulted in the temporary abandonment of that area. This was due primarily to old drill holes made by oil well drillers and salt miners which were not well logged or located on existing maps.

An acceptable site must be located where there are no intercepting holes unless they are definitely located and plugged, which is not a formidable task. There are three general areas in the United States with bedded salt formations that meet the geologic criteria for a radioactive waste repository. These are in central Kansas, west central New York, and southeastern Michigan. An evaluation of these sites indicates that while all three might be suitable, the Kansas area on balance is the most favorable, particularly because of the depth of the salt formations, the thickness and extent of the salt deposit, and the tectonic stability of the area.

Such a facility, as presently conceived, would consist

of a high-level storage operation and an "alpha" or "low-level" operation. The "alpha" facility would provide storage of plutonium-contaminated solid waste from AEC operations. The high-level facility would receive railroad cars carrying casks containing cylinders of waste. The cylinders would be lowered into predrilled holes and backfilled with salt. When all of the floor space had been used, the room would be backfilled with salt.

Beginning this effort early, while the commercial reprocessing industry is still in its infancy, would assure that an acceptable repository is available at the time significant quantities of high-level wastes are available for transfer for permanent disposal. This is expected to occur in the 1980s.

Naturally, Gofman appeared in South Carolina to oppose the Allied-Gulf Nuclear Services fuel reprocessing plant, one of the finest units planned by one of the most highly qualified staffs ever assembled. Gofman tried to explain how 1 per cent of the radioactive inventory of the plant was going to be released and then widely dispersed. He never explained how this release might occur. He expanded the consequences dramatically, once he had assumed that this would happen, stating it would cause the evacuation of most of the East Coast, as far north as New York. Allied-Gulf officials commented on Gofman's statements as follows: "In essence, Dr. Gofman's analysis of a possible catastrophic accident hinges upon the assumption that somehow radioactive materials contained in double stainless-steel tanks, surrounded by four feet of reinforced concrete, and then covered by some ten feet of compacted earth, could somehow get out into the air, where the material could somehow be carried by an imaginary combination of weather and other circumstances to achieve the impact that Dr. Gofman considers possible. We find this simply incredible."

In May 1972, the AEC announced its plan had been altered to employ engineered surface facilities designed to safely isolate waste for centuries if necessary. The wastes could be moved to geologic storage facilities as they are provided. In the AEC and the nuclear waste management field, storage is defined as temporary and disposal as permanent. The volume of high-level waste projected through 1980 is not large, and there is no need for a crash effort to select a permanent disposal method.

(The salt mine or salt dome concept is probably the best final option. Salt structures are the most geologically stable of all known geologic formations. They have been stable for millions of years and will continue to be so for many millions more. Salt absorbs the heat that the waste radiates and in fact becomes more plastic the warmer it becomes. In case of any type of fracture or movement in the surrounding salt medium, the plasticity of the salt will flow enough to create a perfect seal. There is no water in the salt formations and never has been, for this is why the salt is there in the first place. Since it is the most stable geologic formation on the earth, it will remain intact long after the occurrence of a catastrophe which would eliminate civilization and reduce the earth to rubble along with all forms. In other words, salt formations will be the last to go. If a new civilization or a portion of our civilization were to reappear (should total destruction not occur), the wastes would still be safely isolated deep in these salt formations.

Suggestions have been made to propel the waste into

the sun with rockets by trans-solar injection, where it
will be consumed in the sun's fireball. This is a good
idea, but the probabilities of vehicular or mission failure
are much too high. Disposal would require one or two
flights per day. With a failure rate of 1:1000, which was
the recent estimated probability given, once every two
to three years a relatively large amount of radioactive
material could be injected into the stratosphere as fallout. This rules out any possibility of this proposal for
now and sometime well into the future.

Other suggestions include deep arctic or antarctic disposal, surface arctic warehousing, use of huge natural
caverns, uninhabited Pacific or North Atlantic islands,
sealing in concrete and steel vessels to be sunk into the
deepest ocean trenches, such as the Philippine trench,
where it would remain for centuries to decay.

Another proposal would inject the waste into the
earth, well into the molten center where it would be
captured for some several billion years in the molten
core. This suggests more practical overtones. The injection would be made through one of the boundaries of
the various "plates" in the earth's crust which have been
described in recent years. The distance through the
crust of the earth into the molten portion at some of
these plate boundary areas is not great. The "rim-of-
fire" along the Pacific is an example. A distance of four
to eight miles would probably be sufficient to inject material well into the molten mass where the slowly rotating molten core would pick it up, rolling it toward the
core center. If it were ever to surface again, it would
long since have decayed.

A similar and less ambitious but perhaps more feasible procedure consists of drilling 20,000 to 25,000 feet
into selected geologic formations devoid of ground water systems and detonating a nuclear device at the

deepest point to create a large cavern or cistern. Nuclear waste could be emptied into this huge vault and
when filled, a concrete, sand, and earthen plug would
seal the drill hole, sealing forever the material far below
the earth's surface. The technique is simple and
straight-forward and has been done many times to conduct weapons and nuclear device tests. The main technical difficulty involves drilling deeper than the present
weapons test holes have been drilled.) Oil drilling equipment can accomplish these deep drilling requirements,
but only with 8- to 12-inch diameter holes. Weapons
test-hole diameters run as large as 48 inches, and the increased depths may be more costly to attain.

In any event there is more than adequate time available to research the final disposal site and method, and
there is no real problem in assuring its being kept out of
the biosphere. Economics becomes the key as to how
soon and how far we go finally to dispose of it. Mention
should be made of an interim measure which places
certain longer-lived problem isotopes into future reactors to allow escaping or otherwise wasted neutrons to
transform them into short half-lived isotopes and thereby alleviate what some have felt are troublesome storage
problems. It becomes a process of doubtful value when
evaluated on a benefit vs. risk basis and especially on a
cost-benefit basis. While reducing the inventory of certain long-lived, alpha-emitting, high-atomic-number isotopes may appear attractive, in reality it makes little
sense when naturally occurring 226 radium is left alone
in the biosphere. The 226 radium in the water, air, and
foods can never be eliminated. Million of tons of pitch-
blende ore containing 226 radium or 238 uranium,
which decays into 226 radium and then into 222 radon,
exist in the environment. There is no reason to present
radioactive waste from nuclear power plants as an un-

manageable problem on the basis of radiation health
and safety while ignoring 226 radium, which is equally
hazardous but has been "managed" satisfactorily for
ages.

Many of the nuclear extremists go from radioactive
waste storage and disposal to its transportation. They
mainly talk of major accidents during shipping. Though
many people are more concerned about radioactivity
than most other potential hazards, the worst imaginable
transportation accident involving radioactive materials—
a total release of a spent fuel shipment—is roughly
equal to the potential hazard of a tank car of chlorine
which is shipped routinely about the country. In twenty-five years of transporting radioactive material, no
public injury has ever resulted from the release of material. This safety record fits all other nuclear safety records; precautionary measures are absolutely unequaled
in handling any other classification of hazardous material. It is not by chance that the safety precautions work.

The casks which are designed to carry the material
must be built to withstand thirty-foot drops on a hard
concrete surface; to withstand the buildup of G-forces
which can be calculated by bringing a cask to an instantaneous stop from a given speed, for example, 50
m.p.h., or dropping it on a steel spike with a six-inch diameter base. The cask must be capable of withstanding
temperatures exceeding those of a fire of 1,475 degrees
Fahrenheit, in which it must remain for fully thirty
minutes; or not release its contents if dropped in water
of specified psi levels. In the first place the fuel pellets
themselves are uranium dioxide (UO_2), a tough ceramic
substance with a melting point very much higher than
that of metallic uranium—5,000 degrees F. versus 2,100
degrees F. These small cylindrical pellets (1/2″ to 1″),

are sealed into long tubes whose walls serve a fuel "cladding" to make up fuel rods.

The fuel assemblies used in a large water-cooled reactor are about fourteen feet in length and from five to eight inches square in cross-sections and weigh from one-quarter to one-half ton each. Shipping casks vary in their design features. However, a general description of one will illustrate the basic design considerations. Picture a ribbed cylindrical steel cask about sixteen feet in length, several feet in diameter, its total weight about twenty to twenty-five tons. The fuel assembly lies lengthwise in a central cavity and is essentially a steel pipe. The cavity is surrounded by eight to nine inches of lead shielding that is metallurgically bonded to the jacket of the cask. Once the fuel assembly is in place, the opening of the cavity is sealed by a lead plug-and-gasket assembly built into the container head. The jacket of the cask is made of thick steel plate. Transverse steel fins welded to the outer surface act as heat radiators. A single fuel assembly steadily gives off heat equal to several kilowatts, which is comparable to the amount given off by two of the burners of an electric stove. The heat transfers from the surface of the assembly to the inner wall of the cavity pipe, then flows by conduction through the lead shielding to the cask jacket, and finally is dispersed to the outside air by the jacket fins. Regulations require that the exterior surface of the cask jacket be kept below a prescribed temperature limit, and the cask is designed accordingly.

The design of spent-fuel shipping casks and the shipping procedures used are governed by precise and rigid regulations. The principle regulatory authorities involved are the AEC, Department of Transportation, and the United States Coast Guard.

It is of interest, because of what some environmental extremists have said, to mention two radioactive waste nuclides generated by power plants, from an air quality standpoint. The nuclide about which most has been said by the extremists is tritium. It has been calculated that if ten 1,000-Mwe pressurized reactors each discharged maximum quantities of tritium to Long Island Sound, a person obtaining his entire food supply from aquatic animals and plants from the sound would receive an exposure of 0.00007 rem/year. For practical purposes this amounts to a theoretical calculation only. It is far too small to be represented as a meaningful health hazard. The low levels of radiation associated with routine releases from power reactors are not demonstrable but are, rather, an inferred probability from observed high-level dose-effect ratios. The other gas is Krypton-85, a noble or inert gas. It does not represent a significant exposure problem even with the increased number of plants projected. Processes are available to separate the gas and hold it for decay.

It was previously mentioned that a portion of the reactor cooling water is continuously circulated through purification equipment. The principal function of this equipment is to remove dissolved radioactive matter. That is done in much the way that mineral "hardness" is removed by household water softeners, i.e., by passing the water over sand-like resins that soak up dissolved solids by the process of ion exchange. When a given bed of resins has become saturated, the flow is switched to a fresh bed.

The saturated bed is then rejuvenated by washing the resins with a chemical solution. It is then ready for another operating cycle. The wash stream, which now contains the radioactive matter, is pumped to a set of hold-up tanks where it is joined by miscellaneous liquid wastes collected from other parts of the plant: for example, wastes from routine analytical operations, solutions used to clean plant equipment during maintenance procedures, and reactor cooling water that has seeped through valve stems or pump seals, any of which may contain trace quantities of radioactive materials.

From the hold-up tanks, these liquid wastes flow to evaporators which boil them down to sludge-like concentrates. The concentrates contain nearly all of the radioactive matter collected from the several sources described. For disposal, they are blended with concrete, and the mixture is poured into steel drums and allowed to harden, resulting in a rugged, safe-to-handle radioactive waste package. The drums are stored until a sufficient number accumulate and then are shipped to a permanent burial site.

The steam from the evaporators, which contains trace quantities of radioactive matter, is condensed and its radioactive content monitored, and if need be, it is passed through ion-exchange resins.

Diagram of a coolant purification system[38]

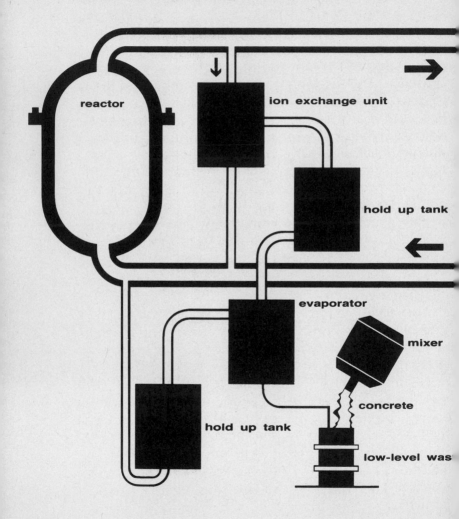

reactor

ion exchange unit

hold up tank

evaporator

mixer

concrete

hold up tank

low-level was

Fusion

Fusion or controlled thermonuclear reactors (CTR) offer the inexhaustible energy source. Unlike the fission process, where heavy elements are split into light elements by the capture of a neutron at room temperature, fusion works in the opposite way, by combining light elements into heavier ones or by "fusing" two hydrogen atoms together. The hydrogen atom has a single electron (−) orbiting around its nucleus which happens to be a single proton (+) to make it electrically neutral. If the electron is stripped away, the hydrogen atom becomes an ion and is said to be ionized. A collection of electrons and ions forms a plasma. A neon light is a simple example of a plasma.[39]

There are two isotopes of hydrogen, deuterium and tritium. Deuterium has one neutron in its nucleus, while tritium has two extra neutrons in the nucleus. Neutrons are electrically neutral and exist peacefully with the positively charged protons in the nucleus. They are the particles around which the whole nuclear industry is centered, for these are the "things" or particles on which all nuclear reactions are dependent, from a more or less empirical point of view. Fusing the lightest elements to create a heavier element always releases energy. Likewise, fissioning or creating two lighter elements from a single heavy one, from the heaviest halfway down the chart of elements, also always releases energy. In the simplest case, two atoms of an isotope of hydrogen, deuterium, are combined to form helium, the next heaviest element, with one neutron left over. This neutron is excess to the process. The reaction also releases kinetic energy in the form of the two new particles.

Since two bodies of like charge are being brought together, they repel each other. This requires that the kinetic energy of the original particles be sufficiently large to overcome this repulsion between like charges. Relatively, this energy requirement is enormous. For this simplest of possible fusion reactions, energies in excess of about 180 million degrees F. are required. If a gas is heated to this temperature, the kinetic energy of the particles is so high that the electrons are stripped away from the atoms, and a plasma is formed from the free electrons and bare nuclei remain.

This brings us quickly and directly to the central problem of a controlled fusion reaction: holding this ionized gas or plasma at these extremely high temperatures long enough for fusion reactions to occur. Holding such a plasma with containing walls of any kind is impossible, for the walls would not only melt, but the atoms released from the wall surface would contaminate the plasma and rapidly cool it. Something is needed to contain the plasma and insulate it from the container. Since a plasma forms a good conductor at high temperatures, this interaction with a magnetic field can be used to provide the force which in principle allows a magnetic container to be made. The plasma is actually held away from, or insulated from, a material wall by a magnetic field, creating an insulator between the plasma and wall, such as with a vacuum, making it possible to release energy by controlled fusion.

The gross properties of the plasma state have received much attention and research, so that few new surprises in the theory are likely to be found. This means that we may not have to wait long for the total picture to produce fusion, just as with fission we did not have to wait for complete understanding of the nucleus. The plasma containment requirements for controlled fusion will dictate how far plasma-state knowledge will have to be carried before fusion power is possible. Confinement of the plasma is related to the amount of energy released by the fusion reaction balanced against plasma production and loss rates. Solving this energy balance depends on plasma concentration or density (n) and the time the plasma is confined (t) in the magnetic "bottle." To produce useful excess energy, this product (nt) must exceed some number yet to be arrived at which varies as a function of the high temperatures mentioned above; plasma densities must correspond to one part in a hundred thousand that of the air we breathe and held for a time like one-half second. During this time, the plasma ions travel about 280 miles and the electrons some 19,000 miles inside the "bottle" and require good confinement. There can be a trade-off in density and time; if the density is greater, the confinement time can be less, and if the density is less, the confinement time must be greater.

The present fusion experiments throughout the world are a few hundred to a few thousand times removed from meeting this requirement. Since the time a hot plasma can be confined is governed in part by the size of the plasma, it has been possible for several years to construct very large devices which would confine them; however, from several points of view, their size is problematic.

Recent developments in plasma containment show that small-sized reactors are probably feasible and have increased the optimism of researchers. The general plasma-confinement schemes of magnetic configurations employ open-ended or closed systems. For closed systems (toroidal) research, as it is generally known, there have been limits in the past on the time we could confine a plasma due to a phenomenon or a law that was

discouraging. Generally, one can think of charged particles confined to magnetic field lines much like beads
confined to a string. The particles can slide along the
lines with ease, but in classical theory they can only
cross the lines very slowly. This analogy holds up quite
well, but in practice, for a number of years during research, the plasma somehow found a way to cross the
magnetic field; hence it was not confined as beads and
was lost. Since 1966 various instabilities which allowed
the plasma rapidly to escape to the container walls have
been overcome, allowing a steadily increasing confinement time through several different approaches.

To summarize the research in closed systems, the
confinement time has been pushed beyond the anomo-
lous limit which prevented progress for so long. Research is underway to discover the next limit. Results
on fusion models, referred to as Tokamaks, make it appear that the next limit may be beyond what is required
for fusion reactors. Progress is being made in other
areas of CTR (Controlled Thermonuclear Reactors).
Extremely rapid plasma-compression experiments may
stabilize these systems sufficiently long to meet reactor
conditions. These devices confine a plasma whose density is one one-thousandth that of our atmosphere, and
therefore, it must be contained for only a few thou-
sandths of a second to satisfy reaction conditions.

A new large experiment of this kind is being developed at the Los Alamos Scientific Laboratory to test
these theories. Should it be as encouraging as its prede-
cessors, another big step toward CTR will have been
made. These experiments are already at plasma temperatures and densities sufficient for reactors. Systems
which directly convert the kinetic energy of charged
particles to high-voltage direct current with an efficiency
of over 85 per cent are also being investigated. If these

experiments prove the calculations, and if economic considerations permit, then the open-ended magnetic system would possibly be competitive with reactors. These direct-conversion techniques may also be useful in improving the efficiency of closed systems.

Each of the approaches described here is close to satisfying two of the three conditions on plasma temperature, density, and confinement time required for them to qualify as critical. Tests will next be made on these systems to determine if the theories and scaling laws are correct. Should these tests confirm other worldwide measurements, fusion could go critical, and the United States should prepare to extract energy from deuterium and tritium fuels in a large-scale device. The limiting feature is the plasma requirement. Most work to date has been done with hydrogen gas, generally at temperatures below fusion level. Plasma fusion ignition temperatures require additional heating methods. This is one of several problems (density and confinement time) with controlled fusion reactors which can be solved *after* they have gone critical but at a time before they have been run to produce a positive energy balance. If this is successful, how is the energy released in the fusion reactions to be converted to useful power?

The first fusion reactors will run with a mixture of deuterium and tritium gas. Deuterium exists in natural water at about one part in six thousand, while tritium does not, being radioactive and decaying (12-year half-life). Eventually fusion reactors are expected to operate on deuterium alone. This requires an improvement factor of fifty in producing plasma density and confinement time. This possibility remains to be seen. Fusion with deuterium and tritium fuels can produce over eight MW days per gm. with the energy released in the form of the kinetic energy of a neutron (80 per cent) and a

charged helium nucleus (20 per cent). Extraction of kinetic energy from the reaction products depends on
slowing down the neutrons, then breeding tritium for
fuel, so neutrons must be captured in such a way as to
produce tritium. Lithium fulfills both requirements. It
acts as a heat transfer material to take up the neutron's
energy (as sodium in a LMFBR), and it fissions with a
neutron to produce tritium.

The problems of handling neutrons, breeding tritium
in flowing liquid metals, heat transfer, materials radiation damage, and safety are similar to those now being
solved in the LMFBR program. This makes fusion reactors somewhat simpler, though special problems need
exploration before this is possible. Steady progress in fusion research on plasma confinement is underway. The
next three to five years should develop criteria to allow
extrapolation to reactors and for testing in large-scale
experiments. Costs may exceed the present $28 million
annual budget, but a crash program in fusion development will not produce answers to the fundamental plasma questions significantly faster and, therefore, is not
warranted. Problems on reactor aspects of fusion are
only now surfacing. Difficulty in designing a power
plant without knowing all details of the heat source does
not preclude working in parallel with the plasma studies. It is essential that a vigorous program in fusion
technology be carried on to answer the questions. If
properly executed, a few years will see the realistic aspects of fusion reactors better defined, and they can be
given the appropriate national priority.

The most recent and encouraging development is the
possible role lasers may play in applications to fusion.
The laser is possibly the key to many different problems
now faced in the field of energy. The most useful possibility is the heat development potential of lasers. Laser

is an acronym for Light Amplification by Stimulated Emission of Radiation. Actually they do not amplify light; rather they produce or rearrange light rays that are coherent or "in step," and all of one wave length of color. Because of these characteristics, laser light is concentrated even at great distances. A laser beam aimed at the moon, 246,000 miles away, will make only a two-mile wide circle of light on its surface. Ordinary light would spread to a diameter of 25,000 miles at that distance. Lasers can be focused to concentrate energy to pinpoint size as well. It is this feature which makes them more applicable to the fusion process; namely, their use to start the fusion reaction. Lasers made to pulse for only a billionth of a second in succession, each having more power than the total output of Grand Coulee Dam, could be expected to create the 180 million degree required temperature. Additional research is needed to follow such possibilities.

The Chinese Syndrome

The longest and most detailed hearings the Atomic Energy Commission ever conducted concerned the Emergency Core Cooling System. The hearing started in January 1972 and lasted until December 1972. The Emergency Core Cooling System was originally conceived and developed with the expectation that it would replace any need for the containment building and was designed to prevent a loss-of-coolant accident, referred to by some as the Chinese Syndrome. This "theory" asserts that a reactor will melt down, for some reason, with such an intensive fiery mass that it will burn all the way through the earth and erupt on the other side, in China. One antinuclear spokesman, Dr. Stanton Cook, Ph.D., sociologist, described the nuclear mass burning its way through the reactor vessel, thence the extra containment vessel, through the plant wall, etc., out through the entrance to the plant compound, into the courtyard and finally into an always "nearby" stream. With this always "nearby" stream available, the radioactive material enters the regional water system. Fallout somehow results, dropping on all the wheat and corn fields, causing all sorts of sickening problems and in general creating a most hazardous condition. Sternglass stated recently that if the reactor planned for the Beaver Valley in Pennsylvania were to melt down, "you can kiss Wheeling and Pittsburgh goodbye."

The most probable cause of such an accident would be an instantaneous loss of coolant water from the reactor core. The huge main line carrying water through the reactor to the heat exchanger is most often pointed to as the possible site of rupture. The pipe and pressure vessel have been tested to several thousand pounds of pressure and the latest WASH-1250 AEC report calculates a rupture probability of once every 20,000 years for "non-nuclear" piping. This had formerly been calculated at once every 1,000 years. "Nuclear" piping would be of much higher quality in all aspects of quality and manufacture, so the frequency would be much less. Should this coolant pipe become inoperative, the reactor would immediately shut down, and a series of safety mechanisms would automatically be initiated. One mechanism is the emergency core cooling system which would spray large quantities of water into the reactor core to cool the fuel to prevent the melting of fuel pellets. If fuel pellets are allowed to melt, the cladding may rupture, allowing radioactive material in the fuel to be relased through a cracked reactor vessel, damaged by the heat effects from the ruptured coolant pipe. Improbable as this may be, it is the source of controversy and the long hearing in 1972.

The hearing board has not made a final recommendation, but it will most likely propose a reinforcement of the present emergency core cooling system where improvement is feasible. Many felt it unfortunate that the hearings were held in the first place, for the system was considered more than adequate and not a matter for great concern. The best evidence to examine in evaluating the core cooling issue is the record of reactor experience. In the first place, there has never been a loss of core coolant. In the second, nuclear reactor engineers forecast no problems with the core cooling system designed for present reactors. In the third, the only case approaching what might be labeled a meltdown or condition similar to a loss-of-coolant situation demonstrated conclusively that reactor safeguards inherent to nuclear reactor construction (described in the discussion of the Brookhaven Report) performed adequately, long before an emergency core cooling system was needed, even though one was available.

Perhaps the main reason the ECCS issue has remained alive and the subject of extensive hearings and controversy is because it is the only probable credible accident which the opponents of nuclear power can sustain in their series of "if" incidents. With core cooling, the principles are of a sophisticated engineering nature, dealing with the highly improbable, and dependent on an intricate series of succeeding improbable failures of positive safeguards. Coping with such a problem requires a firm grasp on reason and judgment to preclude making illogical and imaginary conclusions. Such conclusions were made by many when they protested the detonation of the first thermonuclear device or "hydrogen" bomb in the Pacific Ocean. They feared and warned that a "fusion-chain reaction" of hydrogen in the bomb would occur with the water of the ocean and result in the destruction of the world. Only three or

four years ago, certain groups of people fled the West
Coast of the United States to an area near Boulder,
Colorado, because they predicted that during an impending eclipse, there would be a massive earthquake in
which a large part of California and the West Coast
would fall into the Pacific Ocean. In both cases the
public was told of the improbability of these events happening and that in neither case was there need for concern. Nevertheless their fear was real and unreasonable,
as it is today with those concerned with the ECCS. One
major difference is that today, in an age of unreason,
the fearful are indulged and the issue is massaged to the
degree that someone is supposed to assure beyond a
reasonable doubt that ECCS failure is impossible rather
than extremely improbable.

In a recent study, WASH-1250, the AEC places the
accident probability of a major accident, including one
such as a loss-of-coolant, at 1:100 billion. These numbers were based on a preliminary report in December
1972, of the WASH-1250 study which used an expected
plant life for a LWR of thirty years.[40] All probabilities
are included, one of which finally calls upon the ECCS
to operate. These calculations indicate the probability
that a primary pipe rupture might occur once every
1,000 years for "non-nuclear" piping. In addition the
"non-nuclear" pipe rupture was assumed to have occurred under "grossly unrealistic assumptions." For example, the assumptions for this "worst case" included
the simultaneous failure of all engineered safety systems, breach of the reactor containment, and no protective measures by individuals in the area of the plant.
The final version of the WASH-1250 report changes this
important point and calculates that a complete severance of "non-nuclear" piping might occur once in
20,000 years, so "that an even smaller frequency could

reasonably be expected of 'nuclear-grade' pipe." The practical application of this is that it essentially decreases the accident probability to less than 1:100 trillion, a probability which is meaningless—meaningless to any one, that is, except environmental zealots out to promote their own interests at the cost of the taxpayers and with the indulgence of a ponderous federal bureaucracy.

Responsible scientists and engineers have made the same honest mistake in reference to ECCS that others have made in reference to the effects of ionizing radiation and the radiation protection standards. In the case of radiation standards, it was recognized early that protective standards were required, and they were the foremost issue in approaching nuclear energy. Admitting that the hazard exists allows some to charge that nothing has been done, or if it has, it is inadequate. In both these cases they are wrong, and most now realize it.

Accident evaluations have shown that the most severe of the credible accidents, from the standpoint of fission-product release, is a loss of coolant. What the critics do not mention is that nuclear reactors are designed with at least three barriers for containing fission products both during normal operation and in the event of an accident. The first and primary barrier is the fuel element cladding. The other barriers are the primary system pressure boundary and the containment vessel that surrounds the reactor plant. The warning systems and manual means of control plus other safeguards inherent in plant design all must be compromised before these barriers are called upon to function. In addition, for pressurized water reactors to be licensed in the United States, radiation doses to people from released radioactivity must be shown to be within the guidelines set forth in Title 10, Part 100, of the Federal Regulations for a "worst case" or maximum hypothetical loss-of-coolant accident. These considerations are overlooked by critics who, upon having responsible scientists and engineers admit to recognizing such a probability, try to make a case that it "will surely happen."

Since this hypothetical situation has never occurred, it is helpful to suggest an analogy to explain the relationship of the ECCS to reactor design. The standard automobile may serve as an example. The source of power and the center of the auto's success as a means of transport is the engine. Among all the design parameters the engine must be built to run without breakdown and trouble for a given number of years. Assume for this discussion that ten years is the accepted design criterion for the engine of a particular car. All parts are then built, assembled, and tested to assure that the most critical part related to engine life will last at least ten years. Tests and analyses determine after use whether the goal has been attained or not, and if not, defects are corrected until the proper results are obtained. At the same time, the car must have other components to make it operate, including a drive shaft. As stated, the car engine is designed to run for ten years and, of course, may then be replaced with a new one and run for another ten years, a total engine use of twenty years. Many people normally replace or rebuild the engine and use the car in this manner. Knowing this to be the case, the manufacturer does not wish to have the drive shaft shear prior to the end of the useful life of the car, because some may wish to replace the engine at least once. Since it is not difficult to build drive shafts which will outlast the engine by many years and to avoid having a drive shaft problem, one is designed of high-grade steel and in large size so it will last for at least fifty years of use. The buyer is assured of no drive shaft rupture during the life of his car with at least two (and theoretically five) engines or twenty years. A critic, however, might assume that theoretically, the engine could be replaced ten times, twenty times, or indefinitely, and therefore the car has an indefinite life—an unlikely situation. In making his arbitrary assumption, the critic calculates that the drive shaft is not adequate, for it is designed to last for fifty years, based on the designed engine life of ten years, or with one engine replacement, twenty years. On this basis the critic makes a case against the automobile and attempts to force a solution by redesigning the drive shaft to last indefinitely, rather than for fifty years.

This is the case with the ECCS. Though the life of a nuclear plant is assumed to be thirty years and the rupture of "non-nuclear" piping is once every 20,000 years and probably close to 100,000 years, if ever, for "nuclear-grade" pipe, the critics in this case are asking for a nuclear piping system which will not fail in 100,000 years for a thirty-year use requirement. The calculation and the hypothesis become meaningless as they have in other assertions made by extremists. Assurances of the type they ask are not possible. For instance, no one can assure that the next time Haley's comet approaches the earth it will not violate all the laws governing it and crash into the earth. We must accept the law of gravity whether or not we understand it. The only case which can be assumed to approach a meltdown occurred in the Fermi reactor (a breeder) near Detroit, Michigan.[41] Analyses and inspection determined that a fuel melting was caused by partial suspected blockage of the inlet nozzle of four adjacent subassemblies of the core by one of two detached segments of the inlet plenum. The two segments were removed. Later analyses determined these segments were unnecessary and all were removed.

Early in 1970, after plant improvement in other areas, the company received permission from the AEC to reload the reactor with fuel and, after re-examining the operators, proceeded with power demonstrations. The reactor attained criticality July 18, 1970, and a followup low- and high-power nuclear test program was undertaken. The Fermi reactor can be operated today at its full licensed power of 200 megawatts. Moreover, it has operated at its full licensed power of 200 megawatts thermal, 65 megawatts electric, for many hours without incident at high efficiency. When fuel replacing and processing became necessary, the reactor was shut down because of the economics of operation and not because of safety considerations.

The ECCS is today the subject of controversy that may continue for some time. It is the basis for the continuing pursuit by Ralph Nader, Friends of the Earth, and the Union of Concerned Scientists, for a moratorium on nuclear power. This combine filed a petition in July 1973 with the AEC asking that the operating licenses of twenty nuclear plants be withdrawn or that reasons be given why the plants should not be shut down. The petition is essentially the same as the suit they filed in June 1973. They filed it after the suit and accompanying request for a preliminary injunction were dismissed by a Washington district court judge. He ruled that "the plaintiffs could have petitioned to intervene in each of the twenty proceedings leading to the licensing of the plants, but failed to do so. They could have petitioned to intervene at the time the interim acceptance criteria were issued in June 1971, but failed to do so." Nader then filed an appeal with the United States Court of Appeals, but it refused to hear the case on an expedited basis. On December 28, 1973, twenty-three months after its first hearing, the AEC issued the final

ECCS criteria. There were no surprises, and the final rules essentially reinforced existing ECCS criteria. As to be expected, the Union of Concerned Scientists is considering court action, in conjunction with the Consolidated National Intervenors.

The ECCS is another case of a "means to an end," not an effort to assist in solving a problem. As with other cases, the ECCS case will demonstrate that the nuclear reactor is safer and more reliable and accident-free, rather than less so.

Chapter III
Energy—Crisis or Conspiracy?

As almost any daily newspaper or weekly magazine reports it, we are facing an energy crisis never before experienced in the United States. A crisis is a time of decision or a turning point, and whether or not we wish to call it an energy crisis, we are at a turning point in how we meet our energy requirements. Most commentators treat it as a nebulous many-faceted problem with no solution. Some suggest that it is part of a grand conspiracy or squeeze play by the energy supply companies. A cursory examination with an open mind and a review of the reports to Congress and resource agencies throughout the nation will show that these suggestions, often made by environmental extremists, are groundless.

The facts show that there is a grave and complex energy problem, but that specific and urgent action can be taken to prevent undue hardship to Americans. Some experts even predict the problem will end human existence as we now know it. The United States Geological Survey warned in a May 9, 1973, report that "not merely United States affluence, but world civilization are in jeopardy." The controversial hypothesis that resource shortages may actually threaten modern civilization won semi-official support from a United States government agency for the first time. The Geological Survey had just published an analytical report of United States sup-

ply and demand in sixty-four mineral resources and
warned that many of them are, or will be, in short
supply.

A study prepared at the Massachusetts Institute of
Technology a little over two years ago, called *The Limits to Growth*,[2] warned that modern civilization would
overshoot the world's ability to sustain it and would collapse unless population growth and industrial production are soon curtailed. *The Limits to Growth*
proposition has been thoroughly debunked by now, but
many are still referring to it as some kind of message
written in stone. The geological study, on the other
hand, produced an analysis of resource availability
which enabled Director V. E. McKelvey to express personal confidence that the world can develop adequate
mineral resources to support and create high standards
of living for thousands of years to come. He based his
view on the "undeveloped potential...in each of the
processes by which we create resources. Our experience
justifies the belief that these processes have dimensions
beyond our knowledge and even beyond our imagination at any time." However, the study notes, "it is by no
means too early to become concerned about future
mineral supplies and to start planning. The real extent
of our dependence on mineral resources places in jeopardy not merely affluence, but world civilization." The
study urged that the environmental problems of mining
enormous volumes of low-grade ores should be tackled
squarely, realistically, and soon, between industry and
the public at large. The cost and availability of the required energy are probably the single most important
factors that will ultimately determine whether or not a
particular mineral deposit can be worked economically.

This requires a no-nonsense and unemotional evaluation and when this is done, the facts available today

show that the nation does not face a shortage of energy resources but, rather, a shortage of available or usable energy and production facilities. Of equal importance is the fact that there is no concerted effort by anyone to decide which path is to be taken in the near future, for every promising option runs headfirst into environmental laws, recently enacted, which prohibit using the most abundant energy resources. Vast resources for energy production are available, waiting only to be developed. Some are more readily available than others and would require less capital to obtain and for this reason a priority of energy source development is appropriate. Within the general framework of practical execution, a sensible list of priorities would appear in the following sequence:

1. Increase depletion allowances to reinstitute the incentives for:
   a. domestic oil and gas exploration, including offshore drilling
   b. Canadian and South American oil and gas exploration
2. Scrap bureaucratic regulations (FPC, FTC, FCC) and obsolete pricing
3. Expedite and simplify nuclear power plant construction.
4. Commence commercial coal gasification
   Commence commercial coal liquification
   Commence subsurface and stripmining improvements to increase production
   Maximize hydroelectric resources
5. Increase research on thermo-nuclear fusion
   Expand natural gas stimulation (rock-fracturing nuclear explosions)
   Investigate solar energy from space stations using laser transmission

Authorize research on hydrogen gas fuel

Research synthetic steam or geothermal sources by
use of large thermonuclear explosive heat-cap-
ture in selected rock formations

Evaluate magnetohydrodynamics

Evaluate geothermal exploration programs

Review possible tidal capture sites and ocean energy
sources

Increase research in metals technology as it per-
tains to fuel cells

This system of priorities will not prevent energy shortages in the immediate and near future. Petroleum and
fossil fuels must provide for the short-term demand, but
they are not available in sufficient quantities to meet
long-term needs. Even if crude petroleum were available in sufficient quantities, the refinery capacity has
fallen behind the ability to provide finished products.
During this period, installation of LWRs must be expedited to produce the electricity which petroleum-fired
sources cannot. Increased use of coal is an urgent requirement. It must be brought into the mainstream of
energy production both as fuel for energy and as a
source of hydrocarbons for the chemical industry.
(Three-fourths of our coal supply will have been eliminated by sulfur limits included in Senator Muskie's
Clean Air Act when all controls are in effect by 1977. If
this were not enough, restrictions on stripmining further depress coal use.) The readiness of the breeder
reactor to take over the plutonium fuel cycle generated
in LWRs will start an era of unlimited electrical energy,
making centuries of fuel available from their operation,
including hydrogen gas fuel production if necessary. Alternate energy sources of the future such as hydrogen
gas fuel, tidal, geothermal, solar, and finally thermonuclear fusion, can then be developed or perfected in a
deliberate manner.

This means a commitment to a future of total electric energy usage. Should thermonuclear fusion as a principal source of energy in a reactor not prove feasible, or should it be delayed more than forecasted, it will not prove disastrous since hydrogen gas as a fuel in the conventional sense offers almost the same benefits, provided the breeder reactor is operational. It is too early to assume that controlled thermonuclear fusion reactors can definitely be made operational, even though most scientists expect that they will be. Breakthroughs are being made daily.

The problem, then, is not one of running out of energy resources, but in making energy available. The quantities of energy resources available in the world are so vast that it is difficult to describe their limits in meaningful terms. They are more than adequate. Available energy will provide for reclaiming minerals we have used or may need. The amounts we have used, in relation to what is available in the world today, are only a drop in the bucket compared to the amounts we could recover and use further to improve our standard of living. The benefits of cheap, plentiful energy can be made available to the rest of the world and its population, regardless of what their numbers may be.

Conditions leading to our present energy problems have been clearly presented many times over the past decades by numerous experts in the energy field, to the appropriate governmental agencies and bodies, describing the detailed nature of the problem, with adequate, timely, and appropriate solutions. The word of these resource experts has had little impact and was mainly ignored. Instead, the energy companies are accused of being deceitful, of extracting excessive profits, of using unfair employment practices, and ignoring social responsibilities. The function of profit is no longer understood. In the past two or three decades the private

sector has increasingly been made the scapegoat for the
failure of congressional and governmental programs.

The results of these programs were accurately and
precisely forecasted by knowledgeable observers. Many
have predicted what the results will be of the much-dis-
cussed consumer protection agency. The consumer advocates have produced one result in common, increased
costs to the consumer and loss of resources. This aggravated the energy crunch. Behind most such programs is
the incipient attack on incentives, the reduction of private capital for investment, and the desire for more and
more local, state, and federal agencies, and regulatory
bodies.

These agencies cannot even agree amongst themselves as to who has jurisdiction. They bicker over
money, policy, and enforcement. The Oregon State Department of Environmental Quality sued the United
States Army Corps of Engineers; fought constantly with
the EPA as to which was "tougher"; fought the Bureau
of Land Management, attacked the Department of Geology and Mineral Industries, Health Department, and
the business community, all at the expense of the taxpayer and for senseless complaints. State officials, including governors and legislators, waffle back and forth
on key issues from year to year, depending on how they
read the voters' response, attempting to do one thing
one year and then to undo it the following year.

Roscoe Drummond wrote of the governors' position
on the energy crisis in June 1973.[3] "The nation's governors are departing their 65th annual conference earnest-
ly preaching a new order of priorities...down with antipollution, up with energy development, and quick....
They see trouble ahead—both economic and political
trouble—and they don't intend to sit quietly and see
the citizens of their states threatened with brown-outs

and black-outs and insufficient energy to warm their homes, harvest their crops, fuel their factories, run their automobiles, and heat their schools. . . . Example: Southern California Edison has not been able to start a major new power plant project in four years. Six such projects were either blocked by environmentalists or bogged down in bureaucratic delay. . . . The Democratic governors made no reference whatsoever to the environment, and the same was true when they called for a quick decision to transport Alaskan oil to domestic markets. . . . Opinion polls now show the energy issue among the top ten of the public's most anxious concerns. . . . At last year's governor's conference in Houston, Texas, there was not a single syllable in any resolution suggesting that an energy crisis was either at hand or around the corner. The governors have come late to dinner, and it remains to be seen whether they will be prepared to act. . . ."

Oregon's Governor Tom McCall is one of the most enigmatic of all. Appealing at times to industry to support his programs of economic suicide, he is able to reverse himself completely the following day and assail industry as creating all the problems. Unable to support his charges with facts or substance, he appeals to the emotions to gain support.

For example, in a talk in Los Angeles,[4] McCall disputed charges that environmentalists are revolutionaries by relating the story of a visit from sixty junior high school students from Warrenton, Oregon. Warrenton is the proposed site of a $175 million dollar aluminum plant, which would provide 800 jobs. The plant is supported by local officials and all other responsible agencies having jurisdiction over the facility. McCall stated that he asked how many of the students wanted the aluminum plant constructed. "Not a single hand went up." They said: "We want things just like they are." But McCall told them Warrenton's economy is sagging and this would help pick up the slack. "I wouldn't label these children revolutionaries or crackpots," said McCall. "They just don't want anyone messing around with their part of the world."

How many of the junior high school students pay taxes or support a home or the schools where they are privileged to gain an education? How many of them even know the air emission requirements which have been placed on the aluminum plant and how many of them care about the fact that less fortunate children in poorer sections of Oregon may depend on the economic consequences of 800 jobs? They have not even matured to the point where they understand the question, let alone an answer, yet a person as important as a governor of a state uses their response to appeal demagogically to the emotional aspects of environmentalism.

Plans for averting an energy shortage have been researched for years, at a cost of millions of dollars. The Mining and Minerals Policy Act of 1970 (P.L. 91-631) was enacted solely for this purpose. The first report submitted in accordance with this law had little impact until real shortages of energy jolted the public into recognizing the discomfort of cold and darkness in the winter of 1972-73. More people listened when someone announced that it would be worse next winter.

The Secretary of Interior stated in the first report, "The dilemmas which confront us today in respect to energy and the industries and operations from which it is derived have not suddenly emerged."

On June 4, 1971, President Nixon sent his Message for Clean Energy to Congress. His message coincided with what the Secretary of the Interior and energy experts had reported previously; it pointed out that certain programs were needed: "Our best hope today for meeting the nation's growing demand for economical clean energy lies with the fast breeder reactor. Because of its highly efficient use of nuclear fuel, the breeder reactor could extend the life of our natural uranium fuel supply from decades to centuries, with far less impact on the environment that the power plants which are operating today. A major bottleneck in our clean energy program is the fact that we cannot now burn coal or oil without discharging its sulfur content into the air. We need new technology which will make it possible to remove the sulfur before it is emitted to the air.

"As we carry on our search for cleaner fuels, we think immediately of the cleanest fossil fuel, natural gas. But our reserves of natural gas are quite limited in comparison with our reserves of coal. Fortunately, however, it is technically feasible to convert coal into a clean gas which can be transported through pipelines.... Research to advance our coal gasification efforts and a number of possible methods for accomplishing this conversion are under development.

"Over half of our nation's remaining oil and gas resources, about 40 per cent of our coal and uranium, 80 per cent of our oil shale, and some 60 per cent of our geothermal energy sources are now located on federal lands. Programs to make these resources available to meet the growing energy requirements of the nation are therefore essential if shortages are to be averted. Through appropriate leasing programs the government should be able to recover the fair market value of these resources, while requiring developers to comply with requirements that will adequately protect the environment.

"The Outer Continental Shelf has proved to be a prolific source of oil and gas, but it has also been the

source of troublesome oil spills in recent years. Our
ability to tap the great potential of offshore areas has
been seriously hampered by these environmental problems.... At a time when we are facing possible energy
shortages, it is reassuring to know that there exists in
the United States an untapped shale oil resource containing some 600 billion barrels in high grade deposits.
At current consumption rates, this resource represents
150 years supply. About 80 billion barrels of this shale
oil are particularly rich and well situated for early development. This huge resource of very low sulfur oil is located in the Rocky Mountains area, primarily on federal
land."

The President's message went on to treat other
sources of energy, geothermal, natural gas, solar, thermonuclear fusion, and magnetohydrodynamic power
cycles (MHD is a more efficient method of converting
coal and other fossil fuels into electric energy by burning the fuel and passing the combustion products
through a magnetic field at high temperatures). The
President also described the necessity for government
reorganization and a streamlining of plant siting procedures.

There is no doubt that the looming energy shortage
was not well presented over the past decade. It would
be difficult to list the agencies, councils, committees,
and companies that have devoted themselves to making
this known to the responsible members of Congress and
government agencies for appropriate actions. They have
been unsuccessful and in many cases deliberately
thwarted by the coalition of environmental extremists
and their sympathizers.

In 1972, 1973, and again in 1974, President Nixon
provided data and pleaded for action to assure the nation an adequate supply of energy for the future. The

results of such pleas and advice were not very productive. Congress instead passed Senator Muskie's Clean Water Act, estimated to cost several billions of dollars, and his Clean Air Act, imposing restrictions on automobiles which have multiplied costs, solved few if any problems, and created new ones. The established emission rates and the auto industry's knuckling under to them have resulted in an increase in gasoline consumption as well as poor performance.

The EPA itself estimates that fuel consumption is up 11 per cent over previous models. That means that late-model autos are burning from 24 to 44 per cent more fuel at a time when oil is the most critically short resource we have. Instead of listening to those who argued that a shortage of oil would raise prices and that the laws of supply and demand would curtail auto use as well as auto size, Congress chose the usual method of establishing a huge new bureaucracy whose rules have encouraged production of some new cars which get only 3.4 miles per gallon. It has been estimated that if every car got twenty miles to the gallon, gasoline consumption would be reduced by 60 per cent. This would reduce the air pollution problem and the use of raw materials at the same time.

Engineers are concerned about the reliability and value of the catalytic converters now being installed on 1975 autos. These devices may not last more than 5,000 miles, and 3,000 miles is probably closer to actuality. In addition, the United States will have to import an estimated one billion dollars worth of platinum from other countries, including Russia, to meet the production demand. The required use of nonleaded gasoline has cut refining capacity at a time when this is the single most critical item in the petroleum bottleneck. Yet industry is condemned for not building more refineries, even though it cannot meet the environmental zealots' demands for refinery location, etc., and cannot obtain the needed capital for plant investment—in the least because huge government spending programs are taking the capital.

The Nature of the Dilemma

Fossil or Nuclear Energy

With the world supply of oil and gas not as plentiful as it once was, the considerable supplies of coal and abundant uranium must be developed to meet expanding energy needs. This assumes moving ahead promptly with development of the breeder reactor and following with thermonuclear fusion power, solar, or hydrogen gas.

The short-run energy crunch will pass with the introduction of the breeder. For example, enough uranium and thorium are in sea water to provide thousands of times as much energy as is available in all the proven fossil reserves. The ultimate development of fusion power will provide an effectively unlimited energy supply. The crisis today is not an energy resource shortage, but a failure to make energy available, plus a regulatory stasis or crisis; a disruption and disorientation of energy supplies based upon regulatory failure at multiple levels of a complex, unresponsive government structure.

The long-run energy supply situation can be summarized best by putting into context the idea of "total energy supplies." Massive energy quantities are often measured in Qs—one Quintillion BTU's. One Q (one quintillion is 1 followed by 18 zeros) is about five times the world's total present annual energy usage of about

0.2 of a Q, and about fifteen times the United States annual energy usage of about .07 of a Q. Rough estimates of available energy resources, measured in Qs, are as follows:

Approximate recoverable energy content—in Q's		
	U.S. alone	World
Oil and gas reserves—proven, probable and potential	1 - 2	20
Coal reserves—represents estimated available quantities; minimum figures shown represent 50 per cent of estimated gross reserves, maximum figures shown represent 100 per cent	30 - 60	150 - 300
Nuclear reserves (uranium and thorium)—proven, probable and potential—entire energy content assumed to be ultimately recoverable (about 60 per cent of recoverable with current breeder technology):		
Uranium available at $15 a pound of U_3O_8	100	225 (at a minimum)
Uranium available at $100 a pound of U_3O_8	1,000	N.A.
Thorium	Inadequate data, probably as plentiful (worldwide) as uranium.	
Uranium and thorium in sea water		200,000-300,000

The only acceptable conclusion based on these totals is an energy economy where virtually all energy will come from some nuclear reaction. Oil and gas will be the first of the old sources to go, to be replaced to the maximum extent possible with conventional nuclear reactors furnishing either electricity or direct heat. These in turn must be complemented as quickly as possible with breeder reactors both to furnish energy and to eliminate the need for substantial increases in enrichment capacity. In this way time can be bought to develop fusion reactors as the ultimate energy resource.

Resolving the tremendous impact the total energy problem will have on electric power demand is essential, since the question is the procedure and timetable by which the switch is made from a fossil fuel energy base of today to the nuclear energy of tomorrow. A discussion of natural fuels for energy is more relevant if applied to the ultimate recoverable reserves, rather than to known reserves. M. King Hubbert of the U.S. Geological Survey (U.S.G.S.) has shown the world and the United States ultimate supplies of present primary energy sources (see Table 2). The energy available from 235 U is based on using LWRs (no breeders) with plutonium recycle and includes uranium reserves at costs up to $100 per pound of U_3O_8.

As indicated on the chart, the use of natural gas and oil is the most disproportionate of all in relation to their supply. Natural gas accounts for 1.5 per cent of the United States energy reserve supply, but 32 per cent of the use; oil accounts for 2 per cent of the United States energy reserve supply, but 44 per cent of the demand. Coal, on the other hand, accounts for 63 per cent of the supply, but only 22 per cent of the demand.

Similar disparities are present in the world picture. This is one reason why petroleum energy sources are in serious trouble, and why the putative conspiracy is meaningless. Consequently, if the world continues a 6 per cent growth rate, all conventional fuels will be gone by the middle of the next century. Should the world rate drop to the United States rate of 4 per cent, the depletion point is extended to the end of the twenty-first century. If the world growth rate of consumption drops from its present 6 per cent to the United States rate of 4 per cent, all world petroleum supplies will be gone by 2020; and according to optimistic estimates, if the United States were forced to supply all its needs internally, the United States would be out of oil by 1995. Importing oil will provide twenty-five years of additional time before the world supply of oil is gone. This does not mean that by not importing oil until internal supplies are exhausted the date of world depletion will be extended, because there is only so much oil, and the specific geographic locations exploited first do not change the total amount left.

This is why the energy crisis hinges on the oil and gas supply. The Federal Power Commission gave official notice of this when it stated that, from 1973 on, gas supply is to be considered fixed or stable while the demand will continue to rise. This means no new customers, uses, or increases in present uses can be handled by the gas industry. The growing deficit between supply and demand will worsen. The reason is clear: the finding to production ratio is no longer equal except for the recent Alaskan oil strike. The present impasse over the Alaskan pipeline makes it impossible to predict when that gas can be used. The lack of new gas discoveries means less than twelve years' supply of natural gas at 1970 levels.

The National Petroleum Council projects that by 1985, the United States will be importing oil at a cost of $25 billion per year. This amount of money added to the present trade deficit places more than half of the nation's most essential energy in the hands of foreign governments. This was well understood by some even prior to the latest Israeli-Arab war. Joseph Alsop wrote in early 1973: "dependence on Arabian oil exposes our jugular vein." In a discussion with Mr. Itzhak Rabin, former Israeli ambassador to the United States, Mr. Alsop was told: "you do not think enough about the oil problem. I have been looking into it for months...it is much worse than you suppose...ten times worse. Your jugular, Western Europe's jugular, Japan's jugular, all run through the Persian Gulf nowadays. Yet you have no means to defend your jugular. This is why your country must cease to be a great power, unless you can find means to solve this terrible problem, which everyone has overlooked for too long. No nation can remain a great power that has a wholly undefended jugular, waiting to be cut by anyone with a willing knife. No nation can be a great power, either, that has an ever more worthless currency—unless it is a totalitarian state like Hitler's Germany or the Soviet Union, which the United States will never be."[6] We now are only too painfully aware of what he meant. The "Yom Kippur War," the oil embargo, and resulting crisis came as a rude awakening to millions.

An understanding of the rational choice of options to meet our energy needs during the next decades is made difficult if one listens to the purveyors of the irrational concept now blooming called "net energy yield." This circular argument rests on the principle that man must remain in, or return to, slavery, and then proceeds by insisting that energy utilization be separated from economics.

The argument, similar to the one "what came first, the chicken or the egg," and no more productive, presents the thesis that some forms of energy are more costly to produce than others and are therefore less efficient. A unique set of equations and conveniently pliable data are used in this analysis, usually dealing in BTUs rather than horsepower, kwhr, or conventional terms. Only those energy sources are to be developed and used which this analysis finds efficient, usually on the fundamental point that fewer BTUs are consumed by a man raising x number of calories of wheat by hand than by using a gasoline-powered tool to produce the same number of calories, even though, theoretically, crude oil is bubbling from the earth at his feet. Availability of energy resources, productivity and time need not be considered in the equation, unless suited to the preordained conclusion. A certain amount of work is required converting energy from one form to another, and the human body is extremely inefficient in energy utilization, but little is said of this by the proponents of "net energy yield" in their movement to return to manual labor.

Although oil, gas, or coal may have a certain resource value, they are worthless if not used; and if not usable, they are no longer resources. Although petroleum converted to gasoline may be only 20 per cent efficient (or 80 per cent inefficient) as far as the net energy recovered, it is *100 per cent inefficient* if not used at all. If it is highly valuable and becomes scarce, wasting it is unwise, but use is tied to the cost of the resource and not to idle suppositions about how not to use it.

The "net energy" argument deals in attractive euphemisms now in vogue and attempts to support these with makeshift analyses and rumors passed on by the usual groups, including the Union of Concerned Scientists, Friends of the Earth, and various Ralph Nader groups. My discussions with proponents of this view show them to be economic illiterates and scientifically naive. Newcomers to the important area of energy production, they have found another convenient podium from which to spout their gibberish.

Many experienced and knowledgeable students of energy and resource development find the arguments of "net energy" spokesmen unintelligible. For example, these spokesmen describe shale oil as a 30 per cent "net energy loser." They arrive at this conclusion by first devising their own "net energy data" and then analyzing the equation as follows: for every 100 barrels of oil produced from shale oil, another 100 barrels is expended to obtain it, e.g., to pay for trucks, transportation, metals fabrication, labor, etc. This leaves a net energy account of zero. It thus discards the fact that 100 barrels of oil are now setting on the ground, available to society. It's the old shell game, or now you see it and now you don't. The net energy analysts have discovered an amazing fact that anyone with knowledge of arithmetic can demonstrate: the oil shale reserves should be cut in half if, in fact, it takes one-half of the total to produce the other half (which incidentally, it does not). It also evades the point that if oil shale is the only source of oil, and oil is needed, then shale is where it must be obtained. The "net energy" energumens now conduct a most unusual computation, for they choose to burn their 100 barrels of oil in an electric power plant, which is 70 per cent efficient, 30 per cent going up the stack as waste heat. They conclude that oil shale is a "30 per cent net energy loser."

This idea is being promoted by extremist groups more and more, becoming a widespread fad through willing politicians and news media outlets. Anthony Lewis of the *New York Times,* not known as an agricultural, nutritional or energy expert, wrote on April 25, 1974, "...the American food system is immensely energy-intensive. Huge amounts of energy are poured into growing crops without much labor, then even more into processing and packaging, and still more at the consumer end into auto-powered shopping, refrigeration and the like. In 'primitive' cultures...each calorie of energy invested produces five to fifty calories of food. In industrialized food systems, it takes five to ten calories of energy to get one in food. If all countries followed our energy-intensive pattern the world would use 80 per cent of its annual energy just to produce food."

Earlier in his article Lewis laments the fact that the underdeveloped nations, including India, most of Asia, and Africa are faced with a worsening food shortage and that we must help by sending them more food; yet he appears to subscribe to the notion that the developed nations do an about-face and "find ways of using more labor and less energy in their food production," as do India, China, and most of Africa. China is most often held up by environmentalists as the shining example of how farmers work so well and so efficiently in the fields, but little is said of the fact that China must import vast quantities of food each year and is falling further and further behind in food production rather than increasing its annual supply, even though 80 per cent of its total population is engaged in agriculture, and even though rice is rigidly and strictly rationed. These spokesmen never suggest that without plentiful, clean energy slavery is man's inevitable fate. As more manpower is used to produce a unit of farm produce, more people are employed in farming and less are left for the processing industries. The total amount of commodities available for consumption drops, and a certain group of people is favored at the expense of the majority. Options exist to provide the necessary energy, and the role of this generation should be to invest our intelligence and thrift wisely in making it available, leaving future generations a legacy of freedom from slavery, rather than a return to the dark ages, as these doom-mongers would have us do. The nihilistic instinct surfaces again in this senseless concept.

Oil and Gas

Total oil and gas reserves of the world have been estimated by numerous authorities. Latest estimates of known and partially explored fields indicate a proven and probable reserve of about 5.7 Qs. Nine per cent is located in the United States and Alaska (including offshore reserves). However, estimates of total potential world reserves, including those in Asia and the Canadian arctic, range from 57 Qs, with 20 Qs a conservative number. In 1972, the United States consumed oil at an average rate of 15 million barrels a day and 25 trillion cubic feet of natural gas. These quantities represented 44 per cent and 33 per cent, respectively, of total energy used in the United States.

By 1985 the yearly requirement for these fuels is expected to reach about 9 billion barrels of oil and 33 trillion cubic feet of gas. Cumulative requirements for the fifteen-year period are expected to exceed 100 billion barrels of oil and 420 trillion cubic feet of gas if the necessary supplies can be made available. The Department of Interior estimates this to be in excess of 18 million barrels a day in 1975, and anticipates an annual growth rate between 4 per cent and 4.7 per cent for the intervening period. Beyond 1975 the projection becomes increasingly difficult and ranges of possible requirements broaden. Near-term projections are complicated by such factors as economic growth rate, an apparent shift toward increased energy consumption relative to real gross national product, and potentials for shifts to other fuels as replacement energy sources.

In the face of these projected needs, what are the total estimated resources? An estimated 3.8 trillion barrels of crude oil and more than 200 billion barrels of natural gas liquids were formed in the earth within the United States and its offshore areas. About one-half of these resources are offshore, and of this portion, about one-half are in water depths greater than 200 meters. However, only 171 billion barrels of crude offshore and 246 billion onshore are estimated to be recoverable under current technological and economic conditions, once they have been found. The United States has produced and used 97 billion barrels of petroleum as of January 1, 1972.

Proved reserves of crude oil and natural gas liquids, both on and offshore, amount to 39 billion and 7.7 billion barrels, respectively. Included are 9.6 billion barrels of crude oil reserves on Alaska's North Slope (others estimate this to be 10 to 20 billion) which will not be available until adequate transportation facilities are developed. Reserves in the rest of the United States continued their decline of recent years. Around 4 billion barrels of petroleum liquids were produced in the United States in 1972. A recent report of the National Petroleum Council included a detailed breakdown of the offshore potential. These estimated 60 billion barrels of recoverable crude oil are available from the shelf and slope, exclusive of the Pacific Coast north of the Santa Barbara Channel and of Alaska outside the Cook Inlet and Bristol Bay areas. The USGS places this number at 160 to 190 billion. If the larger figure is to be achieved, incentives will have to be increased to explore such costly areas as the Gulf of Alaska and the offshore portion of the Arctic Slope. This volume is equal to about two-thirds of all the crude oil produced so far in the United States and one and one-half times the 39 billion barrels of proved remaining reserves, including the Alaska North Slope.

United States reserves can be related to the rest of the world's reserves, on which we have to depend, by realizing that hydrocarbons are unevenly distributed among the world's sedimentary basins, or within basins as well. Although basin classifications are somewhat arbitrary, there are some 500 sedimentary basins in the world. Of these 500 basins, three contain over one-half of all the world's hydrocarbon reserves discovered to date (Persian Gulf, Western Siberian and Gulf of Mexico basins). A few-score basins contain more than some 5 billion barrels of oil, plus gas converted into oil on an equivalent energy basis. Of the estimated proved free world reserves of crude oil, the Middle East has 69 per cent. The remaining free world has 24 per cent, leaving the United States with 7 per cent.

Prudhoe Bay on the North Slope of Alaska is the largest oil field ever discovered in this country. The second-largest field, East Texas with about 6 billion barrels of recoverable oil, was found in 1930 and was not followed by any other discovery of similar size. Whether Prudhoe Bay is also a unique giant in an area with much smaller fields, or only one of several giants, is a matter of great importance to American consumers. Even if construction begins today, Prudhoe Bay reserves will not be a source of supply before 1977 or 1978.

This lack of United States reserves has been greatly aggravated by congressional and governmental bungling. A story filed as recently as May 27, 1973, was headlined "FTC Doubts Natural Gas Shortage." It reported that the Federal Power Commission had issued a study which showed gas reserves to be 9 per cent lower than had been estimated by the American Gas Association. The Power Commission recommended price increases to stimulate exploration and development to ease the shortage. Almost every reputable resource expert and agency has been asking for this action for several years. However, the Power Commission's report was not acceptable to the Federal Trade Commission. The Trade Commission has antitrust responsibilities which in this case involve the question of whether the industry has been withholding data and whether the alleged gas shortage may be related to dominance of competing energy sources by oil companies. In the meantime the nation suffers from energy shortages in every area while the FTC chooses to let the situation worsen. Mr. C. Howard Hardesty, executive vice president of the Continental Oil Company, described the problem more precisely.[7] He places the blame for the current energy crisis and oil shortage with Congress and the administration, which were warned about it long ago. He stated that the irresponsible charges by Ralph Nader and some congressional spokesmen overlooked the real causes of the crisis. "The truth is, the situation is not a new one that occurred overnight. It is a result of four years of failure to plan ahead by the government and the conservationists that brought this upon us. It is a direct result of the needs of our society catching up to and exceeding the supply and our capacity to produce. It is irrational to try supplying the energy needs of this nation with supplementary supplies from the Middle East and other politically troubled areas in the face of the dollar situation, international intrigue, and the imbalance of payments, while at the same time we have all the oil in Alaska and on the continental shelf which we have been blocked from using." Hardesty also asserted that it was ridiculous that United States tankers are limited in size to the point where they are uneconomical to operate in competition with the world fleet of supertankers. He placed the keys to the present oil crisis as: 1. reduced demand by the consumer; 2. foreign supplies for domestic needs; and 3. developing United States off-shore and North Slope reserves.

Nineteen fifty-seven was the turning point in United States petroleum producing history. Oil demand in the United States slowed while imports started pressing on domestic markets, and domestic production capacity became excessive. These conditions started a readjustment of producing capacity toward market alignment. Geophysical work, leasing, and drilling were all reduced at that time. Domestic demand for oil increased in 1967, and the closing of the Suez Canal added new requirements for domestic production. Domestic crude oil prices stabilized and caused an upturn in United States exploration activity. But the previous period of reduced activity in exploration and discovery was difficult to overcome. Since oil and gas are discovered only by drilling where geological prospects have been identified and drilling rights obtained, it was 1969 before there was an increased rate of exploratory drilling. Exploration was temporary and declined again in 1970. Domestic oil operations were not financially rewarding, and as a result petroleum exploration and development in the United States ground to a halt. The increasing difficulty and cost in finding new oil and gas reservoirs sufficiently large to permit economic production, and the long-term decline in the price of domestic crude oil, plus federally controlled well-head prices on interstate gas sales resulted in price levels too low to attract investment for further development. An increased tax burden and uncertainties about federal policy on oil import controls further restricted investment. In the late 1940s some thirty wildcat wells were sufficient for one significant discovery of oil or gas. In the 1960s that number has nearly doubled, and this trend has not been reversed.

The natural gas problem is at least as critical as that

of oil. For decades, more gas was found than used. During the last few years, however, production has exceeded additions to reserves in the lower forty-eight states, and there has been a net decline in total reserves. This discouraging turn of events was the inevitable result of the Federal Power Commission's restrictive pricing policies during the 1960s. The commission held prices to artificially low levels and also effectively deprived the industry of the benefits of percentage depletion on gas produced. Low prices imposed by the commission served to stimulate demand, while discouraging the discovery and development of new gas fields.

The effect of these trends in supply and demand, coupled with the present level of tax and other incentives for exploration, has forced the United States to become more and more dependent upon imported energy. By 1980, it is estimated that 47 per cent of our crude oil demand and 17 per cent of our natural gas demand would have to be supplied by imports if:

1. There is no change in present government policies (including tax rates and percentage depletion rates);
2. Crude prices rise only enough to offset inflation; and
3. Gas prices rise but not enough to offset inflation.

The issue faced on the national level in the short term is how much the United States is willing to become dependent on other nations for our energy. The decline in self-sufficiency may not be totally reversible, but our history clearly shows that if adequate economic incentives are provided, domestic reserves can be increased. Percentage depletion and other tax incentives have proved highly effective in making the United States a major factor in the supply of world energy.

In 1969, with a growing oil demand and decreasing oil

reserves, Congress reduced the rate of percentage depletion for oil and gas from 27$^{1}/_{2}$ to 22 per cent, at the
worst possible time. While it reduced the depletion rate,
it added a 10 per cent "minimum tax" on so-called tax
preference items that include the percentage depletion
deduction. This minimum tax provision further reduced
the effective oil depletion rate to the 18 per cent range.
Three major reasons for declining exploration and development activity are:

1. Price restrictions and ever-increasing costs have resulted in inadequate returns on new investments;
2. Delayed access to potentially productive offshore
   and other frontier areas;
3. Environmental restraints.

The petroleum industry has always been accused of
reaping excess profits, but its total domestic tax burden
is greater than the average for all United States corporations, even with sales and excise taxes excluded. Some
politicians, consumerists, and newsmen bewailed the industry's "windfall and excess" profits in the last quarter
of 1973; but *The New York Times, Washington Post* and
Los Angeles Times reported their own profits up by 45
to 66 per cent. No demands or laws were sought to have
their windfall profits confiscated.

Capital requirements of the petroleum industry have
been a major concern since the 1969 tax changes. The
National Petroleum Council estimates that a 23 million
barrels per day consumption rate in 1980 will require 68
billion barrels of oil during the 1970s.[8] If the nation is to
maintain its current self-sufficiency ratio, 60 billion barrels of reserves should be developed during the 1970s,
up 80 per cent from the 1960s. This would imply expenditures of some $90 billion during the 1970s. This es-
timate makes no provision for extra costs attributable to
inflation, pollution control, or drilling in more costly
frontier areas.

The Chase Manhattan Bank estimates the industry's anticipated capital requirements during the 1970s at $57 billion in the lower forty-eight states, plus some unspecified amount for the North Slope.[9] This will leave the United States 47 per cent dependent on oil imports by 1980. This prediction in constant dollars does not allow for inflation. In order to maintain 75 per cent self-sufficiency, Chase estimated that $100 billion would be required, $130 billion with inflation at a very low 2.5 per cent per year. An examination of oil company profits shows they are not adequately profitable in relation to the amount of money needed for investment to meet the nation's fuel requirements. For example, in 1970, the *Fortune* rating on the basis of *gross sales* included nineteen oil companies in the top 100 industrial companies. On the basis of *net income*, seventeen of the nineteen oil firms also ranked in the top 100. However, on the basis of net income *as a percentage of invested capital*, only one of the nineteen oil companies made the top 100, and fifteen of the nineteen stood lower than 200 in the list of the top 500. This is of great significance to prospective investors, who readily find better investment opportunities in other industries.

The equity of a tax system cannot be determined on the basis of income taxes alone. This is especially true of the petroleum industry, where other taxes are far higher than federal income taxes. The United States petroleum industry's total tax obligations on domestic earnings, operations, and properties was $3.4 billion in 1970. The largest single item, federal income tax, amounted to $1.3 billion, 40 per cent of the total. Domestic excise and sales taxes at the same time amounted to $10.5 billion. The U.S. petroleum industry also paid total worldwide taxes amounting to nearly $27 billion, of which sum slightly more than one-half was incurred in the United States.

Opponents of percentage depletion who claim that the petroleum industry has not paid its fair share of taxes have undoubtedly been influenced by data which have been inserted periodically in the *Congressional Record.* For example, data published in the *Congressional Record* of October 27, 1971, indicated that the 1970 domestic federal income taxes of nineteen companies represented only 8.7 per cent of worldwide net income before United States and foreign taxes in 1970.[10] This figure is doubly distorted and inaccurate. In the first place, the computation defines the tax burden for the industry by relating income taxes to net income before taxes. The proper measure of tax burden is the relation of total taxes to gross revenue. Second, the 8.7 per cent computation relates United States taxes to worldwide income and completely disregards the operation of the foreign tax credit provisions in our tax laws which are designed to avoid double taxation. The foreign tax credit provisions are applicable to all United States taxpayers. They provide that United States income tax will be payable on foreign income only to the extent that the foreign effective tax rate is less than the United States rate. Where the effective foreign income tax rate is equal to or greater than the United States effective rate, no United States income tax is payable on such foreign income, and properly so. If both a host government and the United States were to tax net income at 50 per cent without regard to the taxes levied by the other country, there would be no profits, and the taxes would be confiscatory. If the foreign tax were deductible, rather than a credit, the tax rate on United States companies operating abroad would be about 75 per cent, while their foreign competitors would pay 50 per cent. Few United States firms could overcome such a competitive disadvantage.

Price, Waterhouse and Company compiled tax data

on the oil companies and determined that the tax rate for 1970 was 21.78 per cent of book income, two and one-half times as great as the effective rate indicated in the *Congressional Record*. It has been said that taxpayers in the lower brackets pay a higher percentage of their incomes to the federal government than the big oil companies. This is completely false. In 1969, 54 million taxpayers with adjusted gross incomes of less than $10,000 paid $22.9 billion or 9.56 per cent. The top 4,175,000 of this group paid at the rate of 11.7 per cent.

In any event, it is basically inappropriate to compare individual taxes with corporate taxes. A system that taxes both individual and corporate incomes produces double taxation unless relief is provided to the individual shareholder for the corporate taxes paid. Many countries grant such relief (Canada, France, Germany and the U.K.). The United States does not. The comparison, even if based on correct data, would be valid only if the tax burden of the shareholder and the corporation were combined. The energy crisis is in part the by-product of such misleading allegations as the 8.7 per cent tax figure. Congress should start correcting these past mistakes rather than repeating and compounding them.

Actual and impending shortages of oil and gas cause some people to worry that United States resources are about to be exhausted. In that case, they conclude, it would be a mistake to accelerate discovery, development, and production. They suggest instead that United States oil resources be saved for future use and that we use as much foreign oil as possible when it is available. This superficially appealing proposition rests on two incorrect assumptions: 1. that the United States is about to run out of oil and gas or substitutes, and 2. that the nation can wait until an emergency arises to develop more oil and gas.

On June 18, 1973, Canada halted all exports of gasoline and heating oils to the United States. This shows how vulnerable the oil supplies of the United States would be if a single pipeline were built from Alaska through Canada, as many of the environmentalists are demanding. The same applies if a rail line is to be built to transport any of the Alaskan oil across Canada. It is a prime concern of the administration in opposing the Canadian route as a substitute for the Alaskan pipeline and tanker route. Although Canada may supply only a small portion of United States oil needs, it could be an important factor if the pipeline went through Canada, for the Canadians could control the line. The Canadian fuel curtailment is an early warning of what the United States might expect if a government came to power in Ottawa that was unfriendly to the United States and the fuel interests of the two nations clashed. It is, of course, far down the list of reasons for not building the line across Canada, but a serious argument nonetheless. In addition, a report of late June 1973 showed that the government of Canada was not interested in the pipeline passing through its country. This would, of course, have little effect on the environmental extremist, for only he can decide such things, and the silly desires of the Canadian people are of no importance. It is more significant that in 1974 Canada raised its export tax on crude oil from 45 cents to $6.40 per barrel.

The United States oil and gas shortages can be alleviated best by allowing prices to serve their proper function of balancing demand and supply. Resource experts in government and industry agree that a very large potential exists for additional recovery from known fields as well as the discovery of new fields. Although we have been fortunate in having only minor difficulties up to now, all forecasts point to increased dependency on foreign oil. The ability of the domestic oil and gas industry to meet our needs is shot through with inadequate economic incentives for exploration and development, unreasonable environmental opposition, and inappropriate government policies.

Efficient discipline of responsive markets and prices must be allowed to balance supplies with demand. A solution must be found to the endless procedural delays in administering environmental laws, and the major new sources of supply (the Far North and the outer continental shelf) must be used. To realize these potentials, however, requires leasing practices that make offshore areas available for development at a pace to meet rising energy demands economically. It is in the public interest to have more frequent and larger lease sales, avoidance of the unreasonable portions of conflicting environmental requirements, relief from administrative impediments which have hampered existing offshore operations, and continued access to outer continental shelf lands under regulations that protect the environment but which do not needlessly sacrifice resources obtainable from these lands.

The environment can be protected during all phases of exploration, drilling, production, transportation, and storage. If a spill occurs, effective measures are in hand to limit the spill, to contain and recover the oil, and to clean up and rehabilitate. The records show conclusively that no permanent environmental damage has resulted from the most widely publicized spills. Roadblocks to offshore oil drilling must be removed. Delaware, for example has outlawed coastal development and exploration for a ten mile zone; oil company leases which were legally bought and paid for were summarily canceled or suspended by the Department of Interior in the Gulf of Mexico and off the coast of California; no leases have been sold on the vast and possibly productive Atlantic

shelf. Exploration and research studies should be underway now rather than being blocked by environmental
hysterics and fumbling government bureaucrats.

Offshore drilling is not ipso facto environmentally ruinous; provisions can, and of course must, be made to
prevent harm to coastal water. Nobody wants oil spills,
but during World War II, more than fifty tankers were
sunk off the coast of Florida. The beaches were covered
with oil time and again, yet sea and shore life are normal today.

The Santa Barbara Oil Spill caused the greatest concern yet over the environmental aspects of petroleum
drilling and production in ocean waters. While unfortunate, it was not the ecological disaster cited over and
over again by environmental extremists as being typical
of all marine drilling. Some aquatic birds were killed as
a result of the spill, and some beaches were temporarily
despoiled. But existing research, which has been made
publicly available, indicates that the Santa Barbara spill
did no irreparable damage to sea life or the beach. No
sea lions and elephant seals died from the spill—as originally reported—and the few species of birds most affected by the oil spill have recovered their numbers.

One of these studies, conducted by Dr. Wheeler J.
North of the California Institute of Technology, concluded that the spill was indeed "a cause for concern,
but not a cause for hysteria." He indicated in his report
that there was every likelihood that the Santa Barbara
Channel would remain "as luxurious as it ever was."
Subsequently, a more comprehensive study by the Allan
Hancock Foundation of the University of Southern California by Dr. Dale Straughan and some forty partici-
pating scientists concluded that damage to flora and
fauna in the Santa Barbara Channel was much less
than reported and that the area is recovering well.

A report on the USC study was originally published

by *West* magazine of the *Los Angeles Times*, by Don Dedera. It is enough to make any sober-thinking person vow never again to listen to the unsubstantiated rantings of environmental extremists. By the time the facts were brought out, it had cost the taxpayers millions of dollars. In the Santa Barbara story, a local group was organized called Get Oil Out (GOO). It was led by a very rich lady named Lois Sidenberg. But there were others. *Life* magazine reported "a heartbreaking tally of dead seals as far as the eye could see" at San Miguel Island, and *Life* stated that the channel was "a sea gone dead." *Sports Illustrated* published an article titled "Life With The Blob," three months after there was no blob, and a local editorial stated that "the findings of the three dead whales on beaches far to the north meanwhile underscores fears that the channel spill here could have catastrophic effects on marine life."

In addition, there were all those dire predictions by local and network broadcasters: "Conservationists fear that Santa Barbara Channel will become what they're calling a dead sea. Commercial fishermen now claim their business is going to be destroyed for years. Marine biologists fear the worst for the balance of nature."

Dr. Straughan organized a team to conduct the study at USC. She drew on the faculties of four schools— University of Southern California, University of California at Santa Barbara, University of California at Santa Cruz, and Johns Hopkins University. Counting the paid and unpaid, the professors and graduate students, some forty scientists were enlisted. They included a Catholic nun writing a doctoral thesis and a ranking expert on seals and sea lions. The disciplines ranged from geology to chemistry, from biology to physics, and when money ran low, a grant was obtained to finance publication of the findings.

When the findings were published in two hefty volumes, GOO was badly gummed up. Not surprisingly, there was little follow-up in the national press or network television. This exposé of false reports, corruption, and exaggeration was suddenly not interesting to CBS, NBC, or *The New York Times*. The report stated that far from being a marine desert, the Santa Barbara Channel was found to be still teeming with life. Not only had overall damage by the spill been greatly overestimated, but where damage could be documented, nature was returning to normal. According to Dr. Straughan's team, nonscientists had overlooked these basic facts at the time of the spill:

1. For centuries crude oil has been an influence on channel life systems; natural seepage off Coal Oil Point had exuded 11 to 160 barrels of crude petroleum per day. Certain marine species have adjusted so well to this seepage that they have long since built up a tolerance to it.

2. In winter, when this particular spill occurred, marine life is at a low ebb—a seasonal cycle unrelated to pollution.

3. The worst floods in forty years had taken place just prior to the oil accident, placing sea life under stress from fresh water runoff, storm debris, sediments, and pesticides. Isolating the effects of oil seepage from these other pollutants proved next to impossible.

One by one the pieces of the "dead sea forever" theory were refuted by the USC findings. No ill effects on animal and vegetable plankton could be discerned. The volume of biomass and its distribution did not change significantly between May and October of 1969. No damage from oil pollution could be found on sandy beaches. A decrease in marine life was observed in oiled tide zones, but a decrease in intertidal life was also measured on shores far from the spill (one probable cause: people collecting and disrupting tide-pool creatures). The channel fish catch was actually found to have been greater in a six-month period following the oil spill than in a comparable period the year before. Moreover, the spill had no apparent effect on whales, and the same held true for seals. Oiled and unoiled seals were captured, tagged and surveyed later; data indicated no increase in mortality among those animals that had been oiled. Oil may have caused the deaths of some sea lion pups, but not in the scare numbers reported in the press, nor had the spill decimated the bird population to the extent first feared. Of 18,000 birds in the channel at the time of the spill, 3,500 to 4,000 died from all causes. Yet, by May the bird population had risen to 85,000 because of seasonal migration.

In a summary Dr. Straughan concluded: "Damage to the biota was not widespread, but was limited to several species, and the area is recovering well." Dr. North, who did a definitive study of the wreck of the oil tanker *Tampico Maru* on the Baja California coast, states: "We've found that each spill has its own individuality, shaped by weather, geology, type of oil, the paths it takes, and the kinds of organisms involved. A lot of oil is liberated naturally at Santa Barbara and has been for centuries, and it could be that life sensitive to oil departed long ago. There is one unavoidable fact—all animals are reproducing now in the Santa Barbara area."

Agreement with the Straughan-USC study also has come from laymen knowledgeable about marine environments. After a dispassionate summary of the study appeared in *Oceans* magazine, the editor received a terse letter from Larry Cushman, vice president of the National Association of Underwater Instructors: "Thanks for your accurate summary of Dr. Straughan's report. For a long time after the spill, I had conversations and corresponded with amateur and commercial divers and diving instructors from the Santa Barbara area. None had detected any evidence of marine life destruction underwater, nor had they seen any traces of underwater oil. In the face of the popular and overwhelming barrage of oil-destruction publicity they were simply saying: 'That's not the way it is ... I've been down there.' "

Another noteworthy footnote to the USC study is the experience of Mrs. Ruth Case, manager of the Undersea Gardens, a large barge-aquarium moored in Santa Barbara harbor. A great variety of marine life maintained in the aquarium was entirely dependent on water circulated from the harbor when, at times, oil six inches thick lay on the surface. "Throughout the spill, our loss of life was no greater than we normally have in an aquarium where animals of all kinds feed on one another. The oil floated on top, and it didn't seem to poison anything below."

Dr. Straughan commented as follows: "Santa Barbara crude is a heavy oil, relatively insoluble in water, and low in toxic fractions. For these reasons the spill in the first critical days floated on the water surface and did not migrate through the water column. I'm much more in sympathy with those in Santa Barbara who object to oil development on esthetic grounds. Also, there are people who are so strong in their beliefs they have given up all but one car and have gone to biodegradable products. But these people are not in the majority. What we have are people maintaining a high demand for fuel for cars and boats, and petroleum for plastic products, and saying 'Well, let's import the oil.' I ask, who has the right to rape some Arab's kingdom, ruining that environment with pollution, but keeping his own domain pristine?" Mrs. Sidenberg of GOO, incidentally, flies around the country in her own helicopter and, to the disgust of even the most casual sportsmen, has been reported to troll from the machine.

Underscoring how difficult it is to get facts out to the public through the press, a columnist, D. B. Furgurson from Baltimore, recently wrote of the Santa Barbara spill. He was on a trip around the nation on AMTRAK at the time and happened to be passing through Santa Barbara. Naturally he looked up the chairman of GOO. He stated that GOO was formed after the disastrous spill, but said nothing of the findings of the USC study group. He reported instead that a natural spill or slick of oil was standing offshore at the time, one of the natural slicks that have been reported in that area for generations. Furgurson does not believe that such a natural occurrence is real. He ignorantly ridiculed the local reports that fish and birds seemed to be very pleased to be going about life just as if there was no oil at all.

For him this was a personal disaster. He would only have been happy if there were indeed a disaster with the death of wildlife. He implies that the oil industry is to blame some way: "Whether this slick turns out to be seriously damaging to wildlife and seashore or not, and whether it is indeed a natural rather than man-caused leak is less important to the country at large than the reflex skepticism toward the industry's findings. It is a skepticism that spreads far beyond Santa Barbara, and far beyond the understandable reaction of the chairman of GOO." It is hard to believe, but Furgurson relates this natural oil slick (wildlife welfare be damned) to President Nixon. He writes: "What has been happening in Washington lately contributes, of course, to a feeling of mistrust toward big shots, big government, big business—particularly when they are tied up together as tightly as in this administration." Once again a reporter's ignorance and laziness add to the confusion about the environment.

A Look At Foreign Oil

At the end of 1970, foreign liquid hydrocarbon reserves totaled 575 billion barrels, of which an estimated one-sixth (17 per cent) was controlled by Communist countries. Foreign Free World reserves are ten times those of the United States. The bulk of the Free World reserves are in the Persian Gulf countries with four of these, Iran, Iraq, Saudi Arabia, and Kuwait, accounting for 58 per cent. These four countries, together with Venezuela, Libya, Algeria, Nigeria, and Indonesia are the major petroleum exporters of the world. As an example of the magnitude of Middle East operations, Aramco, one of the major producers in the area, is also one of the most familiar. The significance of this single company's present operations can be put into sharper focus by comparing Aramco's production of seven million barrels a day with the total production by all companies in the United States of some 9.5 million barrels a day. Moreover, Aramco is continually installing new production, pipeline, and marine terminal facilities to support increased production of crude. Supplies of oil from each of these countries have been subject to interdiction, embargo, enjoinment, or other forms of restriction. If our domestic production rate could be maintained with the Alaskan oil, needed foreign imports would be about 8 million barrels a day by 1980 as compared with 3.4 million barrels a day now. Much of United States oil imports now come from Canada and Venezuela. Production in these countries will not keep pace with requirements, and increased imports will have to come from the Eastern Hemisphere. In 1951, Iran nationalized the Anglo-Iranian Oil Company. Exports of Iranian oil were suspended for over three years. The Mideast oil flow stopped during the closure of the Suez Canal in 1956-57 and in 1967, as well as the war crisis of 1973 and 1974.

In February 1971, Algeria expropriated all French oil interests there. The Indonesian oil industry nearly collapsed during the Sukarno regime, and Nigerian oil was stalled during the civil war in 1967-1969. In May 1970, the Trans-Arabian pipeline failed; production in Libya stopped, putting a severe strain on the world tanker pool which increased the cost of oil to consuming nations. As a result, some United States companies did not import their allowed quota of foreign oil but relied instead on increased production from the United States Gulf Coast areas.

At the December 1970 OPEC (Organization of Petroleum Exporting Countries) meeting, a resolution was passed establishing certain "objectives" for its membership. The first Venezuelan action following this resolution was taken by the legislature which authorized the government to set tax prices unilaterally, rather than by agreement with the companies, as had been the practice before.

An agreement was signed February 14, 1971, between the six Persian Gulf members of OPEC, Abu Dhabi, Iran, Iraq, Kuwait, Qatar, and Saudi Arabia, and representatives of thirteen oil companies, to become effective February 15, 1971, through the end of 1975. This agreement was designed to establish financial stability between the oil companies and the governments of Persian-Gulf states. Total revenue to the Persian-Gulf states was to total nearly $12 billion over the five-year period. These Arab states control two-thirds of the world's proved reserves and supply 85 per cent of the crude oil consumed in Western Europe and Japan. The embargo of 1973 and 1974 makes it impossible for the United States to rely on imported oil.

More diverse oil provinces must be sought abroad and increased domestic oil supply, synthetic oil, or other energy alternatives, must be made available. Canada may offer an important exception because the United States provides a natural market for Canadian oil. It depends on the ability of Canadians to reconcile their desire for Canadian industry with their growing foreign capital needs.

Our oil import bill from a current level of around $10 billion will increase to about $30 billion by 1980. Special measures will have to play their part in ensuring that the foreign exchange account is made to balance. Exchange rates cannot provide the answer for fuels because the oil exporting countries have protected themselves contractually against dollar devaluation. The increase of Persian-Gulf oil prices to over $20 per barrel will be a continual obstacle to inflation control efforts.

It is essential to attract investment in the United States of funds flowing into the oil exporting countries. Offsets on the credit side of the energy bill will not approach $20 billion. More of our energy needs will have to be met from domestic sources. Energy users in this country will go short unless investment needs abroad are adequately met. Energy investments in the non-Communist world outside the United States are likely to rise to $78 billion by 1980 (in 1970 dollars). If United States companies become unable to compete in the international oil industry, this country would become dependent on foreign-owned companies. There would then be no assurance of even-handed treatment in a supply crisis.

The participation of United States companies in the world oil industry has positive implications for the United States balance of payments. In 1971, remitted earnings exceeded new outlays by about $1.5 billion. United States taxation of foreign-source petroleum income must not be amended to leave American-owned companies at a competitive disadvantage to foreign-owned companies. Concerns owned by producing-country governments have an obvious advantage in access to supplies, but companies owned by governments or private citizens of the principal consuming countries receive special tax and non-tax incentives at least as valuable as the tax treatment provided by the United States.

The logistical problem is of such tremendous proportions that special consideration must be given to whether or not foreign oil in required quantities can actually be *brought* to the United States. American consumption will require a super-tanker every fifty miles enroute from the Middle East to the United States. The tankers will have to be huge, having a draft of sixty-five feet. It has been impossible so far to obtain acceptance for such tanker ports in United States waters. For this reason most major oil companies have started looking or building in the Bahamas or Trinidad. This is not a good option as far as the United States labor force is concerned, but there is little choice for the oil companies. The same serious situation applies to United States refinery construction.

Two issues relating to future refinery construction in this country have been discussed recently. These are environmental opposition to new refineries and the exportation of refinery capacity, especially to the Caribbean. With regard to environmental objectives for refineries, a December 1972 paper issued by the Department of the Interior, Office of Oil and Gas, called "Trends in Capacity and Utilization,"[11] lists ten refinery

projects with a total of 1.1 million barrels per day crude
distillation capacity, some of which are "blocked by or
having difficulties with environmentalist action." An
evaluation of these projects follows:

Shell Oil Company—Delaware; 150,000 barrels/day
Blocked by passage of a state Coastal Zone Bill at
the urging of environmentalists. Shell had purchased the land and begun preliminary engineering and design.

*Northeast Petroleum—Tiverton, R.I.; 65,000
barrels/day*
Proposal blocked by environmentalists. Cited in a
Life magazine article as an example of local
activists winning a victory over outside industrial
interests.

*Fuels Desulfurization—Searsport, Maine; 130,000
barrels/day*
Construction permit denied by the Maine
Environmental Improvement Commission on the
grounds that the company had no "track record"
and might not be able to adhere to its
environmental protection commitment as out-
lined in the proposal. The Maine E.I.C. later
went on record in favor of a refinery deepwater
terminal and petrochemical complex at the location, given reasonable assurances of meeting pollution control guidelines.

*Supermarine—Hoboken, New Jersey; 100,000
barrels/day*
Proposal entailed building a refinery on the site
of the old Todd Shipyard. Permit denied as a
result of environmental objections.

*Guardian Oil Refining Company— site uncertain;
125,000 barrels/day*
Company is seeking a site in the Hudson Valley

of New York. Unable to find a site due to strenuous local opposition. Considering the battles over the Storm King pumped hydroelectric proposal in the same area, it doesn't seem likely that a site will be found.

Crown Central Petroleum—Baltimore, Md.; 100,000 barrels/day
Proposal has received some environmental criticism, especially with regard to the additional tanker traffic in the Chesapeake Bay which the refinery would generate. Final outcome uncertain.

Atlantic Refinery Associates—Norfolk, Va.; 30,000 barrels/day
Proposal is in the early stages, and would include a "Free Trade Zone." Has met only minor environmental protest so far.

Occidental Petroleum—Machiasport, Maine; 300,000 barrels/day
Proposal entailed a special free trade zone. Objected to by many in the oil industry as favoritism. Construction unlikely.

Georgia Florida Oil & Refining—Brunswick, Ga.; 70,000 barrels/day
Project uncertain due to financial problems. Construction not likely.

Dillingham—Barber's Point, Hawaii; 50,000 barrels/day
Environmental impact statements have been filed with the state authorities. No date set for beginning construction.

Five of the above have been either entirely blocked or seriously hampered by environmentalist actions. Two involve some sort of free trade zone; one is suffering financial difficulties; one is under consideration by the state environmental authorities; and one is in the early planning stage. The five which have met considerable environmental objection represent a potential 570,000 barrels per day crude oil distillation capacity.

In addition to the above specific proposals which have had siting problems because of environmentalist opposition, it seems reasonable to assume that stricter environmental regulation and the threat of activist environmental objections have had a depressing effect on long-range refinery construction plans. Many refinery projects have probably died aborning and never gotten to the formal request-for-construction-permit stage. In addition to the problems with new plant siting, there are recent indications that environmental objections are being raised with regard to the expansion of existing facilities. In the past it has been relatively easy to obtain permits for expansion and modernization; and in light of the fact that many refineries are constructed with eventual expansion in mind, any trend which would limit a refiner's ability to expand would have considerable adverse impact on the industry.

As to the exportation of refinery capacity, there are several factors which make Canada or the Caribbean somewhat more attractive as refinery sites than the mainland of the United States. These are:

1. Availability of deepwater ports capable of handling large tankers.
2. Attractive tax treatment by the host governments.
3. Greater flexibility with regard to where the products are marketed, i.e., some products to the United States, others to Europe.
4. Fewer union problems.
5. Less stringent or nonexistent environmental and safety (Occupational Safety and Health Act) regulation.

With regard to the costs of building a refinery in the United States versus the Caribbean, the dollar figures are not directly comparable because the Caribbean refineries are often "single purpose" or limited product-range refineries. Those in the United States are much more complex, land is more costly, labor is more expensive, there is more regulatory red tape, and there is less marketing flexibility. Mainland refineries have to be designed to accept variations in the type and gravity of crude feedstock and to produce a wide range of products. Caribbean refineries can be designed to use only one type of crude and to produce only a narrow range of products, such as heavy fuel oil for the United States East Coast, or naphtha for Europe.

Another major factor inhibiting domestic construction is the uncertainty with regard to specifications for gasoline (the industry's major product) which will be in effect in the next five to ten years. No one wants to take the risk of building a new refinery designed to produce high octane unleaded gasoline and then have the Wankel or some other engine which can use low octane (below ninety) gasoline come into use. There is also the threat of a large increase in the federal gasoline tax rate as Senator Proxmire hinted in congressional hearings of May 9, 1973 (in the name of saving the environment or building mass transit or closing the energy gap or whatever), which could reduce the demand for gasoline. This may not be very likely in the short term, but it is another example of the uncertainties which face the industry and which have acted to curb refinery construction.

King Coal

Coal, as the most abundant fossil fuel in the United States, exists in recoverable reserves in the continental

United States (including Alaska) in excess of a trillion tons (20 Qs) as a minimum, and as high as three trillion tons or 60 Qs. Mapping and exploration to date support a conservative estimate of 3.2 trillion short tons, 2.8 trillion tons of which are above a depth of 3,000 feet, and 1.6 trillion tons above 1,000 feet.

World reserves are placed at 300 Qs (15 trillion tons), ten to fifteen times the oil and gas reserves. One-half (150 Qs) are considered recoverable, varying with legal and potential mining restrictions, which would provide quantities available to supply world energy needs for centuries at present and projected rates of consumption. The single state of Illinois can provide two to four Qs (100 to 200 billion tons), compared with the present annual United States consumption of one-half billion tons. Thus, Illinois alone could supply our nation's coal needs for a century or more, yet Illinois does not have the largest reserves in the nation. These exist in a concentrated area within Colorado, Wyoming, Montana, and North Dakota.

Government environmental regulations have increased the demand for coal containing less than 1 per cent sulfur. In addition, coal with special ash-fusion temperature qualities and ash content is needed for steam production in some utility plant boilers, and coal for metallurgical purposes requires additional special properties. Low-sulfur coal reserves may be limited, but ways of using the more plentiful high-sulfur coals, though costly, are only a matter of time, until sanity is restored to air emission standards.

The nation was sold on the apparent evils of sulfur dioxide, even though no sound scientific evidence supports the contention that it is dangerous at the levels in question. Only the environmental extremist accepts sulfur dioxide regulation with satisfaction, as another link in the chain that will strangle the energy-producing capacity of our nation. No one dares suggest today that our attitude toward sulfur oxides is unrealistic; no one, that is, but the British, the Germans, the French, the Japanese, and perhaps the Russians.

The EPA, the most scientifically perverse and politically cowed agency in the world, is having to clean up its fact-pollution about the sulfur "problem." On June 18, 1973, the EPA announced it is considering a system for controlling emissions of sulfur oxides that has been vigorously opposed by many of its own officials. The new system is one that the electric power, smelting, and coal industries have been advocating and which has had the support of the White House and several important members of Congress. Known as the closed loop or dispersion enhancement system, it uses taller stacks, or requires shutdown or curtailment of operation when weather conditions such as inversions occur. The third option would be to substitute low-sulfur for high-sulfur coal if it were available. As to be expected, Senator Muskie severely criticized it as being inconsistent with the intent of Congress.

Based upon replies to questionnaires from 85 per cent of the investor-owned electric power companies, sulfur abatement costs are running wild. Over $5.5 billion has already been spent or committed for sulfur oxide abatement facilities. The carrying charges on the expenditures will approach $1 billion annually, while additional excess fuel and operating expenses associated with reducing sulfur emissions in connection with electric power production already exceed $1.5 billion a year. Just how costly this can be is evident from recent bids by seven suppliers for SO^2 emission control devices for the Commonwealth Edison Company's 800-megawatt Powerton station with six coal-fired generating units. The estimated investment costs were $63 to $94 a kilowatt for complete installation. Mr. Gordon Corey of Commonwealth Edison stated that capitalized operation costs will bring these figures to over $100 a kilowatt. This amounts to a total bill of at least $15 billion to convert the nation's existing coal-fired generating equipment into sulfur-free operation, with another $10 billion required for additional generating capacity to be installed by 1980. This amounts to a national sulfur abatement cost (for electricity generation alone) of $2.5 billion annually, not including $30 to $60 billion as investment costs referred to above.

The maximum social value of this expense cannot be justified based on EPA estimates of sulfur oxide damage of $8 billion a year, a figure considered to be poorly documented and badly overstated. One-fourth of the sulfur oxide content of today's air comes from natural sources, primarily decay, with only a portion of the remainder from coal combustion. There is no sense in requiring the immediate commitment of $2 to $2.5 billion a year for a limited reduction of electric station sulfur oxide emissions. A $30 to $60 billion expense for additional reduction shows a further lack of common sense in allocating our nation's limited capital resources.

Until ways are developed to remove the sulfur, or it is established that there is no need for removal, there are enough low-sulfur fuels available, but governmental regulatory problems present the most formidable obstacle in their use.

Stripmining is also declared to be evil, even when accompanied by complete land restoration. One such method called "cut-and-fill" could end the worst abuses of stripmining seen in the past. The operators blast and bulldoze a bench, hauling overburden to a holding area instead of dumping it downslope. The coal seam is exposed, and as the coal is removed, the overburden is replaced immediately. Grass and seedling trees are planted in the recontoured slopes to control erosion and bring back the vegetation. In the western United States, Pacific Power and Light Company has demonstrated conclusively that coal fields can be stripmined, reclaimed, and made more productive and esthetically pleasant than the original land.

Mine safety legislation makes underground mining almost impracticable, but coal is needed and should be used as much as possible. To expedite the use of this valuable energy resource the following coal-use projects are necessary:

1. Economical removal techniques for removing sulfur oxide from stack gas emissions or scientific reevaluation of emission release levels.
2. Coal conversion to low-sulfur, low-ash fuel.
3. Coal-gasification processes.
4. Liquid fuels and related products from coal.
5. Use of coal for power generation such as fluidized bed boilers or coal-fired fuel cells.

Use of coal as petroleum involves several techniques, all following the initial step of converting the coal to methane gas. The procedures for making gasoline, oil, or fuel oil are then quite simple. This first step, however, is the one which requires a considerable expenditure of energy. Reports of huge volumes of water being required are used by opponents of the process, who fail to explain that air cooling is an alternate method if water is not available. Also, a nuclear steam source is ideal for furnishing the necessary energy for this first step, should coal itself not be used, which seems unlikely.

Coal conversion to clean (low-sulfur, low-ash) fuel is a huge step toward solving our energy problem, if indeed sulfur must be removed. A continuous, catalytic-hydrogenation process can convert coal to a fuel having 0.2 per cent sulfur content. A pilot plant has been operating which produces a synthetic crude oil from coal for conversion to gasoline and other liquid fuels. Conversion of this plant to a simplified version of the "H-coal process" could produce low-sulfur heavy fuel oil commercially. Another solvent extraction process dissolves coal, filters out the ash, removes sulfur, and results in a comparatively high-heat-value solid or liquid fuel.

Some coal research is now under way, mostly by the U.S. Bureau of Mines. According to Mr. Walter Lewis, one of the most knowledgeable and effective persons in the field, these include:

1. Combustion improvement. A 500 lb./hr. experimental combustor has been built to investigate the combustion of pulverized coals and chars. This study is important because virtually all processes for converting coal to liquid fuels produce chars as a by-product.

2. Synthetic Pipeline Gas from Coal. A process for converting coal to pipeline-quality gas (essentially methane) has been developed and tested in a pilot plant with a wide range of United States coal samples. Referred to as the "synthane" process, it employs a catalyst, Raney nickel, flame-sprayed onto metal tube surfaces. Successful demonstration of the process for commercial use would provide a fuel from coal to replace natural gas.

3. Non-polluting oil from bituminous coal containing 3.3 per cent sulfur was converted to a fuel containing only 0.3 per cent sulfur in a one-step process currently being developed by the Bureau of Mines. The product may be employed directly as a utility fuel. The bureau is studying the applicability of

this process to a range of United States coals to determine its economic potential for converting the nation's considerable reserves of high-sulfur coal to low-sulfur utility fuels compatible with air pollution regulations.

4. In 1968, the Bureau of Mines constructed and began testing a large-sized pilot plant for gasifying coal under pressure. Low BTU gas yields were obtained with caloric values of about 140 BTU per cubic foot. This is a modification of the Lurgi process, which is currently in commercial operation in Europe. It is particularly important for the near term because of the pressing need for clean-burning fuels from coal. The Commonwealth Edison Company has proposed a Lurgi gasifier at its Powerton Station located near Peoria, Illinois, and expects the Lurgi process eventually to produce low-sulfur gas for under a dollar per million BTU. The process is well established and though providing a relatively low-quality gas (150 to 200 BTU/cubic feet), it may be upgraded. Here, as elsewhere, social and regulatory problems constitute the real stumbling blocks. Initiating reasonable solutions to the problems of underground working conditions, disposal of tailings or restoration of strip land will require the exclusion of environmental extremists from the decision-making process.

America is highly dependent on coal for electricity; over 50 per cent is generated from coal. Electric power went off for more than thirteen hours in parts of New York City during the summer of 1972, reminding the city's population of its dependence on electricity. This failure was basically caused by inadequate transmission equipment, but it underscored the possibility of a major breakdown in electrical service because of regulations that are making it impossible for many utilities to burn coal. With coal enough to last for centuries, we suffer from restrictions that prevent using much of what is readily available. As if this were not enough of an obstacle, Senator Mansfield pushed a bill through the Senate in December 1973, which prevents any stripmining of coal on government-owned land. Over 50 per cent of all low-sulfur coal in the western United States is on federal land. Though the need and availability are clear, Stewart Udall and others were asking for a complete ban on stripmining as late as March 1974. Coal is our most precious commodity. By synthesizing petroleum and gas from it, we can supply the petrochemical industry as well as fuel for trucks and aircraft. The critical position coal holds in our nation's energy future must be recognized. It is the energy source which will allow the transition from a petroleum-based economy of today to the ultimate nuclear energy economy.

Options—Real or Fancied

Oil Shale and Tar Sands

Since United States annual oil and gas well production (with Alaskan oil) will not exceed .046 Qs and since our annual usage is .053 Qs and growing, United States wells cannot meet oil and gas needs. But oil shale reserves in the western states can supply our total petroleum needs for many years. These shales occur beneath 25,000 square miles (16 million acres), 17,000 square miles (11 million acres) of which contain oil shale for potential commercial development. Over eight million acres (72 per cent) are public lands managed by the Secretary of the Interior.

The Green River deposits consist of high-grade shales, at least ten feet thick, with about twenty-five gallons per ton, comprising a reserve of 600 billion barrels of oil. Eighty billion barrels of this exist in the more accessible higher grade deposits. They are available with present methods of extraction and near economic competitiveness with petroleum of comparable quality. The United States Department of Interior estimated in 1970 that this reserve would provide a twenty-year supply at present use rates. *Research News* (September 8, 1972, pages 875 and 876) estimates a potential supply equivalent to 2,500 times our present annual energy usage. Research and development by the United States Bureau of Mines since the 1940s and by industry and universities have provided the technological framework for commercial oil shale operations using mining-surface methods. In-situ retorting, in which shale is heated underground, is being tested. Recovery costs and prices are estimated at something on the order of $4.75 to $6.85 per barrel, or 70 cents per million BTU. While transportation and environmental costs will add significantly to this, it is unlikely that the end result will be sharply higher than today's 90 cents per million BTU price of No. 2 low-sulfur oil delivered to Chicago.

In an address to the American Institute of Chemical Engineers in 1972, Mr. R. C. Gunnes took a different view when he said: "Until government leasing and development policies are further clarified, we are unlikely to see much progress in this direction." This is borne out by the result of most government-sponsored projects and agencies' actions, which generally fail. Experimental work on shale is being conducted by the Laramie Energy Research Center, Laramie, Wyoming, on in-situ retorting, occurrence, the nature and evaluation of the oil shale resources, and by-product minerals associated with oil-shale. Environmental extremists have opposed most aspects of oil-shale recovery and processing. Finally in 1974, the government, ignoring temporarily its motto of "nothing ventured, nothing lost," leased land in Colorado for shale oil development.

At the same time it is well known that the largest petroleum reserves exist in the various "tar sands" throughout the world. Tar sand deposits of the United States are located in Utah, with lesser deposits in California, New Mexico, and Kentucky. The Athabasca tar sands, virtually next door to the Midwest in Canada, are one of the world's largest oil deposits, with 200 to 300 *billion* barrels of potentially recoverable oil. About 64 billion barrels is mineable down to a 2.5 to 1 overburden depth. The mining and recovery process has been proved by Sun Oil's CGCOS project. Texaco has also completed the drilling and construction phase of a pilot project on the Athabasca sands of Alberta and has started fluid injection into the tar formation. The purpose of this experimental project is to develop economical methods of recovering oil from tar sand deposits that are buried too deep to be recovered by surface mining. The importance of such projects is apparent because estimated reserves in the entire area approach the 300 billion barrel figure, or about seven times the total proved recoverable reserves of the United States. The Great Canadian Oil Sands plant (45,000 barrels per day) has operated since 1967. Other companies are waiting to begin construction of plants as soon as the Canadian government settles on the terms and grants the permits. The life index (reserves/consumption rate) of the Athabasca tar sand reserves as related to the 1980 Midwest demand is more than 100 years. There are other Canadian tar sands which are being explored, but the Athabasca deposit is the world's largest. All together, tar sand deposits are vast and constitute what may be the largest reserve of hydrocarbons on earth. Estimates go as high as a 40,000-year supply at present use rates. Supply and demand must provide an economic base which will make it worthwhile to recover this oil. It will more than likely become a major source for the chemical and industrial field after electric generation by the breeder makes the use of petroleum unnecessary for energy production.

Solar Energy

Although radiation energy from the sun falling upon the earth's surface is enormous (sunlight falling on an area the size of Lake Erie in one day is equal to the energy from all fuels man has so far burned on earth), the concept of direct use of solar heat is feasible only under ideal, yet-to-be-described conditions. Solar heating and cooling, collecting and storage devices are not economical, essentially because no industry exists to build them; geographic location is important for successful use of solar heat; architectural design of buildings must be considered in the successful use of solar heat; and lack of continous reliability of such heat makes an alternate back-up energy essential under most conditions. Still, as Dr. Aden Meinel of the University of Arizona has shown, there are advantages to be exploited and solar research may be profitable, especially in the area of low-grade heating and cooling systems in areas of high sunlight. Specific solar heat system costs are high; a solar water heater costs three times as much as a conventional heater, a solar water pump some twenty times more than an ordinary gasoline pump, and a solar cooker costs sixteen times more than a comparable fuel-burning stove. Aluminum back-up panes used in most solar heat systems would place massive new demands on aluminum refining and supply systems. Aluminum smelters are one of the environmentalists' prime targets.

Farrington Daniels calculates the feasibility of large-scale solar power plants collecting enough solar energy to generate 1,000 megawatts of electricity. Solar collectors covering forty-two square kilometers (about eighteen square miles) of earth surface are required. To supply the current United States electric generation capacity of 335,000 megawatts we would have to cover roughly a total of some six thousand square miles of land—an area larger than the states of Connecticut and Rhode Island combined.

A more advanced method for converting solar radiation into electricity is accomplished with solar cells (photovoltaic cells). The theoretical maximum conversion efficiency for present cells ranges between 15 and 28 per cent, depending on the specific semiconductor used. The use of intermetallic compounds (cadmium telluride, gallium arsenide, indium phosphide, and aluminum antimonide) will allow construction of cells with greater efficiency but are far from being practical at a reasonable cost. Spacecraft electricity using silicon solar cells can generate one watt of power at a cost of $200, which is 2,000 times greater than conventional generating equipment. In addition it takes major investments in transmission to get the power from the sun to the load. The use of space stations and lasers may change this in the future. Development of solar plants is expected to be on about the same time scale as fusion, so that even if the development is successful, they will not be available until after the turn of the century. World energy consumption rate in 2,000 = 1Q. Solar energy available per year = 5,190Q.

Geothermal Steam

Geothermal energy, which has been receiving wide publicity, can furnish but 0.009 of a Q per year. This is the theoretical limit on the available energy from the world's known geothermal steam resources according to M. King Hubbert, of the United States Geological Survey. The only geothermal site now in operation is The Geysers, located in Sonoma County, California, owned by the Pacific Gas and Electric Company.

Geothermal heat has been developed and used extensively in Iceland, Italy, and New Zealand where it is competitive with other energy sources. Exploration and development of geothermal projects are in progress in Japan and several Latin American countries. The Geothermal Steam Act of 1970 approved by the President on December 24, 1970, provides leasing authority, a listing of known geothermal areas, and the opportunity to proceed with geothermal development. Under favorable conditions, geothermal energy may be locally important to several areas in the western states; however, it probably will be insignificant as a factor in national power capacity (less than 1 percent of total through the year 2000).

A quite different estimate of geothermal resources is presented by some, who view the use of heat deep within the earth as a vast and feasible source of untapped energy. This is no doubt true and the only problem, once again, is to gain access to it. This concept involves penetrating the earth's crust in the regions where it is thinnest. Water is then injected into the earth's molten core, creating steam which is then captured on its return. This could be a significant source of steam if drilling can be perfected to allow such a deep penetration through several miles of the earth's crust. Such a technique would provide energy in large quantities and should last far into the infinite future until the earth cools.

The same principle is involved in the synthetic geothermal steam process, which employs thermonuclear devices of huge proportions. Such devices contain only small amounts of radioactive material and are quite economical to build and detonate. They can be detonated deep within selected rock formations in mountainous areas or deep beneath the earth's surface. On being detonated, the tremendous amounts of released heat create a huge molten mass within the rock formation which remains sealed for ages so radioactivity, even though present in small quantities, is of no concern. In such detonations the heat creates a molten sphere enclosed in a self-formed shell, analogous to an eggshell, which acts as an insulating containment and prevents much release of heat or molten materials. It is a rather simple procedure (to hard-rock miners) to drill a shaft to the edge of the "shell," or even into it if desired. Waterlines can then be extended into the molten core, or as far as necessary to produce steam, which can then be put to use. Frozen areas of the world might open this synthetic process to uses not yet considered feasible. The limits of heat depend on the size of the device detonated, provided the proper formations are available.

Hydroelectric

The total hydroelectric power potential of the United States, excluding pumped storage, is an estimated 178.5 million kilowatts, capable of generating about 700 Kwhr of electricity annually. As of January 1, 1971, the developed hydroelectric capacity of the United States was 48.5 million kilowatts. The 130 million kilowatts of undeveloped hydropower capacity are located largely in the western states and Alaska. Only about one-sixth of the potential sites are in the area east of the Mississippi River. These factors will retard development, and conventional hydropower will supply a smaller share of electric output in the future, accounting for only 5 per cent of the total electricity output by the year 2000.

Pumped storage projects are expected to grow rapidly and supply nearly 200 billion Kwhr of electricity in the year 2000. The pumped storage concept uses electric power from other sources during off-peak periods to return water to the reservoir serving it, which is then used to generate power for peak-load periods. Environmental extremists oppose almost all hydro and pump storage projects. A Consolidated Edison pump storage project has been delayed several years by environmental extremists while the area of New York served by that utility is critically short of energy.

Coal-Fired Magnetohydrodynamics (MHD)

Coal-fired magnetohydrodynamics (MHD) is one process for power production from fossil fuels that environmentalists consider compatible with environmental requirements; unfortunately it offers little practical application. In this process electricity is generated directly by moving liquids or gases through a magnetic field rather than indirectly by means of turbines and rotating generators. An increase in powerplant efficiency to 50 or 60 per cent is theoretically possible with lower discharge of heat to cooling waters and a reduced emission of sulfur and nitrogen oxides. A great deal of technical progress from first-generation plants is first necessary to increase efficiency and lower the capital costs per kilowatt of generation capacity.

MHD requires very high temperatures, a super-conducting magnet, regeneration of "seed," and removal of nitrogen oxides. The United States Bureau of Mines conducted an experiment to solve problems associated with the high-temperature combustion of "seeded" coal in the MHD generation of electric power. The study involved the combustion of coal seeded with potassium carbonate using oxygen-enriched air at 4,000 degrees F. Recovery of "seed" and its cost, removal of sulfur and nitric oxides were also studied. A review of the materials that melt about 4,000 degrees as shown in the attached chart, and the amount of research needed on this system relegates it to a very low priority. It is often referred to as feasible and desirable alternate to nuclear power by opponents of nuclear energy.

Tidal Energy

Tidal ranges suitable for possible tidal power exist only in the Northeastern United States and Alaska. Any use of tidal power in the United States would necessitate the development of turbines able to operate economically under low hydrostatic heads. Tidal power has a constant monthly tidal range average, but it does not coincide with the cycle of power needs. This can be overcome by pump-storage plants using surplus power generated by tidal, hydroelectric, fossil fuel, or nuclear plants in a power system developed to use tidal power for peak loads and to improve the economics of more conventional power generation systems.

The total tidal energy resource available amounts only to .09 Q per year, and this assumes such unlikely and decidedly impractical construction projects as damming Chesapeake Bay and other port facilities throughout the world. Environmental extremists would

Only a Small Number of Elements Have High Melting Points

(This chart shows all known elements above iron and major metals melting at lower temperatures)

DEGREES FAHRENHEIT MELTING POINT

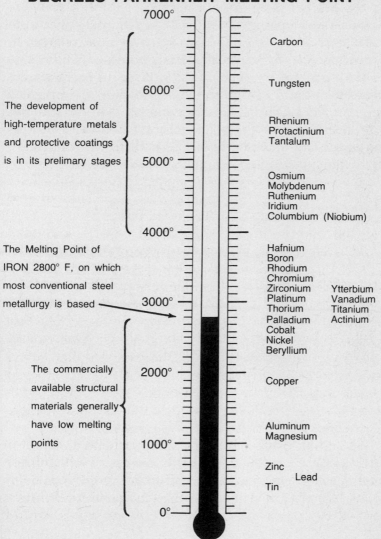

7000°

Carbon

6000°

Tungsten

The development of high-temperature metals and protective coatings is in its prelimary stages

Rhenium
Protactinium
Tantalum

5000°

Osmium
Molybdenum
Ruthenium
Iridium
Columbium (Niobium)

4000°

The Melting Point of IRON 2800° F, on which most conventional steel metallurgy is based

3000°

Hafnium
Boron
Rhodium
Chromium
Zirconium   Ytterbium
Platinum   Vanadium
Thorium   Titanium
Palladium   Actinium
Cobalt
Nickel
Beryllium

The commercially available structural materials generally have low melting points

2000°

Copper

1000°

Aluminum
Magnesium

Zinc
        Lead
Tin

0°

probably endorse the concept of tidal power but would undoubtedly oppose any specific projects as they do hydroelectric ones, especially because of the destruction of estuaries essential to the survival of many forms of sea life. If the oceans are to be considered in the energy picture other than as a source of uranium, the most feasible and unlimited source of ocean energy is the use of ocean thermal gradients as power sources. A power plant based on thermal gradients would cost little more than conventional power plants because the water serves as the medium for the collection of sunlight as well as the means to store the energy. The plants could be located under the water where, by using a heat exchanger, they extract the heat with a "working fluid," possibly ammonia. The cold seawater, moving in from the poles, would operate a condenser to cool the working fluid. These plants could also produce fresh water as well. The concept was discovered by a French scientist in 1881, and in 1922 a shore-based station was built in Cuba that produced twenty-two kilowatts of power. It proved an economic failure because seawater was used as the working fluid. Though transmission of the power would be expensive, it would not be as formidable as transmitting power from solar power units. It represents another source of unlimited power which points to electricity as the ultimate energy form.

Fuel Cells

A fuel cell converts chemical energy released by a fuel and an oxidant through an electrolytic medium into electrical energy. The direct conversion is highly efficient, resulting in efficiencies up to 75 per cent. The fuel cell used in space is a low-temperature converter using hydrogen and oxygen.

A commercial version which operates on fossil fuels is a high-temperature converter. It provides electric power under near silent conditions and with a minimum of mass, but the amount of electricity delivered is also minimal, and the cost of electricity must not be a critical consideration. The use of high-purity hydrogen as the fuel with oxygen is feasible only for special purposes at this time.

The general use of fuel cells, competitive with alternative power sources, will necessitate the use of cheaper fossil fuels in high-temperature (HT) cells. A practical power-generating system to produce electric energy from coal and air has been designed, but purification processes and metal catalysts make the near-term use of hydrocarbon fuels in small power units for a mass market remote. Use of fuel cells will occur when efficient, high-temperature units using impure, low-cost fuels are developed, or when construction is simplified to ensure long, reliable life.

The Dilemma Forestalled

Replacing all imports of oil and liquified natural gas with energy from nuclear power plants in the near future cannot solve the energy problem. Exporting enriched uranium will not provide an effective payments offset for oil imports. A capacity to furnish 25 per cent of the free world's enriched uranium outside the United States by 1985 would equal the total output of one gaseous diffusion plant, worth about $.5 billion. This does little to offset the $25 billion in oil imports.

The import problem must be treated on a massive scale and in two phases. First, for the short term, domestic production of oil and gas must be increased by every possible means, including offshore drilling, deep-well drilling, use of oil shale, tar sands, and synthesizing oil and gas from coal. Second, for the long term, other ways must be provided to meet the energy demands now met by oil and gas.

A goal of replacing all oil and gas uses by the year 2000 is reasonable. The first step is to examine the present use of primary fuels. A report, "Patterns of Energy Consumption in the United States," issued in January 1972, reveals that in 1968 transportation consumed most of the oil, while the industrial sector used most of the gas. Coal and gas were most used by the electric utility industry, with oil filling only 10 per cent. In 1971 the use of oil by the utilities had risen to 16 per cent, a move which aggravates the oil import problem.

Since electricity is an energy form rather than an energy source, each economic sector can be analyzed as to how much energy it consumes in the form of electricity versus its direct consumption of primary fuels. A comprehensive analysis has been done by Philip Ross of the Westinghouse Electric Corporation.[12] It reveals that no sector now uses much energy from electricity. The electric utilities supply only 9 per cent of the total of end-use energy. The greatest end-use of energy is by direct consumption of oil, gas, and coal.

For nuclear-electric energy to replace these dwindling and limited fuel supplies, a quantum jump in electric capacity must be undertaken. Electricity can easily be substituted for all direct fuel applications. It will be difficult to replace only in the transportation sector and for petrochemical raw materials. By excluding petrochemicals and the transportation industry (trucks and aircraft), the remainder, including passenger cars, trains, and industrial vehicles, can be switched to electric energy. On a long-term basis, what happens if nuclear-electric energy is substituted for fossil fuel energy sources?

The projected generation capacity to year 2000 grows from 380 GW (1 gigawatt = 1000 megawatts) today, to 670 GW in 1980, and 2,000 GW in the year 2000. Assuming all new capacity is added after 1980, what must be added to this current projection if all residences shift to electric heat? For residential purposes today, a large fraction of gas and oil is used for space heating, while the remainder is used in water heating, cooking, air conditioning, clothes drying, and other minor uses. Electricity can substitute for all these and at the same time provide significant savings in BTU inputs in the home.

One approach to home heating will involve the heat pump. The heat pump is the "breeder reactor" of house heating, since it puts out more usable heat than fuel combustion. It is an air conditioning system operating in reverse. Depending upon climate, efficiency ranges from 150 per cent to 250 per cent, compared to 50 per cent for a gas or oil furnace. This more than offsets efficiency differences in the conversion and delivery systems and is why it takes more natural gas or oil to heat a house with a furnace than it does when that same fuel is used to generate electricity to drive a heat pump. About 600 GW will be needed to supply the energy to all electric residences in the year 2000.

In the transportation industry, electricity can be substituted for gasoline or diesel-powered automobiles, trains, and industrial vehicles. The electric car requires much less fuel than a gas-engine passenger car. In addition, the electric plant kilowatt-hour installed capacity versus crude oil BTU input is down by a factor of seven. The net result is that switching to electric-powered cars would require an additional 280 GW of new electric generation capacity by the year 2000.

Process steam in the industrial and commercial sectors is perhaps the largest actual energy end-use substitution. There is no problem in furnishing process steam from a nuclear reactor directly. There is only a logistical problem in getting the steam to the user. In the future, industrial plants may be built in clusters or parks around nuclear steam generating facilities as the ideal solution to the problem. This switch in energy source adds a requirement for 800 GW.

Direct-heat end-uses can be met with electrical resistance and induction heating. Neither is as efficient as a heat pump; still none of their heat goes up the flue, so the waste heat applications require 700 GW of installed capacity and at the same time save an equal number of equivalent GWs by eliminating energy "up the stack."

The hydrogen economy, now being discussed to a great extent, is an energy form, not an energy source; and as such, energy must be expended to get it. Two major systems have been proposed for using hydrogen. Both involve using the output of a nuclear power plant to extract hydrogen from seawater and pump it through existing pipelines to a utility point for use. Two systems are suggested as ways to use the hydrogen fuel. One uses a hydrogen fuel cell to produce electricity, while the other transforms the hydrogen to a liquid state for use as a conventional motor fuel.

To compare electric transmission to each of these forms of hydrogen use, assume the output in each case will be used to power a car. One unit of useful work requires slightly less than six units of nuclear fuel using the all-electric route. But using hydrogen in a fuel cell requires in excess of fourteen units, while liquified hydrogen combustion requires seventy units. There are two reasons: 1. extra steps are required in each of the hydrogen systems which create waste energy; 2. an electric car is inherently more efficient than one with an internal combustion engine. As relatively wasteful as it is, there may be necessary places for a hydrogen fuel in end-use applications where form is critical. For instance, liquid hydrogen may be the only fuel available in the future for trucks and aircraft.

Electric space heating in nonresidential areas can also take advantage of the economical use of heat pumps. Space heating applications require 300 GW in all, while 850 GW are saved. Two minor categories left, water heating and miscellaneous, add about 130 GW.

The total electric capacity required by year 2000, substituting it where possible, is about 2,800 GW more than presently planned, for a total capacity of 4,800 GW. This requires an annual electric generation growth rate between 1980 and 2000 of 10 per cent instead of 6.5 per cent. The capacity would double every seven years, with yearly additions triple previous estimates, reaching 600 GW in the year 2000. At year 2000 electric power requirements, increasing step by step with each substitution, will reach a total of 4,800 GW.

The requirement for total energy inputs from this point of view is equal to 245 thousand trillion BTUs, more than three and one-half times the 1970 consumption. Uranium will provide 65 per cent, with coal providing the balance of five and one-half times the 1970 consumption rate. Such a growth rate in coal use is one and one-half times greater than the present growth rate of total energy input.

No present plans or estimates for adding generation and transmission at this capacity exist for serious consideration. An executive of Westinghouse Electric Corporation stated: "We should place our emphasis and efforts on fusion power, not on MHD; on clean burning of coal, not on geothermal systems; on electric energy storage, not on synthetic natural gas (SNG); on heat

pumps, not on more lumens per watt; on superconduct-
ing generators, not power from trash; on electric cars,
not on Wankel engines."

A Solution: The Economics of a
Nuclear-Electric Era

In view of what we have read and what has been stated in the resource documents of reputable agencies and
experts, the only acceptable solution to the long-range
energy supply problem is the nuclear-electric energy
era. To produce the energy from nuclear sources, the
economics must fit the needs. The breeder reactor and
fusion are the only energy sources capable of meeting
such future energy requirements. The breeder reactor
offers 1,500 times the energy available from today's total
natural fuel sources. Breeders reduce the vulnerability
to fluctuating uranium ore costs and eventually obviate
the need for expensive enrichment facilities required by
present-day LWRs or HTGRs.

The fusion reaction opens the possibility of virtually
unlimited energy resources due to its use of deuterium
in the oceans as its basic fuel. Though problems must
be solved before fusion becomes a reality, most authorities expect to demonstrate scientific feasibility in the
next decade and to achieve a demonstration plant by
2000. Present research deals with the deuterium-tritium
reaction which requires lithium 6 to replenish the tritium required for the reaction. Lithium 6 world reserves
are some 70,000 metric tons. This supply limits the
available energy to about 230 Q, slightly less than our
known supplies of natural fuels. In this regard it is both
intriguing and significant that the deuterium-tritium fusion reactor is like today's nuclear fission reactor in that
both can only use a small fraction of the energy avail-

able in their basic fuels. The breeder reactor is the way out of this dilemma, in the case of today's fission reactor, just as the more difficult deuterium-lithium machine is the solution in the case of the fusion reactor. In any event there are vast quantities of uranium and thorium to meet any energy need for several thousands of years.

The delivered price of yellow cake (U^3O^8) in the United States is about \$6 per pound compared with \$7 a few years ago. The world market price is lower, about \$5 per pound. Uranium reserves are high, in spite of little prospecting in recent years, but the quantity of economically recoverable uranium depends upon reactor technology. The LWR uses an intermediate nuclear technology which will help meet today's energy needs but ultimately will be replaced by the breeder. Recently, Commonwealth Edison and TVA joined in a venture with the Atomic Energy Commission to develop the first commercial-sized breeder generation plant in the United States with financial aid from most of the electric utility systems. With today's technology, uranium prices of \$8 to \$10 a pound, possibly \$15 or more, for yellow cake are feasible. But the breeder is expected to use uranium recoverable at \$100, possibly much more per pound. Reserves of U^3O^8 available for LWRs are estimated by the AEC at 273,000 tons (at \$8 per pound) and 430,000 tons at \$10 per pound. Estimates of total reserves in the United States are much higher, 1.6 million tons recoverable at \$15 a pound, with an ultimate energy content of 100 Qs.

World uranium reserves are considerably higher than the United States reserves. Mr. Henry Linden of the Institute of Gas Technology recently stated there were just under four million tons of U^3O^8 in the Free World reserves recoverable at \$15 a pound. These seem low:

for example, 50,000 tons for Australia are unrealistically small. The conservative estimates indicate uranium reserves recoverable at current or moderately higher price levels are sufficient to last until the year 2000 in LWRs. Further prospecting is expected to turn up reserves well in excess of these figures when exploration resumes in earnest. The ultimately recoverable energy content of even such conservative four-million-ton estimates will approximate 250 Qs. The twofold improvement of the breeder now takes on added significance. Not only will it recover fifty times as much of the energy in uranium than the LWR, but it will make feasible the exploitation of more expensive, but vastly larger uranium and thorium reserves, ultimately opening up the almost limitless resources of our oceans. For example, at $100 a pound, a price certainly acceptable with the breeder, a recent estimate puts our domestic U^3O^8 reserves as high as twenty to twenty-five million tons, equivalent to 1,000 to 1,500 Qs, nearly 8,000 times the world's present annual energy usage.

Thorium reserves are not as well explored, but the Department of Interior estimates domestic thorium to be at least equivalent, in tons, to uranium reserves. World reserves are substantial. The eventual energy potential of thorium is considered equal to natural uranium, since the latent energy content of the two is about the same pound for pound. Actually, using the reactor technologies available today, a pound of thorium can produce several times as much energy as a pound of uranium.

For the short run, using LWRs and HTGRs, economically recoverable uranium and thorium will provide 3 to 5 Qs; adequate to fuel them until the breeder is ready. Then, uranium in a breeder will provide much more energy than all of the world's recoverable fossil reserves, no less than 300 Qs. A much higher figure, 1,000 to 1,500 Qs for the United States alone, is more realistic, but either quantity is enough energy to meet the world's total needs (at the present annual consumption rate) for thousands of years, long after fusion or solar energy is available. In addition to this, the uranium and thorium dissolved in sea water contains energy equivalent to 200,000 or 300,000 Qs as a minimum, a thousand times the world's total estimated fossil reserves (coal, oil and gas) of 200 to 300 Qs, and several thousand times the quantity of such fossil fuels as will ever be economically recoverable. There is enough nuclear energy to outlast man.

The real problems for nuclear power licensing and pricing stem from a regulatory crisis rather than an energy crisis. The AEC has improved licensing, but little confusion has disappeared. Construction and licensing lead times are much longer for nuclear than fossil plants, ranging between five to eight years. In 1965, four to five years was the expected maximum. The increased lead times and delays are partly due to technical delays, but they result mainly from environmental evaluations, licensing hearings, and court proceedings, with resulting massive design changes and reconstruction work.

The adversary process may resolve controversy, but is wasteful in making business decisions, especially repetitive business decisions, and particularly when some adversaries are hellbent upon delay and stoppages rather than a resolution of differences. The AEC must impose more responsibility on parties seeking to intervene in licensing. Those seeking only to delay or halt projects are working in opposition to the public interest and ought to stipulate their contentions in detail and be prepared to follow prescribed procedures.

In the past, licensing boards have allowed intervenors

broad latitude due to ignorance of the rules. But intervenors must be held responsible in the conduct of their
cases. Nuclear plant delay leads to extra costs, often av-
eraging over $100,000 a day, a social waste which is by
necessity passed on to the consumer. Gordon R. Corey,
chairman of the Finance Committee, Commonwealth
Edison Company, stated: "In fact, I would put the total
costs of such delays already experienced at more than a
billion dollars."[13] The recent awakening of the public
and media to the effects of power shortages have helped
overcome some regulatory delays.

The other important regulatory problem is one of
rates: how to attract the enormous amounts of capital
needed to finance the nuclear age. The outlook for the
future is the key to this problem: i.e., are nuclear or fossil-fueled units likely to provide the bulk of the nation's
electric power of the future? Less than 5 per cent of the
total electric power generation today is nuclear. It will
take major shifts in public opinion and some heroic
technological effort for the nation as a whole to shift to
nuclear power. Estimates place the overall nuclear percentages at 28 per cent by 1980 and 45 per cent by 1990,
and if electric substitution is made, almost 100 per cent
by year 2020. What will really happen depends on siting
and licensing situations in the future. Licensing and environmental problems are being resolved. Generic treatment of questions to avoid repetition at each hearing by
environmental extremists will make it more difficult for
them to delay purposely or halt projects rather than resolve conflicts. There has been much talk in recent
years about the need to provide additional enrichment
capacity; little has been done about it. Only recently
Westinghouse, Bechtel, and Union Carbide announced
feasibility studies for the first privately owned enrichment plant in the United States. The development of

the breeder must be expedited. The Dounreay Reactor in Northern Scotland includes a small 13-1/2 Mw breeder unit which has been producing power for the British grid for about thirteen years. The United States' EBR II at Idaho Falls has been turning out 15 Mw since 1964. A second British prototype breeder (250 Mw) has just recently gone into service at Dounreay. The British have no doubt about the effectiveness of the breeder and are confident about "going commercial" with a British model soon. Cost figures are surprisingly low.

In the United States, on the other hand, the mere passage of time required to prepare environmental impact studies, to perform environmental reviews and evaluations, to allow ample time for all intervenors, and finally to build the breeder reactor itself will take us into the 1980s before the 350 Mw demonstration plant is operational. It will then be five or ten years more before the record of that plant's reliable operation will permit industry to order breeders. It may be the mid-1990s before commercial breeder plants take on real significance.

Meanwhile, the demand for electric power will continue to skyrocket. Despite talk of limiting electricity usage, there is no evidence of a slackening off, and no indication that load projection formulas of the past are not valid for the future. Electricity is a clean fuel, a precise, easily controlled energy source, and the only energy form which can use our most abundant energy reserves, uranium, thorium, and eventually hydrogen. Therefore, use of electricity will continue to rise faster than other energy forms, as central-station power preempts more of the energy market. The nuclear reactor share of central station power will grow in turn.

The future outlook for nuclear power is favorable. The short-run construction, scheduling, and licensing problems should be resolved with agreed-upon environmental requirements and minimal back-fitting delay. The electric power industry is the most highly capital-intensive industry of all. Sharply increasing construction costs are particularly hard to cope with, and no capital to pay such costs will be available unless electric rates are raised to pay for it. Prices of electricity and other forms of energy should be raised to provide adequate supplies. Most people depend upon an adequate supply of energy, particularly electricity, and few would prefer to return to candles, firewood, horses, hand labor, and stagnant air rather than pay the increasing costs of electric power.

Chapter IV
Cases for Lunacy

The Tussock Moth

The Tussock Moth infestation of a vast section of Northwest forest over the past three years is one of the most bizarre incidents in the chain of ruinous decisions imposed throughout the nation by environmental extremists. When examined in detail, it so defies logic and reason that any attempt to describe the all but willful killing of this forest requires a determined hold on one's self-control. It is helpful first to present several overriding facts to provide an understanding of the issues, facts which should have made all that follows impossible:

1. The Tussock Moth infests and kills large sections of forests if not controlled.

2. DDT is the only effective and safe insecticide known to control and eliminate the Tussock Moth.

3. The loss of forests (which could have been prevented) of major proportions represents one of the most obscene acts toward nature and the environment imaginable. Only fanatics blinded by their "cause" could precipitate such an act. The economy of the region and loss of international trade, especially at a time when there is a log export ban under consideration, are important consequences, but only secondary.

Comments by Dr. Norman Borlaug about DDT, its effectiveness, and its relative toxicity, have been presented in Chapter One. The action of former EPA administrator William Ruckelshaus, in announcing the ban on the use of DDT effective December 31, 1972, defies explanation or understanding. This came not long after he had stated that DDT did *not* constitute a hazard. Nevertheless, following almost eight months of hearing testimony and a thorough review, the EPA lost sight of the fundamental questions, and the fate of DDT was sealed.

Still, the EPA refused to succumb immediately, reporting that the benefits of DDT far outweighed the risks and hazards. It is the author's judgment that the decision of William Ruckelshaus to ban DDT represents the decision of an intellectual cripple. His decision expressly contradicted:

1. The massive weight of testimony received in the hearings and the hearing officer's recommendations.
2. His own agency's select Scientific Advisory Committee.[1]
3. The decision and many recommendations of the Department of Agriculture.
4. Nobel prize-winner Dr. Norman Borlaug and the World Health Organization.
5. The most prestigious entomologists and entomology centers of the United States and the world.
6. The most eminent toxicologists and toxicology centers of the United States and the world.

The groups which opposed the use of DDT and consigned 449,550 acres of timber to death are the same groups that, on the other hand, seek the preservation of our timber reserves and forests to protect them from man's legitimate use.

One group, the Oregon Environmental Council, in its advertising campaign and in its brochures, states in large red print, "Trees can't talk." It goes on to say, "we do it for them." But it adds, "Talk isn't cheap! Your membership and your contribution will...." In regard to the trees of the Blue Mountains, the Oregon Environmental Council adopted a very different view for some reason. Here is what it said to the U.S. Forest Service about using DDT to save the huge forest of firs: "There is virtually no discussion of the effects of DDT on insects other than the target species, yet the broad-scale toxicity of this insecticide to insects is always a source of concern...." Suddenly the welfare of unnamed insects assumes more importance than the trees. The insects will also have a tough time of it if the trees all die, but the Oregon Environmental Council can not see beyond its role of preventing man from beneficial management of his resources. The OEC goes on to state that "at a minimum it will disrupt predator-prey relationships among insects and arachnids (spiders) for a period."

Though the environmental extremists *repeatedly* charge that DDT is highly poisonous, in fact it is unique among pesticides because of its lack of toxicity. This is what all the massive data and literature are trying to tell these zealots; namely, that DDT is *not* toxic to humans and animals above the level of insects.

But that would make no difference to the environmental extremists. They recommend the use of Zectran, which has been reported by Innes, et al. in 1969 as having teratogenic activity. Zectran with DMSO, given subcutaneously, caused increased fetal mortality in mice. Tumorogenicity bioassays on mice showed Zectran as a compound needing additional evaluation. Oregon State University classifies it as a dangerous

insecticide. Approved respirators must be used when ap-
plying it, and areas treated with Zectran must not be
populated sites.

In the intellectually incredible standard of the environmental extremists, the lives of insects and spiders are
placed before the lives of millions of large fir trees. The
welfare of people and their environment depends on
keeping these firs alive and growing. Thanks to these so-
called "protectors" of nature, the cost in dead trees and
timber resources in the Tussock Moth-infested areas is
$27,000,738. This does not count intangible costs which
environmental extremists apply to other situations.
These include recreational, wildlife habitat, watershed,
and soil erosion losses. (Some are discussed later.)

The U.S. Forest Service submitted an Environmental
Impact Statement on the Tussock Moth and received
back a significant number of replies.[2] There were nine-
ty-four in favor of using DDT and saving the trees.
These included:

> Oregon State University, Agricultural Chemistry
>   Department
> Western Forestry and Conservation Association
> Washington State Sportsmen's Council
> Washington Forest Protection Agency
> Washington Department of Natural Resources
> Southern Idaho Forestry Association
> Society of American Foresters (Puget Sound)
> Society of American Foresters (Blue Mountains)
> Oregon State Forester
> Oregon Forest Protection Council
> North Idaho Forest Association
> Northeast Oregon Resources Council
> Western Environmental Trade Association

Those opposed to saving the trees included:
> Environmental Defense Fund
> Oregon Environmental Council

Sierra Club
Wilderness Society
National Audubon Society

There were only nine opposed to saving the trees.

In addition, there were seventeen county and local government agencies in favor of saving the trees, and none opposed. In private responses, 812 wrote in favor of saving the trees and only seventeen wrote opposing saving the trees.

The reasons given for the overwhelming support for control of the Tussock Moth and saving the trees are:

Reasons	Number of Signatures
Prevent timber losses	490
Protect watershed values	379
Prevent scenic losses	333
Prevent negative economic impact	328
Prevent loss of jobs	260
Prevent recreation losses	75
Prevent general loss of forest values	48
Stop build-up of increased fire danger	48
Reduce human health hazard	46
Protect wildlife	30
Reduce effects on private land	20
Prevent general environmental damage	18
Prevent spreading of moth	13

Many respondents gave reasons why they were for or against the use of DDT:

Reason in Favor (98 Per Cent)	Signatures
Benefits outweigh harm	986
Best or only alternative	160
Previous results safe	99
Minimal environmental damage	54
Prevents further outbreak	53
No long-range damage	19
Little effect on wildlife	15
Best economic alternatives	7
Fastest of alternatives	1
Little effect on livestock	1

Reason Not in Favor (2 Per Cent)	Signatures
Affects non-target animals (insects)	30
Harmful ecosystem effects	21
Adverse effects on water	12
Lasts too long	9
Expensive	7
Human health hazard	7
Insufficient knowledge about DDT	3
Target would develop immunity	3
Would set bad precedent	1
Other controls not explored	1
Reduces natural enemies of moth	1

In the Pacific Northwest during 1970, Tussock Moth larvae were observed during ground surveys throughout eastern Oregon, but no visible damage was noted. The only damage reported in Washington in 1970 was on shade trees in Spokane. In 1971, severe defoliation was spotted at widely scattered locations in Washington near Cashmere, Riverside, and Oroville. The outbreak at Cashmere collapsed by the fall of 1971. Egg surveys in the fall of 1971 near Riverside and Oroville indicated these populations would cause additional damage in 1972.

Field experiments using new insecticides such as Zectran and pyrethrins were tried as possible replacements for DDT. The results were encouraging, but additional tests are necessary before either can be recommended for operational use. Defoliation continued to occur in Washington in 1972. Scattered outbreaks were reported in various counties and on the Colville Indian Reservation. A total of 22,459 acres were defoliated.

During 1971, the Tussock Moth continued to remain at subepidemic levels on the Umatilla and Wallowa-Whitman National Forests, and Winema National Forest in Oregon. In 1972, the population in two of these areas exploded to epidemic proportions. Visible damage developed on 173,600 acres. The outbreak extended northeast fifty-seven miles from LaGrande, Oregon, into southeast Washington. No DDT spray was used.

The Douglas Fir Tussock Moth winters in the egg stage, and in late spring after the host tree has begun new growth, the eggs hatch. Egg hatch extends over a period of several days depending on the environment. The tiny, newly hatched larvae are fuzzy, longhaired caterpillars about one-eighth inch long. Their long hair and light weight allow them to be carried long distances by the wind. Mature larvae are up to one and one-quarter inches long and very colorful. The body hairs of the larvae are barbed and cause a skin rash on some people. These hairs are used to cover the cocoons and egg masses and serve to protect the moth from some predators.

The Tussock Moth prefers to feed on Douglas fir, White fir, and Grand fir. It will occasionally feed quite heavily on subalpine fir. Larvae have been found feeding on Ponderosa pine, Western hemlock, and Western larch after the preferred hosts have been defoliated. The moth is a native insect of western North America and has periodically caused extensive tree mortality in the coniferous forests of Canada and the United States. Biotic conditions favorable for explosive moth outbreaks are unknown. Tussock Moth outbreak histories indicate populations of this insect can reach high levels within a three-year period and cause heavy mortality in Douglas fir and true fir stands.

Based on extensive biological data collected in the Oregon and Washington area during the fall of 1972, which appeared to be the second year of this outbreak, it was estimated that insect populations within the total forested area, which included National Forest, state, private, and other federal ownerships, would cause significant tree defoliation and mortality unless weather, food supply, or other biotic factors, either singly or together, cause a collapse of the insect outbreak prior to the start of heavy feeding.

The USDA-Forest Service, the Oregon State Department of Forestry, and the Washington State Department of Natural Resources evaluated all possible treatment alternatives, including "no control." Based upon the response to the Draft Environmental Statement and a recent analysis of biological control agents, they concluded that DDT was the only effective control. There is no registered or suitable insecticide available at this time for the control of the Tussock Moth. The analysis included a thorough review of the many responses to the statement and an in-depth study of data from areas where DDT treatments have been made in a western coniferous forest environment for the control of the same or similar insect pests during a number of previous outbreaks.

Anticipating that the use of DDT might become necessary, the Forest Service and the states of Oregon and Washington applied to the EPA administrator, William Ruckelshaus, on April 20, 1973. The EPA report indicated that the ruling against DDT was made on the ground that insect populations would probably collapse and that DDT could contaminate air and water; it was EPA's view that the benefits did not outweigh the risks. Therefore, DDT could not be considered as a control alternative. Although the EPA indicated that chemicals other than DDT could be used to control this outbreak, there are none that are either proven effective or registered for this purpose.

This precipitated a proposal to accelerate salvage logging efforts to get as many of the usable trees out as possible and to increase fire protection in order to minimize the risk of much greater losses that could result from greatly increased fire hazard in the diseased area.

The pleas of the residents of the area had no impact on the EPA. The city of Walla Walla, Washington, was one of the more seriously affected. Residents presented a detailed regional impact statement to the Forest Service and the EPA; it had no effect on the final decision. The Walla Walla impact statement included the following summation: "If the infestation is not brought under control in the Blues, the Walla Walla area tends to lose its timber industry at a cost of over $7 million dollars annually to the community in jobs, retail sales, bank deposits, and support services. There is, also, potential tax loss to area counties from forest receipts. A loss of watershed forest would mean a loss of one-third of our water storage capacity and a cut in our irrigated crops and reduction of crop land production to serve our processing industry. The flooding and erosion problems will increase also. Recreationally, the infestation will have a negative aesthetic impact on the many campers, sightseers, and travelers who go into the Blues. The Blues are the only areas for summer and winter activities for the lowland semi-arid cities...; [these benefits] will be lost if the forests continue to be denuded.

"The defoliation is expected to affect the deer and elk herds the greatest. In 1971 the monies spent to harvest the elk and deer totaled $2.1 million, which does not represent the monies spent by over 58,000 hunters who did not get their deer or elk in 1971.

"There is no doubt [that in] timber, agriculturally, recreationally, and from many other ways, the continued infestation by the Tussock Moth in the Blues will have a negative impact to our economy now and for a long time after.

"The dollar figure for an additional impact totals

a conservative $1,543,409. Add this figure to the $5,653,200 income from logging and mill operations, and we have a total annual potential loss of $7,196,609 to the area economy. If this does occur, the forest may not be ready for harvest for another thirty or forty years which could result in up to 280 million dollars loss to the area economy during those years.... We urge action be taken now and that DDT be released for use on this crisis situation."

William Hazeltine, Ph.D., Entomology, and a forestry consultant, commented on the Tussock Moth after a detailed study of the area.[3] "I realize the decision to not control the Tussock Moth is now largely political; however, this does not excuse any political authority from being responsible for this massive waste of a natural resource."

The four-pound Environmental Impact Statement with all these facts, prepared at an estimated cost of $1,000,000, had no substantive effect. In April 1973 the EPA refused the emergency request to use DDT. Matt Gould, director of environmental control for Georgia-Pacific Corporation, said, "it was a political decision; there is no secret that the EPA did not take into consideration scientific, technological, or economical aspects in reaching its decision. They knew that unless the spraying was done in the last two weeks of June, 400,000 acres of firs will be devastated by the moths. The U.S. Forest Service and the Oregon State Forestry Department recommended early this year that DDT, the only known chemical control for the moth, be used. This document was rewritten in Washington, D.C., and the original destroyed."

The city of Walla Walla, Washington, again appealed to the EPA to allow DDT to be used. This request was turned down on June 14, 1973. Ernest Bonyhadi, the lawyer for the watershed interests said, "there was an open door at the agency, but not an open mind. Although the evidence was overwhelming in our favor, EPA has almost a blind faith in the ban on DDT."

Referring once again to the EPA-consolidated DDT final hearings, findings, conclusions, and orders published on April 25, 1972, the hearing officer stated: "The right of cross-examination spurred a genuinely sober assessment of the facts available, particularly on the question of the benefits and risks of DDT; and it exposes those few instances where the purpose was to generate more heat than light on the subject.

"There were some appalling instances of incredible inactions such as the publication of a paper containing faulty information which, after discovery, was never corrected and apparently is still being relied upon. However, practically every witness from the scientific community responded readily to this first-of-a-kind subjection of his professional work on DDT to the crucible of cross-examination;...the thoroughness with which the topic of DDT was explored and analyzed has not made easier my task in evaluating, in a short space of time, the conclusions that result therefrom." The conclusions of the Hearing Examiner Sweeney were:

D. CONCLUSIONS OF LAW

Based upon the evidence and the Findings of Fact in this case, I made the following Conclusions of Law:

9. DDT is not a carcinogenic hazard to man.
10. DDT is not a mutagenic or teratogenic hazard to man.
11. The uses of DDT under the registrations involved here do not have a deleterious effect on fresh water fish, estuarine organisms, wild birds or other wildlife.
12. The adverse effect on beneficial animals from

the use of DDT under the registrations involved here is not unreasonable on balance
with its benefit.

13. The use of DDT in the U.S. has declined rapidly since 1959.

14. DDT as offered under the registrations involved
herein is not misbranded as defined...because
it does not create a risk that is unreasonable on
balance with the benefit.

17. There is a present need for the continued use
of DDT for the essential uses defined in the
case.

E. OPINION [of Hearing Examiner Sweeney]

There was presented a lot of testimony, both oral
and written. Much of it was pointed to a showing
of the global extent of the presence of DDT. The
purpose of expending so much expert opinion to
make that point is somewhat obscure to me. During the hearing, an article appeared in a scientific
publication stating that I did not understand the
"subtle" case against DDT. Well, the only "subtle"
aspect about the worldwide approach is the apparently assumed theory that no "cause and effect"
showing is necessary to apply the global impact to
the uses under the registrations at issue here.... In
my opinion the evidence in this proceeding supports the conclusion that there is a present need for
the essential uses of DDT; that efforts are being
made to provide a satisfactory replacement for
DDT; and that a cooperative program of surveillance and review can result in a continued lessening in the risks involved.

Finally, Dr. Hazeltine treats the subject of wildlife effects of DDT especially applicable to the Tussock Moth
case:

The speculated effects of DDT on birds need much more detailed evaluation, particularly the individual egg residue and eggshell correlations.... A manuscript submitted to *Nature* presents data and references to support the conclusions that:

a. It is no longer reasonable to allege DDT or DDE as the cause of Brown Pelican, Peregrine Falcon or Bald Eagle egg thinning.

b. There are data showing nearly perfect correlations of DDE and shell thickening for Brown Pelicans. This shoots down conclusions based on correlations of residues and thinning.

c. Statistical manipulations to make data look conclusive are sometimes used inappropriately.

d. Egg shells for Bald Eagles in the U.S. started to thin before DDT was commercially available (1945).

e. The Mallard Duck model showed an average of 13.2 percent thin, and an average residue of DDE of 146.6 ppm per weight.

f. The Kestrel (a sparrow hawk) fed DDE feed for a year laid eggs which were a net 7.6 percent thin, Peregrines apparently reproduced satisfactorily when thin shells were 20 percent thin.

g. USDI researchers question the correctness of concluding DDE as the cause of thin pelican and other bird eggs.

h. In the United Kingdom, the Peregrine population increased for eight years after their egg shells were thin.

i. Arctic Peregrine eggshells were as thin in 1952 as in 1969, yet the population was reproducing satisfactorily until 1969, when the population crashed.

j. There is apparent bias by scientists on the DDT-eggshell stories.

k. Sea gulls eat thin pelican eggs, yet the sea gulls have normal thick egg shells. Sea gulls are as high or higher on the food chain than pelicans, so the food chain story needs overhauling.

This paper points out why DDT is no longer a reasonable candidate to blame for eggshell thinning of predatory birds. And of all the anti-DDT stories, the osprey decline due to DDT or DDE residues seems to be one of the most bizarre. The maximum egg residues of 10 ppm were reported on the East Coast (AMES, P.L. 1966) where the birds were reported in trouble. A July 1970 *New York Times* story reports thirty-four young produced from thirty-eight nests in 1970. Declines of 50 per cent in fifty years were reported prior to 1882 (Bent, A.C. 1937). This decline occurred up to the publication of Bent's book. Risebrough and others have reported suspicions that P.C.B. caused chick deformities in Terns from the same areas where the osprey on Long Island are presumed to feed.

In sum, alleging DDE as the cause of osprey reproduction problems is speculative and worth very little in weighing risks from control of Tussock Moths with DDT.

Spofford (p. 327 in Hickey, J.J., 1969, *Peregrine Falcon Populations*) showed increases of Osprey passing the Hawk Mountain Sanctuary in Pennsylvania, since 1950. Kestrels (sparrow hawks) increased after 1946 low numbers.

The most amazing aspect of the entire DDT issue is that DDT is not endangering the public health and has an amazing and exemplary record of safe use. It has a very high toxicity threshold in man. Nor does it cause a toxic response in other mammals and is not harmful unless taken in massive suicidal overdoses. It would appear that the main concern of the EPA in sacrificing the Blue Mountain firs was to keep intact the Oregon Environmental Council's vital "insect-arachnid" (spider) predator-prey relation. There simply is no logical explanation to this irresponsible and absurd act.

Norman Podhoretz, in the February 1973 issue of *Commentary*, says of the environmental extremists, "an important element in the otherwise puzzling enthusiasm of the left for the ecology movement—puzzling because conservationism has in the past appealed almost exclusively to conservatives—is, I would guess, that it has created a substitute line of attack on the corporations and a new argument for controlling them in the absence of any significant popular feeling against their strictly economic power."

In thus carrying out their attacks, the spider and insect protectors and red-eyed fanatics dull the understanding that needs to be made clear to all by those who propose reasonable solutions to difficult problems.

Finally, on February 27, 1974, the EPA issued the United States Forest Service an "emergency exemption" to the DDT ban to control the moth, but with some ill-conceived restrictions including, of all things, placement of warnings in public places in sprayed areas of the date, time, and duration of such spraying. No reasons were given for this senseless requirement. A research program costing approximately $600,000 was also required to pile additional evidence on top of existing data as to DDT effectiveness.

To anyone who remains skeptical as to what the author and others are saying about the environmental extremists and what they are inflicting on the nation today, I suggest a trip to Walla Walla, Washington, or La-Grande, Oregon, and a drive through the once beautiful Blue Mountains, where the Tussock Moth has been allowed to kill the firs. It will remove any doubt as to the veracity of what this book reports and the disastrous results of the activities of the environmental zealots and their allies.

The Clearcutting Issue

Clearcutting is a technique of forest management, referred to as even-aged silvi-culture. Without its use, it would be difficult, if not impossible, to perpetuate some of the nation's most important tree species, and they would not grow in the volume and quality now in evidence. Clearcutting is not a pretty word, which explains to some extent why the term is controversial. Professional foresters refer to it as "even-aged management" or "regeneration cut," because the environmental effects of this forest management practice are quite the opposite from what many people have been led to believe. Before discussing the environmental extremists' position on clearcutting, a brief explanation of what it is will be helpful to those unfamiliar with this technique of forestry.

While clearcutting is only one of many harvesting techniques, it is the preferred method for shade-intolerant species like Douglas fir because it assures maximum results in regeneration. Trees of this type grow best with full exposure to sun, which clearcutting provides. Since the environmental benefits that forests can provide depend to a large extent on the quality of trees that can be grown, it is ironic that clearcutting is opposed in some quarters on environmental grounds. Under sound forest management clearcut tracts are replanted and soon restored by a verdant cover of young trees that blend well with surrounding mature trees. These older trees are often themselves the result of regeneration following clearcutting. In fact, the mature even-aged forests of the U.S., born of forest management, are the envy of the world, some of them looking more "virgin" than a virgin forest.[4]

What do the environmental extremists have against clearcutting? The main thrust of their complaint stems from the appearance of a clearcut forest. It is not the forest it was before. The trees have all been cut and removed so all one can see are stumps and the remains of stumps from the harvesting process. It looks much like a stand of wheat that has been harvested, leaving only the cut stems. They have no other substantive arguments. They choose not to view the forests as resources for timber and do not wish to recognize that the harvest of mature forests is necessary to protect this valuable natural resource for the future of a huge industry in this country. Based on this one objection, the esthetic one, the environmental extremists went to work to stop clearcutting.

In early 1972 a proposal for an Executive Order was considered which would have severely restricted clearcutting on federal commercial lands. The order, which would have had the force of law, contained subjective criteria that would have impaired the ability of federal agencies to use even-aged management for timber growth and regeneration. Subsequently, the proposal was dropped by joint decision of the Secretaries of Interior and Agriculture and the chairman of the Council on Environmental Quality. Shortly thereafter, the Senate Interior Public Lands subcommittee, chaired by Senator Frank Church of Idaho, issued a report on federal forest management practices, including clearcutting, which it had investigated in hearings held in the spring of 1971. At that time bills were introduced in the Senate and House proposing a two-year moratorium on clearcutting on federal lands while a study was made of the practice. The subcommittee's report included guidelines for the Executive Branch, particularly the Forest Service and Bureau of Land Management, regarding the application of clearcutting on public lands. The subcommittee recognized the role of the national forest in providing timber for the future needs of the nation and the key part clearcutting plays in this effort. The subcommittee recommended against any ban and said it "does not question that under appropriate conditions, clearcutting is a necessary, scientific, and professional forestry tool." The report continued, "clearcutting is generally an essential means of achieving even-aged forest management. It can be applied judiciously and with expertise with favorable results...." Almost immediately after the report was made public, Forest Service Chief Edward P. Cliff announced his agency's approval of the suggested guidelines, calling them technically sound and generally compatible with a series of studies and reports which have been completed by the Forest Service and others, all involving extensive public comment. Unfortunately, the issue is far from dead and could be revived in Congress, particularly if some members feel the Senate-suggested guidelines are not being satisfactorily applied to public lands. There even may be attempts to restrict clearcutting on privately-owned lands.

To be better able to act in the public interest, people must become aware of all the facts, environmental, social, and economic, relating to the practice. America today has about 75 per cent as much forest land as existed here when Columbus landed. The total area is 758 million acres. Of that total, about one-third, 248 million acres, is set aside in parks, wilderness areas, watersheds, or is not suitable for growing commercial timber. This third of the American forest equals the size of Norway, Sweden, Denmark, Austria, Switzerland, Holland, Belgium, and Israel. The remaining 510 million acres of the total forest base is the commercial forest. This forest land produces raw material for wood products, contributes to the net oxygen gain, and provides recreation for millions of Americans.[5]

It is commonly assumed that commercial forests in America are owned by a few large timber companies. This is not the case. The biggest single owner of the commercial forest is government, both state and federal. About 142 million acres of the commercial forest land is publicly held, 28 per cent of the total. Private individuals, about four million persons, own almost 60 per cent of the forest, or about 303 million acres. The forest products industry comes in a distant third, with about 13 per cent of the commercial forest, 66 million acres. In spite of this, the land owned by the forest products industry produces about one-third of the timber required for wood products, because it is intensively managed to increase yields. Industrial forest lands average about fifty-two cubic feet of new wood growth per acre per year. This is about twice the average growth realized on public lands. Both industrial and government growth averages far exceed the productivity of lands held by individuals but not managed for timber production.

The United States Forest Service is fully capable of increasing the growth rate of national forests. In fact, much of the research and development work on which modern forestry practices are based was done by the Forest Service. However, Congress has not provided the funds necessary to practice the high level of management achieved on industrial lands. For example, over the last eight years, only 40 per cent of the funds requested by the Forest Service for timber growing have been approved by Congress. At the beginning of this de-

cade, more than five million acres of federally owned
land were lying idle, in need of restocking. Another
thirteen million acres were in need of improvement
work. This is acquired land, or land that has been dev-
astated by natural catastrophe, such as fire, insect damage, or disease. Nearly half of the total area of the
eleven western states (359,197,200 acres) is in federal
ownership. Alaska (not included in that total) is 96.9 per
cent federally owned. Environmental groups are pushing hard for the government to buy more of these
lands. There is a bill now in Congress which would provide for the expenditure of from $50 to $60 million to
buy Indian lands near Klamath Falls, Oregon.

This resumé is not intended to imply that little or
nothing has been done with out national forests. But
environmental zealots hope to maneuver the public into
thinking that the responsible representatives of government and industry wish to maintain the status quo; that
is, unless they are forced into it, they will not change
existing practices. This is not necessarily the case. Tra-
ditionally, our greatest areas of progress have been the
result of business and government acting jointly to allow
the enterprise of private citizens to function freely. National forests were created early in the twentieth century because of public insistence that our forests be
protected. Misuse of some forest lands in the East created fear that the same might occur in the West.

The Forest Service was formed as a branch of the
Department of Agriculture to administer these lands.
The service's management procedures on forests were
extended to regulate the flow of navigable waters as well
as timber production. Watershed protection, improvement of fish and wildlife habitat, establishment of out-
door recreation facilities, the purchase and development
of wilderness areas, and the control of grazing and min-

ing activities were then added and called the "working forest" concept. The 1960 Multiple Use, Sustained Yield Act provided that wild and scenic rivers, hiking routes, endangered species of wildlife, and plant life having an esthetic consideration be a part of Forest Service activities.

The increasing pressure from conservationists to set aside more and more wilderness area and reduce the acreage that can be harvested, impinges upon management practices necessary to increase yields from such areas. Good forest management and resources production require that certain timber be harvested, and if it is not, the results are unproductive. Slightly more than fourteen million acres of additional forest land are now included in the wilderness area grouping. No timber harvesting is done on this land. In addition 108 sites covering some 911,000 acres have been designated as archeological, historical, botanical, geological, scenic, or natural areas as well.

At the same time, there is a marked increase in the demand for softwood timber products. Increased housing construction since 1970 has caused a sharp increase in lumber requirements. This can be met with no danger to our forest stands if the resources are properly managed. The projected demand by 1980 of twenty billion board feet requires increased annual investments in the national forests as well as private holdings, additional investments in reforestation, stand improvement, access roads, fertilizers, and faster-maturing species. The sales of standing trees total more than a quarter-billion dollars each year, and timber produced from these lands is the raw material base for more than a million jobs, generating an estimated $15 billion toward the gross national product.

Log exports, especially to Japan, have caused public

concern recently. Unfortunately, the issue is being settled on a political rather than on a forest management basis. The problem may soon be to whom mature timber can be sold. The demand for plywood and raw logs is already falling, and they may soon be difficult to sell at an adequate profit.

Regardless of the log export situation, forest management practices dictate how available timber is used. For example, even-aged timber management requires that at some stage a final harvest cut be made and this may include clearcutting. This type of harvest cut is one stage in a series of actions necessary to assure regeneration of a vigorous and healthy forest of certain species. Whether this requirement for a final harvest cut coincides with the demand on the national or international market is something the forest managers may or may not be able to control.

Road construction is another factor; the harvest or reforestation of many of the large stands ready now requires an adequate road network. Construction of roads has been made difficult by the actions of poorly informed environmental groups. Even though the areas needing roads are not within wilderness or natural areas designated for preservation, environmental zealots are opposed to road construction on the basis that it will open these areas to the public and damage the natural setting of the forest.

However, the main controversy between forest management personnel and the environmental zealots continues to be clearcutting. Those not familiar with the different techniques of forestry or harvesting may think that foresters clearcut all their forests. This is not the case. Other methods of harvesting include group, patch or stand clearcutting, shelter-wood and seed-tree cutting, selection cutting, intermediate cutting and salvage cutting. Each has a special use and may be better for a certain type of species of tree in certain areas.[6] The inability of some species to regenerate and grow in the shade of other trees or in competition with other species often requires clearcutting in one form or another. For example walnut, black cherry, yellow poplar, aspen, birch, Douglas fir, Lodge pine, and most other conifers benefit from clearcutting. Conversion of existing forest stands to genetically improved stands for timber and other purposes depends on clearcutting. It is superior to other types of harvest where protection of seedlings is not needed and may be detrimental to germination. Land management considerations may help determine its use, for instance, where the trees that are left for shelter will be extremely susceptible to wind after other trees are cut, and volumes of defective and unusable material contained in the stand would make disposal of slash impossible without damage to remaining trees.

In the case of certain species such as old-growth Douglas fir, several features are applicable in regeneration by clearcutting. This species will not develop and grow below 50 per cent full light conditions, doing best where light intensity exceeds 75 per cent and in mineral soils. The moist and warm conditions which prevail on most Douglas fir sites, particularly on the coastal areas of the Northwest, produces a heavy brush undergrowth. Complete logging of such areas followed by slash burning is essential to prepare the site for regeneration. Shelter wood cutting in such a stand favors a rapid take-over by a low-growing brush and does not accomplish the site preparation necessary for prompt tree regeneration and survival. More than 50 per cent of forest lands in the west is located on steep slopes which makes selective cutting impractical. And finally, large-sized timber is common in old-growth Douglas fir stands. A single tree four feet in diameter and 220 feet tall may weigh more than 30,000 pounds, and single logs weighing in excess of 20,000 are not uncommon. Machinery to log such areas is necessarily massive, relatively immobile, and expensive. Partial cutting in heavy timber such as this, and on steep slopes, produces an unacceptable degree of damage to the remaining trees. Clearcutting is the most effective way to control and prevent losses from insects and disease and the only way to make use of timber recently killed by insects and disease. Dwarf mistletoe disease is most effectively eliminated this way.

Wildlife benefits from clearcuts, because it diversifies the forest environment. Wildlife requires openings in the forest for the production of food and for play, and dense cover for protection, reproduction, and rearing their young. Clearcuts are used to increase and regulate water flows from forested areas. Research has shown that soil erosion most commonly results from logging roads improper in their location, construction, and maintenance, and not from logging practices. By the yardstick of scientific knowledge and decades of experience, clearcutting is one of several ecologically and economically sound tools of forest management. Concern for protection of the environment is widespread, but poverty is not a contributor to a quality environment. In this regard, in the Northwest alone, preventing the use of clearcut logging would result in the loss of fifteen billion feet of harvest over a five-year period, representing an annual loss of approximately 20,400 man-years of employment in the lumber industry and an additional 43,600 man-years in supporting industries for the same period. In spite of all this the Sierra Club and other environmental groups almost succeeded in having an executive order issued which would have stopped clearcutting. They did succeed in wasting large amounts of the taxpayers' money in a senseless and useless campaign of obstruction. The Forest Service maintains that the harvest can be increased, consistent with the objectives of sustained yields, environmental quality, and multiple use objectives. Its improved management and research programs should be started without delay. This means construction of access roads, improved use, more thinning and salvage, more effective protection of forest from fire and insects and disease, and reforestation and timber-stand improvement.

A good example of some of the benefits of this type of management, specifically of clearcutting, can be seen in the magnificient old-growth forests which exist today in the west. Wildfires long ago were followed by natural reseeding, which is nature's method of "clearcutting" the land and regenerating the forests. At the same time, there are undesirable esthetic impacts from clearcutting as in other types of harvesting, or for that matter almost anything done in a developing nature. Benefits versus cost and risks must be dealt with and balanced. There are ways to minimize the impact of timber harvesting on other resource values so they do not degrade the ecosystem. The objective is to minimize the adverse effects and optimize total benefits. Forestry experts insist there is a definite place where clearcutting must be used to protect our harvestable resources.

Nevertheless the environmental zealots continue their demands that clearcutting be prohibited. Senator Metcalf of Wyoming once again has introduced his bill to ban all clearcutting. This is one more example of the misuse of the conservation ethic, resulting in the needless destruction of our timber resources and wildlife.

The Alaskan Pipeline

The widely discussed, urgently needed Alaskan pipeline was in limbo from 1968 to 1973, due to a technicali-

ty in the law. Section 28 of the Mineral Leasing Act
provides that the Secretary of Interior may issue a permanent right-of-way not to exceed 25 feet on either side
of a pipeline. This was no problem. For almost 100
years revocable land-use permits have been recognized
by the government as the valid mode of granting the
privilege of using public lands outside permanent pipeline right-of-ways for temporary construction purposes.
When a line is finished, these temporary permits are re-
voked and the land must be repaired to original condition at no cost to the government.

Nonetheless, on February 9, 1973, for the first time
ever, after 50 years of operation under Section 28 of the
Leasing Act, and in face of the most critical oil shortage
in U.S. history, the Court of Appeals for the District of
Columbia held that Section 28 prohibits the temporary
use of public lands outside the 54-foot right-of-way for
any pipeline purposes.[7] The court rejected the argument
that in the context of the statute the phrase "right-of-
ways" refers to authority for the permanent use of federal lands and does not include revocable special permits for the temporary use of lands for construction
purposes: in the court's view, for the first time ever, the
special construction permit sought by Alyeska (the nonprofit company set up to construct and operate the line)
is a "right-of-way" within the "plain meaning" of the
statute.

In concluding that Section 28 bars the issuance of a
special construction permit to Alyeska, the Court of Appeals rejected what it recognized to be the long-standing
(100 year-old) and consistent administrative construction
of Section 28. It should be noted that the Bureau of
Land Management has also permitted the use of land
outside statutory rights-of-way for the construction of
pipelines, a practice formalized since 1960 (though the

issuance of special construction permits and special permits have been granted by many federal agencies for various purposes over the 100-year period).

The ruling was made in favor of a group of environmental zealots: the Wilderness Society, Environmental Defense Fund, Inc., Friends of the Earth, Canadian Wildlife Federation, and the Cordova District Fisheries Union. The objections of these groups had been answered in great depth during the previous five years, but to no avail. This formidable group of doom-mongers is also supported by the National Wildlife Federation, Sierra Club, Trout Unlimited, D.C. Wilderness Committee, Zero Population Growth, National Audubon Society, Izaak Walton League of America, and the United Automobile Workers.

Their position rules out any national security aspect. These zealots insist the "West Coast would not need Alaska North Slope oil even in the case of a prolonged cutoff of all foreign oil." Their answer to the possibility that Canada might preempt part of a Trans-Canada line and thus reduce the quantity of Alaskan oil is to refer to Canada's energy minister who two years ago indicated that "Canada expects to guarantee a throughput level for Alaska oil equal to that contemplated."

The strangest aspect of their argument is their objection to the Alaskan route on environmental grounds and earthquake hazards, while at the same time supporting a Canadian route four times as long over the same geologic area of the North. The extremists discount the all-important refining differences of the West and Midwest and, most of all, disregard the economics, including capital requirements, balance of payments, and the best interests of the Alaskans.[8]

They have only one goal, to stop the pipeline and thereby prevent the oil from reaching the United States, deliberately ignoring our national interests. In the last three years, our reliance on foreign crude oil has increased while our domestic reserves have decreased; at the same time foreign crude prices and transportation costs have greatly increased. We face a choice of becoming more dependent on other nations (which entails more strain on the dollar), or developing domestic reserves. It is estimated that at least ten billion barrels of oil can be produced from the North Slope reserves. This equals the reserves in Louisiana, Oklahoma, Kansas, and half of Texas combined. North Slope oil is a high-grade oil with a lower than average sulfur content.

It will cost $3 billion to build the trans-Alaskan oil pipeline, but even more not to build it. With the pipeline in service, at full capacity of two million barrels a day, United States-owned oil will displace foreign oil and reduce dollar outflow by $3.3 billion yearly. Each day's delay in bringing Alaskan oil to the mainland economy results in a balance-of-payments loss of $9 million, a cost sure to rise. In the mounting United States energy crisis, Alaska's North Slope offers a major new source of basic energy fuels, oil, and natural gas.

Costs of labor and materials to carry out the largest privately funded construction job in history go up daily, prodded by inflation. The involved companies have already spent over $400 million on the line project, and the ultimate cost escalates almost $200 million each year.

It is impossible to place a price tag on the frayed nerves of the millions of Americans sweating out the energy crisis, while huge reserves of natural gas lying under Alaska's North Slope cannot be tapped until the oil starts flowing. The United States, desperate for new sources of natural gas, is talking to Algeria and the Soviet Union, even though gas imports would further aggravate our balance-of-payments problems. Gasoline rationing is already at hand, with some gas stations curtailing hours or even closing down altogether. Only a mild 1972-73 winter in New England and the Mid-Atlantic states forestalled a serious shortage of home heating oil, and the 1973-74 winter produced grave and widespread fuel scarcities, and gasless Sundays.

The nation's need for North Slope oil grows every day, and so does the cost of getting it out of the earth and into the country's economic mainstream. A finished $9 million environmental statement for the trans-Alaskan pipeline gathered dust on the shelf. The nation was held in bondage by environmental extremists, in this instance acting in a most dangerous and irresponsible manner.

The natural gas picture is the most serious. By 1980, the annual shortfall will be almost thirteen trillion cubic feet without North Slope production. Liquefied natural gas being considered for import is extremely costly when compared with domestic wellhead prices. Discovered gas reserves in the Prudhoe Bay field alone can provide more than a trillion cubic feet of gas per year for United States consumers. These reserves will add 15 per cent to total available domestic supply in 1980, but only after the trans-Alaska pipeline begins delivery of the oil to market.

The time requirements have been anything but reasonable. Regardless of all the reasons for past delay, after four years of congressional and public hearings, native claims legislation, project descriptions, a preliminary draft and a $9 million, 175 man-year Final Environmental Impact Statement, technical and environmental stipulations and litigation, the Court of Appeals said "Stop" because for this first time ever, the Interior Secretary did not have the authority to grant a right-of-way for a pipeline which he had found to be in the nation's and the public's interest. The secretary had been able to authorize construction of pipelines on public lands up to this time with no apparent dissatisfaction with respect to any of its provisions.

A chronology of major events relating to the proposed line shows the extent of public involvement as well as the hopeless and endless strangling of this project.

July 1968 Atlantic-Richfield and Exxon discover oil at Prudhoe Bay and propose an Alaskan pipeline.

April 1969 North Slope Task Force established within the Department of the Interior. Pipe ordered at a cost of $100 million.

May 1969 Interior's Task Force is expanded to an all-government group by authorization of President Nixon.

June 1969 Application submitted to Bureau of Land Management. Trans-Alaskan requests permit for 390 miles of construction road.

Aug. 1969 Department of Interior holds public hearings on the project at Fairbanks, Alaska.

Sept. 1969 Representatives of the pipeline make presentations to Senate and House Interior Committees.

April 1970 Two suits filed in Federal District Court, Washington, D.C. (Judge George A. Hart, Jr.) result in preliminary injunctions barring the secretary from issuing permits which would allow pipeline construction to begin.

Aug. 1970 Alyeska formed as a nonprofit contractor to construct and operate the trans-Alaskan pipeline system.

Jan. 1971 Draft Environmental Impact Statement for the pipeline released by Interior, (eight federal agencies subsequently comment on the draft).

Feb. 1971 Interior conducts public hearings on the draft statement in Washington, D.C., and in Anchorage, Alaska.

July 1971 Alyeska submits its Project Description (a three-volume document with 26 volumes of appendices) to Interior.

Sept. 1971 Judge Hart allows Alaska and Alyeska to intervene in two cases pending before him.

May 1972 Secretary Morton announced his decision to grant right-of-way permits for the pipeline.

Aug. 1972 Judge Hart, ruling on behalf of Interior, Alyeska, and Alaska, dissolves preliminary injunction. Plaintiffs appeal the decision.

Feb. 1972 The Court of Appeals rules that the secretary did not have the authority to issue Special Land Use Permits.

April 1973 Supreme Court upholds the Appeals Court by denying a petition for a *Writ of Certiorari*.

July 1973 U.S. Senate passes law to permit construction of the pipeline.

A federal task force on Alaskan Oil Development, established by President Nixon in May 1969, formed a Technical Advisory Board which, in turn, established the Menlo Park, California, Working Group, representing several federal agencies and Alaska.

The Working Group conducted the following essential action:

1. Prepared a six-volume Environmental Impact Statement, at an estimated cost of $9,000,000; considered to be the most comprehensive and detailed study ever conducted under the environmental law. Preparation of the statement required eighteen months and involved consultation with and contributions from more than

twenty federal and state agencies;

2. Closely examined other alternatives, including possible Canadian routes, other transport systems, and other sources for the energy;
3. Prepared a three-volume detailed analysis of the economic and security aspects of the system;
4. Conducted a sweeping geologic and engineering analysis of the proposed pipeline system across Alaska; and
5. Developed the strictest environmental and engineering stipulations ever drafted to safeguard a project of this kind.

The department organized a professional federal team to validate designs submitted by the oil companies and exercise continuing surveillance over construction to assure strict quality control of the pipeline system and minimum environmental disturbance.

Three significant and separate groups of public hearings were held on the proposed line:

The first, on August 29-30, 1969, in Fairbanks;

The second, a series, nine in number, held by the House and Senate Interior and insular Affairs Committees, and by the Fish and Wildlife subcommittee of the House Merchant Marine and Fisheries Committee between August and September, 1969; and

The third series, over a period of seven days in February 1971, on the preliminary environmental statement in Washington, D.C., and Anchorage, Alaska.

The hearings resulted in more than 12,500 pages of testimony.

The U.S. Fish and Wildlife Service prepared a separate report on the impact of the pipeline and marine terminal sites as early as March 1970. Their summary of possible effects were:

1. Problems associated with construction and maintenance. These include erosion and siltation, barriers to fish movements, physical damage to spawning areas and fish, and entrapment of fish.
2. Chronic problems associated with permanent change including disturbance of wildlife, interference with big game migrations, entrapment and interference with local movements of animals, increased harvest, sewage and solid waste disposal, and thermal pollution.
3. Potential for oil pollution is the greatest danger of this project to fish and wildlife resources and their environment.

A pipeline was decided on because it is stable, controlled, and can be carefully monitored.[9] The oil will enter the line at the Prudhoe Bay oil field, then flow on to the Brooks Range. From there the pipeline will cross an arctic desert. The earth is frozen year-round except for a thin surface layer which thaws for about four months each summer. Short, squatty spruce trees begin to appear in the southern Brooks, and these get larger and more luxuriant toward the south. Most areas along the route are drained by rivers and streams which thaw in the spring and freeze again in the fall.

From Prudhoe it follows the Sagavanirktok River and Atigun Valleys and across the Brooks Mountain Range through the 4,800-foot-high Dietrich Pass. On the southern slope of the Brooks Range the line will follow the Dietrich and Koyukuk Valleys and cross the hills and muskegs of the Yukon River. The line will pass through more rolling hills, skirting ten miles east of Fairbanks, then south to the Alaska Mountain Range. The line will reach an elevation of 3,500 feet as it crosses through the Isabel Pass before descending into the Copper River Basin. After it crosses the basin it will enter the Chugach Mountains, reaching an elevation of 2,500 feet as it goes through Thompson Pass. From Thompson Pass it descends through the Keystone Canyon to Valdez terminal—a total distance of 789 miles.

In terms of topography and related physiographic features, the north-south route of the pipeline is analogous to going from eastern Colorado across the Rocky Mountains and the Great Basin, and across the Sierras and the coastal range through California and to the Pacific Ocean. Initially, the 48-inch diameter pipeline will be able to transport up to 600,000 barrels daily, moved by five pumping stations. At full capacity, twelve stations will operate to move two million barrels a day. This means there will be approximately 11,000 barrels (42 gallons per barrel) per mile. The anticipated initial throughput will move at slightly more than 2 m.p.h. At full capacity, the oil will travel at just over 7 m.p.h.

The entire pipeline will be monitored 24 hours per day by a computerized control center at Valdez. The line can be shut down in less than six minutes. Remote-controlled cut-off valves will be installed at each pump station and at other special locations such as major river crossings. Additional valves will be placed at strategic points along the line with an average spacing of about fifteen miles. These valves can be closed to "compartmentalize" the pipeline if required. During regular operation the oil pressure will vary from point to point, ranging from practically 0 to 1,180 pounds per square inch. System controls will be provided to prevent or minimize pressure increases if the line is shut down quickly.

A pipeline over this route is by far the safest and most efficient way to bring this oil to market. Conditions in the Arctic Ocean are less than ideal for tanker operations. Ice and an extremely shallow undersea shelf make close-in loading impossible. A fleet of 60,000 tanker trucks running 24 hours a day would be required to transport as much oil as the pipeline. A railroad system to move as much oil as the four-foot pipeline would require a 100-car train leaving every 23 minutes, 24 hours a day. Railroads and highways also require more total area than a pipeline, since they must go around or through steep hills, while a pipeline can easily surmount a 30 per cent grade. Use of jet tankers and submarine tankers were also considered and rejected.

The much discussed alternate Canadian route down the MacKenzie River across Canada and into the Midwestern U.S. would be more than four times as long as the Alaskan route. A trans-Alaskan line will take three years to build and a gas line which must await completion of the oil line could be in service in six years. A trans-Canadian oil line would take nine or ten years; a gas line three or four. Midwest refineries are geared to process light oil from the Southwest, not the relatively heavy Alaskan oil. The Midwest's fuel needs are linked not only to increased supplies of crude oil via pipeline, but to increased refining capacity. At present the refineries from Chicago to Buffalo and St. Louis can handle 2.2 million barrels of oil daily. About one-third of this comes from Canada, the remainder through seven pipeline systems from Texas, the Rocky Mountains, and by river barge. Conversion of a 100,000 barrel-per-day refinery costs $50 million. Midwest refiners would spend on the order of $1 billion in processing equipment which already exists on the West Coast. When the trans-Alaska line is built, it will serve West Coast needs, and Alaskan gas will serve the Midwest and Northeast.

It is difficult to understand why anyone mindful of

our already heavy dependence on foreign oil suppliers
would want to place the responsibility for delivering
Alaskan oil to the United States in foreign hands, even
if those hands belong to our good neighbor, Canada.
Some Canadians may want the pipeline, but some definitely do not. Canadians would require at least 51 per
cent Canadian ownership of the $7 to $10 billion
facility; deliveries through the pipeline would generate
substantial revenues for the operators, which in turn
would produce tax receipts for the Canadian government. A Canada line would be built by Canadian labor
and materials; it would not only carry Alaskan oil, it
would also transport oil from Canada's MacKenzie Valley. Its cost is almost double that of an Alaskan line.

On the other hand, if a Canadian line were built,
some other projects such as a gas line to the MacKenzie
Delta or the James Bay hydroelectric plant would probably not be undertaken. It is not reasonable to assume
the Canadians would give up one of these in order to
facilitate construction of a pipeline through Canada to
deliver United States-owned oil to the United States.

Several other questions arise: whose oil would have
priority, Alaskan or Canadian? What would happen if
the oil flow from Alaska's North Slope filled the maximum capacity of a Canadian line? Would Alaskan production be curtailed to make room for Canadian oil?

Any cutback in Alaskan oil output would be made at
the expense of the citizens and government of Alaska.
The Prudhoe Bay oil field is on land owned by the state,
which would collect taxes from oil production and can
take one-eighth of the oil free of any development costs.
Two per cent of the state revenue would go to Alaskan
natives under the Native Claims Act as partial compensation for their lands. Alaska is counting on North
Slope oil to help finance new schools, roads, sewer sys-

tems, and other public programs to increase its standard of living.

Environmental issues sealed the fate of the trans-Canada line. Being four times longer, it would cross more of the fragile Arctic terrain and span more rivers. The environmentalists point to dangers associated with United States tankers plying waters off the coast of British Columbia en route to and from West Coast refineries. Ironically, they say nothing of tanker traffic (some ten ships weekly) moving regularly along the East Coast of the U.S. carrying South American and Middle East oil for Canadian refineries.

The idea of larger tankers or "supertankers" brings to most people's minds the thought of larger and more disastrous oil spills due to collisions, but studies of groundings show no correlation between the size of the ship and the amount of oil spilled. In summary, the use of supertankers would reduce the probable volume of oil spilled each year by as much as 50 per cent compared to moving the oil in smaller tankers.

At the Valdez terminal all crude oil will flow through steel loading arms into tankers. There will be no rubber hose connection in the entire system. Tankers creating a water pollution problem in Valdez harbor have been a major issue. Ballast water will be pumped into treatment facilities where oil will be separated from the water and removed. Alyeska will load only those tankers whose masters certify that no ballast was discharged at sea prior to docking. Ultimately even these procedures may become unnecessary as the trend continues toward ships with separate cargo and ballast tanks and piping systems. Another major issue has been potential oil pollution along the West Coast. Thousands of tankers travel up and down the West Coast every year without incident. These tankers will be American flag vessels so it will be possible to enforce these safety controls. North Slope oil will add about eighteen large tankers a week to West Coast traffic.

When the project was first conceived, a series of ecological studies in the Arctic and sub-Arctic was undertaken to show what effects the pipeline might have on the environment.

The amount of technical preplanning and the extent of environmental studies produced in preparation for this project are unprecedented and were largely aimed, directly or indirectly, at preventing oil spill pollution. The pipeline engineers faced environmental problems of two kinds:

1. Those which could affect the integrity of the pipeline and could cause oil spills. (These were permafrost, erosion, possible seismic action, and river scour.)

2. Those which concern the disturbance of fish, wildlife, and vegetation by the construction or mere presence of the line.

The extreme ambient temperatures encountered from one end of the line to the other, -60 to 90 degrees F., were accepted as a design, construction, and operation difficulty only, and river scour and erosion were considered as normal design problems for a pipeline. The project was then left with two unusual problems to consider, permafrost and earthquakes.

Since the oil in the pipeline is hot, permafrost is probably the most critical factor unique to this pipeline project. Insofar as pipeline design is concerned, this situation converts itself into a problem of soil mechanics. The line must be designed in such a fashion that it will not cause thawing of the permafrost to the extent that settlement will overstress the pipeline. Permafrost is permanently frozen material, from solid rock to muddy ice.

Most of Alaska is underlaid with permafrost, which may extend from a few feet to hundreds of feet below the surface. In the coldest regions the permafrost is close to the surface, separated by a thick seasonal freeze-thaw layer and surface vegetation commonly called tundra. It serves as insulation to limit permafrost thaw in the summer.

The oil could enter the line at a temperature as high as 140 degrees F., depending on production rates and how the oil is handled before delivery to the line. Because of the heat generated in pumping and friction between the oil and inside surface of the pipe, the oil will remain warm while it moves through the line. More than half the pipeline will be buried in a trench about six feet wide and seven feet deep. Testing of thousands of core samples has resulted in the selection of a route through dry stable permafrost (well-drained soils or rock). Since the warm pipe will not thaw the permafrost in these buried areas, it will not create an unstable situation. In scattered areas of wet permafrost the pipe will be elevated above ground or specially handled. A raised gravel pad will provide a working area. This gravel insulating technique is used in construction which completely overlays permafrost on the North Slope and in Fairbanks.

In the southern parts of the route the permafrost is sporadic or nonexistent, and the pipe will be laid like any pipe through a remote area.

Earthquake-effects designers have evaluated the seismic activity along the line. The system is designed to withstand the most severe earthquake ever recorded in Alaska history. Beyond this, safeguards such as remote controlled cut-off valves and emergency clean-up crews will be on a standby basis. Dikes will be built around all tank facilities, and the Valdez terminal itself is to be built on an area of solid bedrock high above potential tidal waves.

The system has been designed to withstand direct earthquake effects, including shaking of the pipeline by seismic waves and movement of the earth where the line crosses a known active fault; the effects of slumping earth supporting the line; liquefaction of the supporting soil; and landslides.

Soil borings along the route were used to study thaw consolidation, thaw settlement, slope stability of recently thawed permafrost, thaw plug stability, pile, and anchor tests.

Two classes of earthquakes were utilized for seismic design of the line:

1. Contingency-plan earthquakes.
2. Operating earthquakes.

Contingency-plan earthquakes have a Richter magnitude equal to or greater than any known historic earthquake which has occurred within a distance of 100 miles of the pipeline. These earthquakes are associated with long-term average frequency of one every 200 years or more. The pipeline is designed so that in the event of a contingency-plan earthquake the line might experience substantial deformation but will not reach the point of failure with resulting large oil loss.

Operating earthquakes are defined as earthquakes which induce acceleration at the pipeline of half of those resulting from the contingency-plan earthquake. The line is designed to remain operational during such earthquakes. In general, three construction modes have been used, conventional burial, elevated, or special burial.

Bedding and padding is used for protection of the pipe and for coating. Protection from corrosion is provided by epoxy coating and cathodic protection.

Where the pipeline is placed above ground, it will be supported on piles or pile bents. Lateral movement will be accommodated on the supports between anchors to relieve thermal stresses. The elevated mode will sustain the earthquake and thermal forces. Thermal insulation will be provided to maintain the pipe temperature above −20 degrees F. and to slow the oil cooling rate during a shutdown in order to speed up restarting of the line. In certain relatively short sections of the pipeline route through ice-rich permafrost, the pipeline will be buried in the conventional manner except that mechanical refrigeration will be installed along with the carrier pipe to insure that thaw bulbs do not develop.

The seismic design for pump stations, terminal facilities, and tankage has considered both "operating" and "contingency" earthquakes as described above. Oil spills are not expected to occur even in the event of a contingency-plan earthquake.

At Valdez the design has considered that a tsunami (seismically generated wave) may result from earthquake motion. All facilities are out of reach of these waves except the fixed and floating berths which are designed to resist forces resulting from a twelve-foot wave when a ship is in berth and a twenty-foot wave without a vessel alongside. The design criteria are consistent with experience in the great Alaskan earthquake of 1964.

The permanent pipeline right-of-way will occupy approximately 5,230 acres or 8.2 square miles from Prudhoe Bay to Valdez. The total area of Alaska is 586,412 square miles. Other new techniques, developments, and findings have been used:

1. Various fast-growing perennials and annual grasses, to reseed the areas after construction, are in-

tended to hold the soil and provide biotic insulation until the natural vegetation grows back in 5 to 7 years.

2. Gravel pad surfaces will overcome the effects of loss of insulating vegetation during construction.

3. When the line crosses a river it will be by a specially designed bridge or be coated with four inches of concrete and buried several feet below the deepest probable scouring of any unusual flood.

4. Construction will be timed to avoid fish spawning periods.

5. Sediment basins and diversionary channels to minimize siltation will be used.

The caribou have caused some public concern. Some 450,000 of them summer and calve on the North Slope. These animals, which migrate through the Brooks Range on routes that parallel the pipeline, may cover as much as 25 to 40 miles a day. In most cases, above-ground sections of the line will be short enough so that caribou movement will not be impaired. Where sections may be too long, special ramps are provided. Experience has demonstrated that caribou have no difficulty crossing raised gravel roads, well-drilling pads, or airstrips. Intensive studies conclude that rare species such as Dall Sheep and Peregrine Falcons will not be affected by the line. Although Dall Sheep lamb and graze in the Atigun Canyon area, construction will be timed to minimize disturbance to the sheep and falcons that nest in adjacent regions. Contracts stipulate that trash, garbage, and debris must be removed before payment for services will be made. No one connected with the oil industry or the line construction is licensed to hunt during active assignment to the project.

In summary, the environmental effects were well defined from the start by the U.S. Fish and Wildlife Service.[10] These effects were discovered to have beneficial aspects in many cases by the U.S. Department of Interior. But this was not really what the opposing groups had in mind. For instance, during a presentation in Washington, D.C., a spokesman for the environmental zealots told an audience that the Alaskan native should not be allowed to buy snowmobiles with the royalties from the oil sales, for he could then widen his travels. This would make it easier for him to hunt and kill caribou, which are the focus of environmental concern but the principal source of food for Eskimos. A former native Alaskan in the audience pointed out that the use of dogs by Eskimos requires killing twice the number of caribou, for the dogs must also be fed. The uninformed zealot was defeating his own purpose of caribou conservation while at the same time denying the Alaskan native a chance to conserve and improve his food supply. This says nothing of the many other benefits which the Alaskan natives will derive from this project, permitting them to join modern society with equality—benefits such as education, training, and job opportunities provided by the line, coupled with benefits from anticipated land claim settlements, oil royalties, and severance taxes. This will improve the present condition of many Alaskans who have never seen a doctor, a paved street, a flush toilet, a two-story building, or a toaster. Their feelings are borne out by the signs they displayed when the Senate took its first action in July 1973, which read "Sierra Club Go Home."

Finally in November 1973, Congress passed the special act authorizing the construction of the pipeline. President Nixon signed the bill into law on November 16, 1973. The permit was issued to Alyeska on January 23, 1974. In spite of this special act of Congress authorizing its construction, it is difficult to estimate the completion date for this project. Many speculate that it has been delayed by as much as five years. The $9 million environmental impact statement prepared by the special task force, with additional input from more than twenty state and federal agencies, was not effective in permitting the construction of the line. It emphasizes the sad fact that environmental impact statements have no effect on the completion of controversial projects. Their preparation has become nothing more than an exercise in futility. They have become another means to the end, a halt to energy production. In the meantime, the vital substance of the United States is being depleted by environmental extremists, in the name of the "spider-insect prey relation" or whatever "issue" can be contrived to thwart the needs of the nation.

An abstract of the executive summary of *The First Annual Report Under the Mining and Mineral Policy Act of 1970*, published in April 1972, provides data for a perspective in planning future resource usage.[1] Resource development is, in the first instance, tied to the standard of living. The United States requirement for new mineral supplies to maintain our standard of living represents the following percentages of world production at this time: petroleum, 32 per cent; natural gas, 57 per cent; coal, 16 per cent; steel, 19 per cent; aluminum, 35 per cent; copper, 27 per cent; and proportionate quantities of some eighty other minerals. Pressures to raise the standard of living are increasing in many developing nations, while the industrialization process is accelerating, and therefore, the search for mineral deposits is intensifying. On the other hand, the highly advertised need for cleaner air, cleaner water, land reclamation, and improved health and safety has constrained mining, mineral processing, and energy generation and transmission. But just how much? Is the announced shortage of energy resource material and other serious deficiencies associated with it, just another campaign of scare and emotion? Hardly. It is in fact a troublesome situation which can readily be documented by facts and figures. The most reliable of all indices available are capital investment and production. Do these show an increase, status quo, or a decline?

We find that investment in domestic mineral development has dropped sharply because investment in foreign mineral development is potentially more rewarding, despite the fact that foreign subsidiaries of United States mineral firms have been nationalized. United States primary demand for minerals in the year 2000 is projected to rise to $117 billion (at 1970 prices). At the same time, a twenty-year trend indicates United States primary production of minerals in 2000 will be $53 billion, a deficit of $64 billion. It is mandatory that a necessary social and economic environment be created to assure development of mineral resources, within valid environmental constraints, to meet minimal future mineral and energy requirements.

To assess accurately the current United States mineral position, both the recent past history and anticipated future developments must be considered. The USDI report considers a fifty-year period, the two decades 1950-1970, 1971, and the projected period to 2000. Any such consideration must take into account that the geographic distribution of minerals varies widely, and the demand and use patterns for some are unique, reflecting special properties. There is also a degree of interchangeability and suitability, largely dependent upon relative price and availability. Accordingly, to assess the overall mineral position, attention must be directed to the following:

1. the entire mineral industry as an aggregate
2. the major components, energy, ferrous metals, nonferrous metals, and nonmetallics
3. the peculiar characteristics of individual mineral or chemical elements.

The current mineral position is reflected in the following data. In 1950, the domestic primary demand was two billion tons valued at $14 billion. Values of domestic primary production were $12 billion. Imports of crude minerals and processed materials of mineral origin were under $2 billion, and recycled mineral scrap was also under $2 billion. By 1971, domestic primary demand had risen to four billion tons valued at $42 billion. Value of domestic primary production was $30 billion. Imports of crude minerals and processed materials of mineral origin had risen to $10 billion, while recycled mineral scrap was just over $2 billion.

While the $30 billion value of domestic mineral production in 1971 was the highest on record, it was some 3 per cent less than in 1970, in terms of the 1970 dollar. Of even greater concern was the widening gap between domestic demand and domestic production, a gap which has been gradually developing over the 1950-1970 period. Looking to year 2000, a reasonable growth rate from now to then is of the order of 4 per cent. Based on present knowledge of future mineral and energy demands, and based on 1970 prices for minerals, in the year 2000 domestic primary demand will be eleven billion tons, valued at $117 billion. Based on the same forecast data, the value of domestic primary production will be $53 billion. As to imports of crude minerals and processed materials of mineral origin, there is no way to make a reliable forecast, except to show that domestic production versus domestic demand leaves a deficiency of $64 billion.

This can be broken down into major mineral groups, and when this is done, energy becomes the first consideration. Over the two decades 1950-1970, United States demand for energy doubled. Energy, as the largest component of total United States mineral demand, accounted for 63 per cent of total mineral demand in 1950; 55

per cent in 1971; and a projected 46 per cent in 2000.
The sources of United States energy supply have
changed over the years; they will undoubtedly change
further as shown in the table below prepared by the
U.S. Department of Interior.

Per cent contribution to United States energy			
	1950	1971	2000
Coal	38	18	14
Petroleum	39	44	35
Natural gas	18	33	26
Hydropower	5	4	3
Nuclear power	0	1	22

In this regard, domestic coal and petroleum production fell in 1971 from 1970 levels. This drop reflects a
persistent decline in the rate of development of new domestic reserves, and this scarcity of domestic energy
minerals is due primarily to environmental and associated factors, rather than to the availability of such minerals. This applies to all mineral groups, as can be seen
from data on each:

Metals

During the period 1950-1970, domestic demand for
metals tripled. Metals accounted for 28 per cent of total
mineral demand in 1950, 36 per cent in 1971, and are
projected at 43 per cent in 2000. In terms of economic
significance and tonnage, steel is the most important
metal in use and has been for the past two decades. Domestic production of raw steel in 1950 was 97 million
tons, 47 per cent of the total world production. By 1971,
United States production of raw steel was 120 million

tons, representing only 19 per cent of world production because of vast production increases in other areas. Significantly, 1971 imports of steel exceeded 18 million tons. The steel industry is highly dependent upon imports of several major ferro-alloying metals, notably chromium, manganese, and nickel. (The United States is a significant source of several lesser ferro-alloying metals, notably molybdenum, vanadium, and tungsten.)

Demand for iron and ferro-alloying metals is expected to grow at a 2 per cent rate to year 2000. On a tonnage basis aluminum is now the second major United States metal. Domestic production of aluminum rose from 719 thousand tons in 1950, to four million tons in 1971. Bauxite is the ore of aluminum; United States reserves are 13 million long tons which were imported, as well as 2.5 million tons of alumina, the intermediate between bauxite and aluminum. Only relatively small quantities of aluminum scrap are recycled, 180 thousand tons in 1971. Primary demand for aluminum will rise at a 6 per cent rate, to exceed 26 million tons by 2000. Copper is now the third major United States metal on a tonnage basis. Copper recovered from United States ores rose from 921 thousand tons in 1950 to 1.4 million tons in 1971. United States reserves are 81 million tons of contained copper, and mine production had increased to virtual self-sufficiency in 1971. Domestic production of zinc declined, while that of lead increased. A number of other important metals are by-products of copper, lead, and zinc mining: antimony, arsenic, bismuth, cadmium, gallium, germanium, gold, indium, selenium, silver, tellurium, and thallium. The value of metals in ores produced domestically in 1971 was over $3 billion. The value of all metals and metal products shipped from metallurgical plants was $25 billion.

Nonmetallics

This group accounted for 8 per cent of total mineral demand in 1950. It is projected to reach 11 per cent by 2000. Nonmetallics include large-tonnage, low-value items such as sand, gravel, stone, clay, and intermediate processed materials such as electronic crystals and synthetic high-hardness abrasives. They are generally produced in response to short-term demand. Domestic reserves for most major nonmetallics are large and domestic production in 1971 totaled nearly $6 billion.

The situation presents problems which must be solved, and the place to start is to allow private enterprise to do what it has been trying to do for at least a decade. Industry and government must work together to assure a continued and expanding flow of mineral raw materials at reasonable cost from dependable sources. Obviously, the one and one-half million square miles of the dry land area of the United States and the adjacent continental shelf are among the most reliable sources of supply. The mineral resources of the United States are vast, but the distinction between "resources" and "reserves" is critical to solving mineral supply problems. A resource is a material known to exist in the earth's crust or judged by skilled geologic inference and extrapolation as likely to exist. A reserve, however, is generally a smaller quantity which can be produced by known technology and at current prices. The conversion of resources into reserves requires improvements in the technology, or higher prices, or both. Because of inflationary pressures, technology must be improved so domestic mining, minerals, metal, and mineral reclamation industries can operate with greater productivity and efficiency. Private development of domestic mineral resources must be encouraged. Patent and antitrust policies, exchange regulation, land use, tax, and trade policies must be reviewed. Obstacles to increased private development must be removed rather than erected in greater profusion. The United States is committed to major goals, including abatement of unemployment, improved urban living, better education, and better recreational facilities. These goals can be accomplished only through continued economic growth, which in turn can provide needed supplies of minerals and energy at low cost.

The Stakes Involved

In its 1972 report, the USDI isolates what it feels are the fundamental problems involving the United States mining, minerals, metal, and mineral reclamation industries in the implementation of the National Mining and Minerals Policy Act. The primary problem it presents is that *development of the mineral resources of United States is not keeping pace with demand.* The department breaks down the problem into thirteen parts with a special explanation of the environmental effects:

1. Domestic demand for petroleum and natural gas already substantially exceeds readily available domestic productive capacity.
2. Our increasing reliance upon foreign sources of minerals gives rise to three somewhat interrelated problems as follow:
   a. Expropriations, confiscations, and forced modifications of agreements in foreign countries already have severed the flow to the United States of some foreign materials produced by United States firms operating abroad and have made other materials more costly.

b. United States industry is encountering far greater competition for foreign mineral supplies.

c. Increasing dependence on foreign sources for important mineral supplies places increasing constraints upon the conduct of United States foreign policy and at the same time threatens the stability of the United States economy.

3. Investment in development of domestic mineral properties is falling far behind.

4. Environmental regulation threatens major disruptions of some domestic mineral production. "The impact of environmental controls and growing requirements for major capital investments for expensive control equipment (some of which is not yet technologically ready) has been severe. Under present-day pricing conditions, the costs to install this new equipment cannot be recouped, and this has radically changed the economic status of several existing operations. A pattern has also been set in economic evaluations of future operations which raises uncertainties with respect to any new or expanded refining or smelting facilities. For example, while new zinc smelting capacities amounting to a net gain of 1.3 million tons will be added to world totals between 1972 and 1975, none is planned for the United States.

"The need for lessening the impact on the environment by the mining and minerals processing industries is recognized by industry and government alike, and there is no doubt that significantly more improvement will be achieved. However, the present difficulties in recovering the costs involved must be resolved, and with a balanced approach to the cost-price squeeze, reasonable environmental controls and a viable minerals industry will likely result."

5. Actual and prospective withdrawals of land available for prospecting and exploration may adversely affect domestic mineral development.

6. For many nonenergy minerals, domestic demand in the past few years has been cyclically lower. Concurrently, domestic producers have experienced increased import competition.

7. The trend toward increased importation of processed materials of mineral origin increases balance-of-payments problems and further reduces employment and investment opportunities in the domestic mining and mineral processing industries.

8. Instability of government stockpile objectives and potential disposals of government inventories overhang domestic metals and mineral markets and producers in periods of lower demand.

9. Mining suffers from a shortage of skilled manpower.

10. Failure of United States transportation facilities to keep pace with modern developments is making the movement of mineral commodities in domestic and foreign commerce more difficult and more costly.

11. Fundamental research affecting mineral production and use is being cut back when, instead, it should be expanding.

12. United States government organization and its information base for the implementation of the National Minerals Policy is inadequate.

13. The United States mineral industry is restricted by government regulations from organizing for effective operation in the modern world.

The only effective solution is to let private enterprise take charge again and bring back to this nation the degree of productivity, peace, and world leadership that it enjoyed before our slide toward statism. With proper relief from the burdens and restraints it now carries, private enterprise could solve the formidable array of problems. In a few years, the United States could be restored to health. But the medicine is bitter to the statists, who will cling to power even if our survival as a nation is threatened. Their resistance must be overcome by the whole truth about our economic and even moral condition. Only then can the terrible burdens of overtaxation and overregulation be scrapped, to let the creative energies of free Americans lead us to a national renaissance.

The latest examples in Uruguay, Chile, and Argentina leave the statist totalitarians no positive argument to support the ideal they relentlessly preach. The advocates of communism can only view the dismal failure of the Soviets and the straining dynamism of the Eastern Bloc nations to escape it as hard evidence of the bankruptcy of this "idealistic" nonsense. That Marx and Lenin were incompetent dawdlers in ideology is well established; that they were totally incompetent and irrelevant in economics is illustrated in every nation of the world where their scheme is or has been an experiment. In the field of resource management, socialism is especially disastrous. Socialist economics are notorious for waste, inefficiency, pollution, and wholesale ecological damage.

Unfortunately, history suggests that politicians are reluctant to change the course of events, even if they know that their continued actions will lead to the downfall of their nation. Few have tried and even fewer have been successful in their attempts to bring about necessary changes.

There are some decision-makers and legislators with vision, who know what is happening to the nation dynamically and understand what lies at the end of the trail. They constitute a minority at this time, but their ranks are being bolstered by newly enlightened citizens every day. The following excerpt from the *Congressional Record*[4] by Rep. Philip Crane of Illinois, is the view of one who knows:

One need not look far for examples of the "chicken little" syndrome. We are told the sky is falling in on us at every turn. The Friends of the Earth hint darkly that all mankind will perish before the end of the century through pollution of our environment. Zero Population Growth, on the contrary, alerts us to the prospect of billions upon billions of people standing upon one another's shoulders by the end of the century. Others warn of a crisis in health care or suggest that millions of Americans are starving to death and lacking adequate housing. . . . The same people who dun us daily with horror stories of this nature are usually in the vanguard of the "truth in advertising" campaign.

With the capable tutoring of the anticapitalist mentalities, free institutions and free enterprise become convenient scapegoats. . . . Our crisismongers accuse the businessman of a calloused unconcern for the air we breathe, the water we drink and recreate in, our wildlife, our purple mountains and our fruited plains.

There is a romantic longing for the blissful era of medieval feudalism. Such reactionaries would not only repeal the twentieth century—in the name of progress—but would repeal half a millennium. There is a horrifying logical consistency between the goals of people of this persuasion and those of Zero Population Growth, as there are roughly three billion more people on this earth today than could be sustained on a feudal economy.

Having defined the crisis and established the cause, the solution that immediately springs into the simplistic minds of the kneejerk statists and collectivists is to launch a preemptive strike by the federal government with massive infusions of taxpayer dollars.

If the fruits of this cacophonous coalition were not so porten-
tous, we might dismiss them with a knowing grin or a bored
yawn. But we live at a time when today's lunacy is tomorrow's law. . . . After the dismal experience of the past 40 years
of federal involvement in such areas as agriculture, welfare,
housing, Indian affairs, or the postal system, one might sup-
pose that we would have learned some painful lessons of history. On the basis of that history we might safely formulate a
law: Problems increase in direct proportion to the degree of
attention given them and the amount of money spent on
them by the federal government.

The Founding Fathers viewed the role of government in negative terms. Its primary function was to prevent trespass and
otherwise stay out of our way. "A wise and frugal government"—Jefferson said—"which shall leave them otherwise
free to regulate their own pursuits of industry and improvement, and shall not take from the mouth of labor the bread it
has earned. This is the sum of good government."

By the 1960s, an Indiana senator could publicly announce
that—"The people should depend upon the government like
children depend upon their mothers."

Those who advance such a view argue that under socialism
there would be no pollution of the air, for the state would be
in control and if the "people" are in control there would be
no greed, and thus the proper precautions would be taken to
insure pure air, clean rivers, and the like. This argument
makes internal sense, as all ideological arguments do, but it
has one major flaw. It is simply not true. A look at the world's
environment shows the fallacy of such thinking. Victor Zor-
za, the Eastern European correspondent for the British newspaper, *The Guardian*, makes this point: "In the West, the
strength of the profit motive is often said to drive capitalists to
press on with production regardless of damage to the environment. In Russia, it is the weakness of the profit motive that
gets the blame."

We should be proud of our system and defend it vigorously.
Far too long American businessmen have tended to apologize
for their successes, to sit silently by as capitalism was attacked
by those who argued that, somehow, government control of
the economy would produce a more "equitable" sharing of

the nation's resources....They failed to point out that capitalism was simply freedom applied to economics, that under a system of free enterprise it was the consumer, the individual, who voted with his dollars in the marketplace and determined in this manner exactly what would be produced in the economy. In the socialistic, communistic and fascistic economies supported by the advocates of collectivism it is a small band of bureaucrats who make this decision.

Some Signs of Change

There is hope that reason and common sense will prevail over the insanity of the environmental extremists. The following *Excerpts of House Report No. 93-275*,[3] of June 12, 1973, from the House Committee on Appropriations shows that the majority of the committee is beginning to realize that it has been sold a bill of goods in previous years, which it is not willing to continue buying:

The Need for Scientific Studies [page 11] The committee is concerned that many decisions, such as the banning of DDT and DES, may have been made without adequate scientific facts.

The following table provided the committee indicates that the substitutes for DDT are more toxic than DDT. The figures in the table show how much of a chemical must be used in order to cause acute oral toxicity in rats; in other words, the smaller the figures in the table, the more toxic the chemical. Therefore, the table shows that DDT is the least toxic of all the chemicals listed.

Comparative Acute Oral Toxicity for Rats or Various Chemicals

$(LD_{50}$ (mg/kg))

Chemical	Males	Females
DDT	217.0	----
Methyl parathion	14.0	24.0

Guthion	13.0	11.0
Azodrin	17.0	20.0
Lannate (methomyl)	(24.0)	----
Ethion	65.0	27.0
EPN	36.0	
Trithion (methyl)	98.0	120.0
Di-syston (disulfeton)	6.7	2.3
Demeton	6.2	2.5
Bidrin	21.0	16.0
Endrin	18.0	7.5
Monitor	15.6	13.0
Thimet (phorate)	2.3	1.1
Phosphamidon	24.0	24.0
Thiodan (endosulfan)	43.0	18.0
Parathion	13.0	3.6
Temik (aldicarb)	.8	.6

Source: Extension Service, U.S. Department of Agriculture.

Similarly, the committee asked the Food and Drug Administration how much of a banned substance a human would have to consume to equal the amounts given experimental animals. The acting commissioner of the Food and Drug Administration replied as follows in a letter of May 17, 1973: ...the following are ingredients that have been banned as a result of the lack of proof of safety, and because they induced cancer in laboratory testing of animals. The equivalencies of required intake by man of affected products are, of course, just simple mathematical projections. They are intended only to provide a general perspective of required consumption based on the levels of carcinogens used in laboratory experiments.

Cyclamate—A 12-ounce bottle of soft drink may have contained from 1/4 to 1 gram of sodium cyclamate. An adult would have had to drink from 138 to 552 12-ounce bottles of soft drink a day to get an amount comparable to that causing effects in mice and rats.

Oil of Calamus—In order to get an amount comparable to that which caused effects in rats, a person would have to drink 250 quarts of vermouth per day.

Safrole—A person would have to drink 613 12-ounce bottles of root beer-flavored soft drink or eat 220 pounds of hard candy per day to get an amount comparable to that which caused effects in rats.

1,2-Dehydro-2,2,4-trimethylquinoline: polymerized—A plasticizer used in packaging material. If all foods in the diet were to be packed in this material, a person would have to eat 300,000 times the average daily diet to get an amount comparable to that which caused effects in rats.

4,4'Methylenebis (2-chloroanaline)—A plastic curing agent used in food contact surfaces. If all foods in the diet were exposed to this material, a person would have to eat 100,000 times the average daily diet to get an amount comparable to that which caused effects in rats.

DES—Based on findings of 5 per cent of liver samples containing 2ppb [parts per billion] of DES, and assuming that 2 per cent of the average diet is beef liver, a person would have to consume five million pounds of liver per year for 50 years to equal the intake from one treatment of day-after oral contraceptives. . . .

Examples such as these, which translate abstract scientific studies into their real-life equivalents, help illustrate why common sense is needed. The regulatory agencies under this bill should try to include such examples in future decisions so that the public will not become unduly alarmed.

TITLE III ENVIRONMENTAL PROGRAMS *Research Studies* [page 49]

The committee recommends $715,000 for research studies, the full amount of the budget request. This year, as was the case last year, the Council on Environmental Quality was unable other than in very general terms to tell the committee how they planned to use the request research funds. Therefore, as part of their fiscal year 1974 research studies program, the committee directs the Council on Environmental Quality to perform the following studies:

The impact of exports of basic raw materials (such as timber, coal, ores, or metals and scrap iron) on domestic prices and the competitive position of American industry.

The economic impact on American consumers of actions taken by the government to restrict or ban certain chemicals.

The cost-benefit implications of automobile emission control standards.

The impact of environmental standards and regulations on domestic energy consumption, including increased dependence on foreign sources.

The extent to which American industry is moving to foreign countries because of environmental considerations, and the extent to which American agriculture and food processing are moving to Mexico and other foreign countries.

Major Legislation Affecting EPA. EPA is currently charged with administration of all or parts of the following major legislation:

The Clean Air Act

The Federal Water Pollution Control Act

The Solid Waste Disposal Act

The Federal Environmental Pesticide Control Act of 1972

The Noise Control Act of 1972

The Marine Protection, Research, and Sanctuaries Act of 1972.

Basis for Committee's Recommendations [page 52] When environmental concerns reached national prominence a few years ago, it was common practice to speak of "spaceship earth" and to think of the environment as a "closed cycle." People began to realize, many for the first time, that a relationship exists between the air, the water, and the land. People also began to realize that whatever pollutants we remove from one must go into one or both of the others. How, then, should we approach the problem?

Logically, we should attempt to reduce pollution to its most unobjectionable form. Furthermore, we should set our priorities for doing this. We should attempt to first take care of that which represents a hazard to human health and then set about to take care of that which is merely undesirable. Again, being logical and using our common sense, we would look at the undesirable in terms of how we could spend our money to get the greatest amount of environmental improvement per dollar invested.

Congress recognized the need to do something about our environment and passed the National Environmental Policy Act. The stated purposes of the act are: "To declare a national policy which will encourage productive and enjoyable harmony between man and his environment; to promote efforts which will prevent or eliminate damage to the environment and biosphere and stimulate the health and welfare of man; to enrich the understanding of the ecological systems and natural resources important to the nation."

Then followed a period when the Congress passed many additional laws. These laws reflected the feelings of the nation and the Congress and express their earnest desire to improve and restore the environment. However, these new laws for the most part did not address the total environment, instead they addressed an individual environmental problem. We have passed air laws, we have passed water laws, we have passed solid waste laws, we have passed noise laws, we have probably passed too many laws. By passing these laws we have tended to some degree to look at the environment with tunnel vision. Because we have approached the problem of improving and restoring the environment on a piecemeal basis, we in many cases have forced or encouraged the Environmental Protection Agency to look at the action and ignore the reaction, thereby totally disregarding the premise on which the environmental movement was based—that we must deal with the total environment. An example of this dilemma can be found in the opinion written by Judge Winner, U.S. District Court, Denver, Colorado, in the case of *Anaconda* vs. *Ruckelshaus.*

"Compliance with the administrator's proposed emission limitation would create additional pollution problems and air pollution problems having to do with the quarrying, transportation, and the hauling of limestone and other similar materials. These problems are directly related to the resultant production of a staggering quantity of unsalable sulfuric acid which would threaten water pollution. None of these problems has been studied or considered by the administrator or by any member of his staff."

Increasingly, we are seeing more and more examples of our failure to consider our "total environment." Likewise, many actions have been taken where there is reason to believe that the costs may outweigh the benefits.

$287 Billion to Clean Up the Environment [page 53] Testimony before the committee this year indicated that in order to meet the pollution problems and the solid waste disposal over the next decade the country will have to spend about $287 billion. By setting standards that are perhaps too high, we have forced massive expenditures that may result in only modest improvements. Not only is there a problem of cost, but the Congress has passed laws based on technology that does not exist, acting much like the person who contacted the Patent Office and asked for a list of things that had not been invented.

The hearing record this year shows strong evidence that actions by the Environmental Protection Agency in carrying out these laws have contributed to the energy crisis, have increased the damage from floods because of the delay of flood and soil conservation projects, have increased the cost of production of food, thereby contributing to higher consumer prices, and have greatly increased the danger to human health by banning DDT, which according to testimony has never injured a human being. In addition, actions by the agency have placed American industry and American agriculture at a competitive disadvantage both at home and abroad.

Energy Crisis. The committee is convinced that the Environmental Protection Agency has played a major role in the current energy crisis. The approval by the agency of overly restrictive state plans, which call for the meeting of primary and secondary ambient air standards at the same time, has resulted in the need for industry to convert from coal to low-sulfur fuels. This increased requirement for oil and gas has been a major contributor to our current fuel problems.

In addition, the automobile emission control standards imposed by the agency have greatly increased the requirements for gasoline, which is also in short supply and will probably require rationing.

The energy crisis has major implications with regard to our country's national security, foreign policy, and balance of trade. These implications were not considered by the agency in setting the standards and approving the plans that led to the problem. The potential impact on the economic and social well-being of this nation of actions by the agency is so great that it is absolutely essential that the agency be required to consider the impact of their actions.

Automobile Performance. Emission control standards issued by the agency, at the direction of the Congress, have created serious problems for the American consumer. By setting deadlines that called for the development of new technology, the automobile companies, according to testimony before the committee, were forced to proceed with the development of the costly catalytic exhaust converters. Had sufficient time been allotted to meet the standards, then the automobile companies could have devoted their research funds to alternative types of clean-burning engines. Instead, deadlines were set that did not provide sufficient time for development of alternative types of engines and the American consumer has ended up with an automobile that costs significantly more to buy, significantly more to maintain, will provide poor fuel economy, with a reduction in performance. The committee recommends an increase of $2,000,000 for research on alternative types of clean burning engines so that the agency can accelerate this important program.

Overly Restrictive Standards [page 55] The committee is extremely concerned that the agency, in some of its regulatory or standard-setting activities, may be placing too little emphasis on the environmental and economic impact of such actions. Increasingly, questions are being raised that certain actions by the agency have been addressed to the elimination of one specific source of pollution without giving sufficient consideration of the overall impact on the environment. Many times these actions have actually proven detrimental. Reportedly, some abatement actions have resulted in a reduction of air pollution while at the same time significantly increasing water pollution or solid waste. Some standards or regulations have resulted in modest reductions in pollution while at the same time causing enormous increases in energy requirements, thereby increasing pollution and raw material usage.

The agency also has to approve many of the state standards or regulations to see that they equal or exceed federal standards or regulations. The committee is concerned that the agency does not consider the economic and environmental impact of these state standards. Reportedly, the agency will disapprove state standards if they are too loose but will approve state plans that are too restrictive. For example, testimony before the committee indicates that in the case of the Clean Air Act, most states designed their plans to attain or surpass the secondary ambient air quality standards by 1975, which is more than the Clean Air Act requires. Reports prepared for the committee indicate that these overly restrictive standards have played a major role in the current energy shortage of the nation.

The committee has also been advised that the Tennessee Valley Authority has had to include $43 million in their budget for cooling towers for a nuclear powerplant under construction in Alabama. These cooling towers are required because the State of Alabama has currently set water temperature standards that require discharge temperatures lower than the natural temperature of the river.

Need for a Sense of Balance [page 55] By not using a commonsense approach and by not thinking in terms of the total environment, by looking at the trees rather than the forest, we may well end up creating an environmental backlash which could put an end to all the momentum we've gained in recent years in our efforts to improve and restore our environment. Therefore, since this committee is the only committee that reviews all of EPA's programs, we have made several recommendations this year which should help to restore a sense of balance to our environmental efforts.

Economic and Environmental Impact Statements. The committee feels that if the agency had considered environmental and economic consequences of both their standards and the state standards which they approved, many of the problems we are now faced with might not have occurred. Therefore, the committee has included funds and language in the bill to require the EPA to consider the environmental impact along with the economic and technical considerations of their actions, except where prohibited by law, as authorized by the National Environmental Policy Act.

To illustrate this point, in early 1974, because of the unjudicious and rigid requirements for environmental impact statements, millions of board feet of urgently needed lumber will not be harvested in the U.S. forests. At a time when the nation's economy is staggering along, when homes are needed and industry is seeking more lumber, this foolish requirement prevents our meeting these needs. Much of the timber which would be harvested to fill this need will decay or suffer a marked drop in quality.

The same newly required environmental impact statements by the Bureau of Land Management on cattle grazing lands of the West will prevent the multiple use of grazing areas which cattlemen have used for years and for which they have paid, and from which the consumer has profited in lower prices and higher quality beef. These same ranchers have improved this once "worthless" government land, so that now, under pressure from environmental extremists, the BLM decides it must not be damaged. The officials respond that since the environmental impact statements are so lengthy, detailed, and subject to court challenge by environmentalists, they simply are unable to render them in time to allow the use of these badly needed grazing lands by western ranchers.

Meanwhile, on the Senate side there are indications that even the most unlikely members are beginning to assume positions which will disassociate them from Senator Muskie and his Clean Air and Water Acts and other absurdities.

The advice and warning of some of the most influential engineers is now proving to be a serious thorn in the side of Senator Muskie.[4] The ideology that underpinned the Clean Air Act in 1970 is starting to fall apart as the facts continue to pile up against all the bases he used for its passage. The decision of the United States Supreme Court in early June 1973 let stand a lower court ruling that the EPA must not permit the "significant deterioration" of air quality even in regions where the lowered air quality would still meet federal standards. Senator Muskie was insistent that this section be included in the law. It is turning out to be a major contributor to the energy shortage. A prime reason is the inevitable delay in construction of new power facilities in areas affected by the decision until such time as further court decisions define just what constitutes "significant deterioration." No one is going to commit the hard-to-get capital to build a multi-million dollar power plant and then find out that it can't be operated. The only good part of the Supreme Court's action is that it may force Congress to pass new laws to scrap or render the 1970 Muskie law inactive.

Even the nescient Senator Philip Hart (who led the panic-stricken movement, complete with hearings, on mercury) spoke in the Senate of the many new factors that have arisen since the clean air measure was hurriedly passed in 1970. "Our energy supplies and the systems...to meet the statutory standards will require increased fuel consumption." He also stated there is still no medical evidence of the degree to which public health will be improved by the act. The cost-benefit ratio is difficult, if not impossible, to compute. Another factor is the added cost of $275 to the price of each new automobile which will be required to bring cars into compliance with the 1975 and 1976 Clean Air requirements. "The consumer putting out those dollars," said Hart, "will be justified in asking precisely what benefits will accrue to themselves and their communities. I am not sure our answers will be very satisfactory, especially to that 30 per cent of the nation's population not living in urban areas." He says little about the fact that he was told this at the time the law was being drafted and that he joined the other frightened members of Congress to vote for the Muskie law.

The prestigious National Academy of Sciences, which has questioned the bases of the Muskie law for some time, is now calling for congressional re-examination of the Clean Air Act. The academy was commissioned by Congress to do an impartial study of the legislation. The NAS gave as one of the chief dangers of the act the fact that the deadlines for implementing the law could force the auto industry into the hasty manufacture of one pollution-abatement system when, given more time, a less costly, more fuel-efficient alternative is surely to be developed, provided one is even found necessary. The ultimate cost of more than $20 billion per year for the system, according to NAS, is a problem of grave consequence, even to spending senators like Muskie and Hart. Additional fuel costs are another major factor. The Chase Manhattan Bank conducted a study which shows the present emissions standards, which are less stringent than the 1976 standard of the Muskie act, account for half of the nation's 9 per cent increase in gasoline consumption over the previous year. A 1 per cent saving in fuel consumption would have ended the 1973 fuel shortage.

Dr. D. L. Ginzton, chairman of the NAS committee on motor vehicle emissions, told Muskie's subcommittee, "it is imperative to examine the standards, the rationale...how they were arrived at...." Perhaps the most embarrassing criticism of Muskie's law is the apparent haste and its lack of scientific and technical quality, over and above the complete lack of common sense. Almost everyone now agrees, for instance, that nitrogen oxide, the most difficult exhaust gas to eliminate, may not be as dangerous to health as the environmentalists insisted when Senator Muskie pushed through the Clean Air Law. He certainly had adequate quality advice to the contrary at the time yet chose to ignore it. Also to be re-evaluated are the standards for hydrocarbons and carbon monoxide. These standards have no basis in fact either.

The same reversal of positions is evident in the April 1973 recommendations of the EPA when it asked Congress to reconsider the emissions standards for 1973 of nitrogen oxides for 1976-model vehicles with a view toward relaxing them. Latest findings show that these standards are unrealistically restrictive and do nothing toward protecting the health and welfare of the nation. Not long after this announcement, the EPA released another report that stated it had further reconsidered the nitrogen standards and found the EPA had made errors in the original measurement and calculations and, therefore, they were being revised.

The New York Times reported on June 11, 1973, that rising home costs are putting the dream of a house out of the reach of many young families. One of the major causes according to Michael Sumichrast, of the Nation-

al Association of Home Builders, is the environmentalists pushing for land-use restrictions. "In the last
twenty-five years, land...has changed dramatically....Much of this is because of environmental pressures, increasing not only the cost of land, but the cost
of land development. It is a significant cost, and I don't
know that we yet have any idea what the cost of the environmental movement is going to be to us as a society."

The paper shortage is becoming critical, as are many
other products dependent on natural resource development. A report in *The Oregonian* of June 17, 1973, stated that the major problem stems from the high cost of
air and water pollution abatement control as well as the
uncertainty of governmental standards.

Juan del Valle of Boise Cascade Corporation, senior
vice president and head of the paper group, said "a lot
of the cash flow that paper companies used to invest in
discretionary expansion has been syphoned off to pollution abatement uses. The costs of operating the pollution abatement facilities have reduced...new capital
available to invest in capacity purposes." Production has
increased, but pollution abatement costs have cut into
what otherwise might have been profit margins large
enough to add productive capacity. The pollution abatement problem has also caused shutdowns of mills.
Three mills have closed within three years and a domi-
nant factor in each case was the costs for meeting environmental requirements. Mr. del Valle also pointed out
the "difficulty of getting pollution abatement permits because of changing standards. It is difficult to make an
investment decision of this magnitude when standards
are changing."

Meanwhile, Ralph Nader conducted a study of the
pulp and paper industry in Maine. As to be expected it

was found "full of inconsistencies." The report asserted that "the old contention by industry that the mills will go broke if made to conform to strict antipollution standards or will pull out of Maine and wreck the economy are increasingly seen as economic blackmail." But the mills *are* closing because of overstrict regulation and so are facilities in every industry under siege from antipollution extremists.

Nader's report was written by William Osborn, the attorney with Nader's Center for the Study of Responsible Law, who is not a forestry expert. A spokesman for Georgia-Pacific Corporation, operator of one of the largest mills in Maine, pointed out that Nader called a water-cleaning system "adequate" on one page but "inadequate" on another. In addition the Nader report charged the company with claiming the water-cleaning system was adequate when in fact the company had already reported the opposite. The company knew the clarifier in the system was inadequate when it was installed as part of the first phase. Construction during the second phase would have made the first system adequate, as the company had planned. The second phase was delayed by, of all things, a court action filed by the EPA, which prevented the start of construction. The EPA action delayed the project for two years. Finally the EPA dropped its suit against Georgia-Pacific on January 26, 1974, when a U.S. District Court dismissed the suit. Nader had no response.

The fact remains that the pulp and paper industry is in serious trouble throughout the nation, according to every expert who has spoken on the subject. No amount of lying and deceitful reporting by anyone is going to change it. Plants are closing and massive emissions control programs, with no reasonable consideration for long-term changes, will close more of them. Such regulation may clean the air and water or it may not, but the interim effects will certainly inflict many more serious and irreversible effects on people.

The Hillsboro Argus, in the center of the pulp and paper industry of the Northwest, discussed the paper shortage in an editorial of June 26, 1973: "In addition to the critical shortage of gasoline, the United States is also faced with a shortage of paper. Part of the reason for this shortage is the inability of some paper mills to meet federal and state pollution standards, resulting in the closure of several American and Canadian mills. Also according to information received from Crown Zellerbach Corporation, there is not a single new paper mill presently being constructed anywhere in the United States or Canada, where the bulk of paper supply comes from. . . .

"Newspaper press manufacturers are reporting cancellations of orders in droves, which will force eventual unemployment in this portion of the industry. . . .Manufacturers of ink, printing plates, film, chemicals, and other raw material necessary for the manufacture of newspapers will also feel the effect of the shortage, and layoffs in these industries can be expected as the supply of paper gets tighter. Or, at best, no new jobs will be created in these areas. . . ."

Nevertheless, Russell E. Train, newly appointed administrator of EPA, persists in restating that oil company advertising is to blame for the energy crisis. He says that antipollution efforts have nothing to do with it. He remarked on June 14, 1973, "I emphasize this point because there is a current tendency to make the environmental programs the whipping boy for our energy problems. . . ." The tendency is there, all right; as consumers and taxpayers, citizens are getting the bill for unnecessary and hysterical environmental programs.

That the environmental extremist is prepared to go beyond mere taxation to achieve his ends is illustrated by Diarmuid O'Scannlain, former director of Oregon's Department of Environmental Quality. "The people, not industry, are now Oregon's principal pollutors....If society cannot voluntarily comply with controls, it might have to accept fetters. We are very close today to having only the latter option," he said in a recent speech. Mr. O'Scannlain and other government officials are quick to seek new ways of clamping fetters on individual freedom through regulation.

Dogberry—Circa 1970

When William Shakespeare wrote *Much Ado About Nothing,* he created Dogberry as a special character for the play. Shakespeare based his characterization of Dogberry the Constable on an assertion not hard to accept, for we have all known some minion of the law who might be "writ down as an ass." Indeed, it was Dogberry who decreed, "for the ewe that will not hear her lamb when it baes will never answer a calf when he bleats." Consider the massive Tussock Moth infestation. At the insistence of the Oregon Environmental Council and Senator Robert Packwood, DDT was shunned, to protect the arachnid-insect relation. In fact, the actions of governmental agencies, officials, and environmental extremists, independently or in concert, have resulted in some of the most bizarre ironies in our history. To wit:

—The former director of the Oregon Department of Environmental Quality, L.B. Day, a politician and environmental extremist, at the insistence of Governor McCall, an environmental opportunist, promulgated a rule which was intended to prevent mining and mineral ex-

ploration and development on Oregon lands by imposing noise limits in the wilderness. These idiotic
proposals would have made it a violation of the law for
a husband to speak above a low conversational tone to
his wife, or would prevent his calling to a member of
the family if lost in the forest.

—At the same time, Day was also going to sue the
United States Army Corps of Engineers and force the
closing of the hydroelectric dams on the Columbia river
because of his insistence on a 5 per cent reduction in
nitrogen level in the water below the levels approved by
Idaho, Washington, and the United States government.
This was in the name of rescuing the salmon and steelhead population of the Columbia river. Day expressed
no concern that at the same time commercial fishermen
and Indians continue to catch salmon and steelhead by
the thousands, using primitive, wasteful, and cruel gill-
nets. He also had admitted that the passage of salmon
and steelhead up the Columbia river for spawning in
1972-1973 was the highest count recorded in the recent
past. Nor was he ready to confess that the best and
most recent research indicates nitrogen levels have little
to do with salmon mortality. He was widely praised and
applauded by the press for his noble stand.

—At the time when the Alaskan pipeline should have
been under construction to increase the flow of oil into
this country, the zealots were complaining of ecological
damage to the State of Alaska, when in fact it involved
a total of 5,230 acres or 8.2 square miles for the permanent right-of-way.

—A "pollution control" initiative (Proposition Nine)
in California was almost passed which would have
stopped all transportation systems and energy sources
using diesel fuel, which is one of the least critical to the
atmosphere. It would have halted all modes of diesel
transport the next day, had it passed.

—The president of the Oregon Environmental Council called on the governor of the state to prohibit further use of electric heat in homes and offices, while at the same time his own manufacturing plant, recently relocated out of the city to a new pristine area in the residential suburbs, is fully air-conditioned.

—Senator Philip Hart introduced the Industrial Deconcentration Bill, S1167, a law which would allow the government to seize corporate property on a whim without any charge of wrongdoing but on a basis of size only or because the company was engaged in certain manufacturing areas defined as concentrated.

—Then, in mid-August 1973, John Gofman appeared on his favorite network, CBS, and recounted the means for making plutonium bombs. He said this was the reason that the United States should stop nuclear power plants, for radicals could steal the plutonium with which to make the bomb. If this were the case, which no one considers sensible, it certainly is not going to stop Russia, China, France, Great Britain, Germany, Japan, or any one else from building nuclear power plants. If the radicals are really serious about building a bomb, and they have the means to do so, they can get plutonium from one of these countries a lot more easily than they can get it here. Other than to scare the listener or reader, why would this probability be a valid reason to stop the United States' nuclear energy program?

—Steel pipe for oil drilling has not been available lately to drillers, while huge stocks rested on the ground in supply depots, unable to be sold since price control quotas set by the government prohibited its sale. Meanwhile it could be sold to foreign buyers, who were able to ship it to American oil companies in Indonesia or the Middle East and sell it at inflated prices.

The list is endless, and each of us has read of similar puzzling incidents which defy completely logical explanations. Looking back, we can all recall similar cases; but they were rather uncommon occurrences and when uncovered, common sense brought about corrective action. Reports of ironic blunders now come to us daily, for they are the modus operandi of the lunatic fringe driving the environmental movement along. When listening to one who describes the terrible effects of a proposed hydroelectric or pump storage project, listen carefully to his reasons and study his background. Then ask if he would be willing to substitute nuclear or even fossil-fired powerplants. Does he retreat to the impenetrable defense of offering no solution or saying that no power is needed? Does he propose alternate workable solutions, or is he just creating heat and no light?

We must ask ourselves, are we responsible for the future of our children and their children, and is this the way to prepare for that future? Resources and energy are needed to clean the rivers, the land, and the air if we wish our children to inherit an earth that resembles the one we were handed.

The answers lie in the thoughtful and studied analyses of scientific and technical knowledge applicable to the wide spectrum of problems which we confront. Man will prevail on earth and he will grow and prosper despite the barrage of disastrous and tragic forecasts drummed at us by the doomsayers. The problems are simply not that difficult to solve. It will be more difficult, though, if we tolerate laws and regulations which say "stop" for the majority and allow the minority of elitists and totalitarians to insulate themselves from their actions at the expense of others. It is probably true that the environmental extremists will be removed from the positions of influence and power they have seized, but by the time this happens irreparable damage to the nation's interests will have occurred. Great and costly damage has already been done. To undo the damage, we must liberate our productive and creative energies from regulatory and bureaucratic chains. We have the facts. Now we must insist on new policies based on good judgment and plain common sense.

Table 2. United States demand for energy resources by major sources, year 1970 and estimated probable demand in 1975, 1985, and 2000 [1]

	1970 [2]	1975	1985	2000
Petroleum (includes natural gas liquids) [3]				
Million barrels	5,367	6,550	8,600	12,000
Million barrels per day	14.70	17.9	23.56	32.79
Trillion Btu	29,617	36,145	47,455	66,216
Percent of gross energy inputs	43.0	40.8	35.6	34.6
Natural gas (includes gaseous fuels)				
Billion cubic feet	21,847	27,800	38,200	49,000
Trillion Btu	22,546	28,690	39,422	50,568
Percent of gross energy inputs	32.8	32.4	29.5	26.0
Coal (bituminous, anthracite, lignite)				
Thousand short tons	526,650	615,000	850,000	1,000,000
Trillion Btu	13,792	16,106	22,260	26,188
Percent of gross energy inputs	20.1	18.2	16.7	13.7
Hydropower, utility [4]				
Billion kilowatt-hours	246	282	363	632
Trillion Btu	2,647	2,820	3,448	5,056
Percent of gross energy inputs	3.8	3.2	2.6	2.6

Nuclear power [5]				
Billion kilowatt-hours	19.3	462	1,982	5,441
Trillion Btu	208	4,851	20,811	43,528
Percent of gross energy inputs	0.3	5.4	15.6	22.7
Total gross energy inputs, trillion Btu	68,810	88,612	133,396	191,556

[1] Preliminary estimates by Bureau of Mines staff.

[2] Latest data

[3] Product demand—includes net processing gain

[4] Includes pumped storage, internal combustion and gas turbine generation. Converted at prevailing and projected central electric stations average heat rates as follows: 10,769 Btu/Kwhr in 1970; 10,000 Btu in 1975; 9,500 in 1985; and 8,000 in 2000.

[5] Converted at average heat rates of 10,769 Btu/Kwhr in 1970; 10,500 in 1975 and 1985; and 8,000 in 2000.

Note: from FIRST ANNUAL REPORT UNDER THE MINING AND MINERALS POLICY ACT, United States Department of Interior, 1972.

Notes
Chapter 1 The Ecological Police State

[1] Kristol, Irving. *The Public Interest*, No. 31, Spring, 1973.

[2] Abelson, Philip. *The Oregonian*, December 16, 1972.

[3] Snow, C. P. *The Two Cultures*, Cambridge University Press, 1963.

[4] Carroll, Richard B. *The National Review*, May 25, 1973.

[5] Rapoport, Roger. *The Oregonian*, December 18, 1969.

[6] *Trends In Capacity and Utilization*, United States Department of Interior, Office of Oil and Gas, December, 1972.

[7] *Power for the Environment*, Atomic Industrial Forum, October, 1971.

[8] *Info*, Atomic Industrial Forum, No. 44, January, 1972.

[9] Carroll, Richard B. *The National Review*, May 25, 1973.

[10] Borlaug, Dr. Norman. *The Oregonian*, March 27, 1973.

[11] Borlaug, Dr. Norman. *The Green Revolution*, 16th Governing Conference, United Nations Food and Agriculture Organization, Rome, November 8, 1971.

[12] Stokinger, Dr. H. E. *Science*, Vol. 174, November 12, 1971.

[13] Berry, Warren. *Los Angeles Times-Washington Post*, October, 1972.

[14] *The Stateman's Yearbook*, Macmillan, 1973.

[15] McCracken, Samuel. *Commentary*, May, 1972.

[16] Podhoretz, Norman. *Commentary*, May, 1972.

Notes
Chapter II The Nuclear Controversy

[1] Fadely, Robert C. Oregon Malignancy Pattern Physiographically related To Hanford, Washington, Radioisotope Storage, *Journal of Environmental Health,* May-June, 1965.

[2] *Comments on Paper by R. C. Fadely,* United States Public Health Service, Division of Radiological Health, August, 1965.

[3] *Info,* Atomic Industrial Forum, No. 51, August, 1972.

[4] Ibid. No. 42, November, 1971.

[5] Ibid. No. 16, February, 1969.

[6] Ibid. Special Issue No. 17, March, 1969.

[7] Ibid. Special Issue, July, 1969.

[8] Ibid. No. 27, May, 1970.

[9] Ibid. No. 23, February, 1970.

[10] Ibid. No. 22x, January, 1970.

[11] Ibid. No. 37, May, 1971.

[12] NCRP Report No. 39, *Basic Radiation Protection Criteria,* National Council on Radiation Protection and Measurements, January 15, 1971.

[13] *Info,* Atomic Industrial Forum, No. 20, October, 1969.

[14] Ibid.

[15] Ibid. No. 21, October, 1969.

[16] Ibid.

[17] *Proceedings, North West Conference on the Role of Nuclear Energy,* pp. 171, 173. 1969.

[18] *Info,* Atomic Industrial Forum, No. 26, April, 1970.

[19] Ibid.

[20] Ibid. No. 32, December, 1970.

[21] Ibid. No. 37, May, 1971.

[22] Ibid. No. 26, April, 1970.
[23] Ibid. No. 27, Supplement, May, 1970.
[24] Ibid. No. 31, October, 1970.
[25] Sagan, Dr. Leonard A. *Comments on the Supplemental Testimony of Ernest Sternglass at the Shoreham Hearing,* May 10, 1971.
[26] *A Compilation of Reviews of the Theories of Dr. E. J. Sternglass,* Atomic Industrial Forum, 1972.
[27] *Thermal Effects,* Atomic Industrial Forum, 1970.
[28] Ibid. No. 27 Supplement, May, 1970.
[29] Ibid. 1972.
[30] Ibid. No. 59, May, 1973.
[31] Ibid.
[32] Ibid. 1971.
[33] Ibid.
[34] Ibid. No. 56, 1973.
[35] Ibid. No. 32, December, 1970.
[36] Ibid. 1971.
[37] Johnson, E. R. *Info,* Atomic Industrial Forum, 1972.
[38] *Nuclear Power Waste Management,* Atomic Industrial Forum, 1971.
[39] Ibid. 1971.
[40] Ibid. No. 61, July, 1973.
[41] *Proceedings, Fifth Annual Health Physics Society Midyear Topical Symposium,* November 3-6, 1970.

Notes
Chapter III. Energy—Crisis or Conspiracy

[1] *United States Mineral Resources*, United States Geological Survey, 1973.

[2] Meadows, D. L., and others. *The Limits to Growth*, Universe, 1972.

[3] Drummond, Roscoe. *The Oregonian*, June 8, 1973.

[4] McCall, Governor Tom L. *The Oregonian*, April 10, 1973.

[5] Hubbert, M. King. *Resources and Man*, National Academy of Sciences, W. H. Freeman, 1969.

[6] Alsop, Joseph. *The Oregonian*, April 10, 1973.

[7] Hardesty, C. Howard. *The Oregonian*, June 12, 1973.

[8] National Petroleum Council, *United States Outlook, An Initial Appraisal*, 1971-1985, vol 1, p. 28, July, 1971.

[9] Chase Manhattan Bank, *Capital Investments of the World Petroleum Industry*, 1969.

[10] *Congressional Record*, pp. 16896-16898, October 27, 1971.

[11] *Trends in Capacity and Utilization*, United States Department of Interior, Office of Oil and Gas, December, 1972.

[12] Ross, Philip N. *Implications of the Nuclear-Electric Energy Economy*, Westinghouse Electric Corporation, December 11, 1972.

[13] Corey, Gordon R. *Electricity and Nuclear Power*, Commonwealth Edison Co., November 20, 21, 1972.

Notes
Chapter IV Cases of Lunacy

[1] *Consolidated DDT Hearing,* Environmental Protection Agency, April 25, 1972.

[2] *Environmental Statement, Cooperative Douglas Fir Tussock Moth Pest Management Plan,* United States Department of Agriculture, Forest Service, Oregon and Washington, 1973.

[3] Hazeltine, William E., Ph.D., *Comments on Environmental Impact Statement, Douglas Fir Tussock Moth Pest Management Plan,* March 9, 1973.

[4] *National Forest Management in a Quality Environment—Timber Productivity,* United States Department of Agriculture, Forest Service, 1971.

[5] *Forests, USA,* American Forest Institute, 1971.

[6] *Timber Harvesting and the Environment,* United States Department of Agriculture, Forest Service, 1973.

[7] Morton, Rogers C. B. *Petition for a Writ of Certiorari to the United States Court of Appeals for the District of Columbia Circuit, in the Supreme Court of the United States,* March, 1973.

[8] *Fact Sheet—Alaska Pipeline Issue,* Alaska Public Interest Coalition, May 25, 1973.

[9] *Summary, Project Description of the Trans-Alaska Pipeline System,* Alyeska Pipeline Service Company, August, 1971.

[10] *Reconnaissance Report on the Impact of the Alaskan Pipeline and Marine Terminal Sites,* United States Department of Interior, Fish and Wildlife Service, March, 1970.

Notes
Chapter V Resources or Reserves

[1] *First Annual Report Under the Mining and Minerals Policy Act*, United States Department of Interior, 1972.

[2] Crane, Philip, Rep. *Congressional Record*, vol. 118, No. 91, June 6, 1972.

[3] Excerpts from 93rd Congress, 1st Session, *House of Representatives Report No. 93-275 on Agriculture-Environmental and Consumer Protection Appropriation Bill*, 1974, (H.R. 8619), Title IV, Consumer Programs, 1973.

[4] *Human Events*, June 23, 1973.

INDEX